If you have ever wondered about what makes some people lie, or if you have had trouble with a "Big Liar" in your life, in a romantic relationship, at work, or a scam artist, this book will answer all your questions. Hart and Curtis expertly present scientific evidence about prolific liars and tips on how to deal with such individuals. This book is engaging, very readable, and full of fascinating case stories.

—**VICTORIA TALWAR, PhD,** AUTHOR OF *THE TRUTH ABOUT LYING: TEACHING HONESTY TO CHILDREN AT EVERY AGE AND STAGE*

Hart and Curtis provide new insights into the understudied topic of big liars. This work provides an accessible account of the psychology of unusually deceptive people.

—**TIMOTHY R. LEVINE, PhD,** AUTHOR OF *DUPED: TRUTH-DEFAULT THEORY AND THE SOCIAL SCIENCE OF LYING AND DECEPTION*

BIG LIARS

BIG LIARS

WHAT PSYCHOLOGICAL SCIENCE TELLS US ABOUT LYING *and* HOW YOU CAN AVOID BEING DUPED

CHRISTIAN L. HART PhD

and DREW A. CURTIS PhD

 AMERICAN PSYCHOLOGICAL ASSOCIATION

Published by
APA LifeTools
750 First Street, NE
Washington, DC 20002
https://www.apa.org

Order Department
https://www.apa.org/pubs/books
order@apa.org

Typeset in Sabon by Circle Graphics, Inc., Reisterstown, MD

Printer: Sheridan Books, Chelsea, MI

Cover Designer: Mark Karis

Library of Congress Cataloging-in-Publication Data

Names: Hart, Christian L., author. | Curtis, Drew A., author.
Title: Big liars : what psychological science tells us about lying and how you can avoid being duped / by Christian L. Hart and Drew A. Curtis.
Description: Washington, DC : American Psychological Association, [2024] | Includes bibliographical references and index. | Summary: "Inviestigates the science behind big liars"-- Provided by publisher.
Identifiers: LCCN 2023006323 (print) | LCCN 2023006324 (ebook) | ISBN 9781433837517 (paperback) | ISBN 9781433837524 (ebook)
Subjects: LCSH: Deception--Psychological aspects. | Truthfulness and falsehood. | Honesty. | Psychology, Pathological. | BISAC: SELF-HELP / Compulsive Behavior / General | PSYCHOLOGY / Personality
Classification: LCC BF637.D42 H37 2024 (print) | LCC BF637.D42 (ebook) | DDC 177/.3--dc23/eng/20230415
LC record available at https://lccn.loc.gov/2023006323
LC ebook record available at https://lccn.loc.gov/2023006324

https://doi.org/10.1037/0000367-000

Printed in the United States of America

10 9 8 7 6 5 4 3 2 1

To my mother, Mary Ann Hart,
The first brilliant person I ever met.

—Christian L. Hart

CONTENTS

PREFACE

> *A man is never more truthful than when he acknowledges himself a liar.*
>
> —Mark Twain

Human civilization rests vulnerably on the foundational assumption that when people speak, they generally tell the truth. No human endeavors of consequence would take shape without trust holding people together in the pursuit of common goals. The idea that humanity is built on faith in the honesty of others may seem absurd when one considers that rampant lying is an indisputable feature in society. Not only is lying common, it is also widely tolerated, and it is sometimes viewed as the right thing to do.

Though honesty is widely touted as a fundamental goal in human interactions, in practice, people do not communicate completely honestly all of the time. In fact, much of the time they do not. When telling the truth feels inconvenient, people resort to less honest communication. They steer conversations away from certain topics, they feign ignorance, they withhold key details, they intentionally use vague or misleading words, or, sometimes, they just flat-out lie. And as you are likely aware, some people lie much more often or with much greater effect than others. We call them *big liars*.

GOALS

Our aim in this book is to provide a general audience with an accessible synthesis of the scholarly work on lying, with a particular focus on individuals in our society who seem to lie extraordinarily. When we (the authors) use the concept of big liars, we are referring to people who lie with much greater frequency than the typical person as well as to people who tell enormous lies that have a substantial impact on the people around them. In essence, big liars are people who lie extraordinarily and for whom lying is a defining feature. We hope to show the reader who the big liars are, what makes them tick, how their lying affects relationships and society, and how they can be dealt with.

There are a great number of books on lying, each with a unique perspective. This one stands apart in some key ways. Many books fail to address the issue that most people are quite honest while a small subset of the population is very deceitful. These prodigious liars pose the greatest threat. Big liars destroy lives through duplicitous romantic relationships, conniving business relationships, and all other manner of disingenuous exchanges. We hope to provide a full account of the grand deceivers in our midst. Additionally, this book presents a scientific rather than a purely anecdotal perspective. Stories are interesting and instructive, but careful scientific analysis can help us see things more clearly, allowing us to separate fact from fiction. There is an overwhelming amount of fascinating scientific findings on deception and liars. However, much of this work is available only in scholarly scientific journals or dense academic books. We synthesize much of the scientific evidence into accessible narratives and weave those narratives with real-life stories into a gripping analysis of big liars.

Each person forms their own moral boundary, deciding when it is best to be honest and when a little dishonesty would be more prudent. Our central thesis is that almost everyone is dishonest sometimes and that dishonesty is usually fairly harmless. We even ponder whether a certain degree of dishonesty may serve important roles in society and in normal social relationships. However, some people step well out of the bounds of normality and use profuse malevolent deception to manipulate others for their own gain. We hope that by closely analyzing those people who use deception as their principal mode in life, we can help readers learn to deal with them more effectively.

Our goal in writing this book was to examine how big liars differ from the more honest types. Researchers now know enough about colossal liars to provide some accuracy in determining who lies, how big liars are created, how big liars operate, how people can become more honest, and how everyone can avoid being manipulated by liars. We offer helpful advice to the many people who are harmed by big liars. We hope to help readers understand the challenges in detecting liars as well as the prospects of reducing or eliminating lying in important contexts and relationships. Perhaps by studying the big liars among us, everyone can also learn a bit about our own strained relationships with honesty and the truth.

STRUCTURE

In Chapter 1, we make the case that big liars are profoundly more dishonest than the typical person. We explore the variables that distinguish big liars from everyone else, examining innate biological differences, differences shaped by the cultures and contexts in which people were reared and live, differences in personal philosophies, and differences in key personality traits. We also posit a theory that explains who the big liars are as well as why they lie so prolifically and monumentally.

In Chapter 2, we try to unravel the origin story of the big liars by exploring their childhood development. We track the emergence of lying early in childhood and the trajectories that lead some to transition into honest adults while others gravitate toward deceit.

Chapter 3 delves into the world of people who play loose with the truth. Storytellers, exaggerators, pathological liars, and psychopaths all spread questionable information. We try to figure out what distinguishes these various groups of untruthful people, ultimately discerning who is a big liar and who is not.

In Chapter 4, we consider the big lies of scam artists and the sanctioned lies of lawyers, doctors, and politicians. We explore examples of big liars who work as law-enforcement officers, corporate executives, salespeople, preachers, and other occupations. As it turns out, most professions have their big liars.

Chapter 5 uncovers how big liars operate in relationships. Some people always hold close to the truth in their relationships, while others are unmoored to veracity and are willing to sail far out into the sea of deceit. We have considerable information about how lying unfolds in different types of relationships, the interventions that can reduce lying, and the ways in which social relationships are fractured by deception. We review research findings about prolific lying in romantic relationships and in other familial relationships and among friends. Our fraught relationship with lies and liars is a natural outcome of a tension between wanting to have fair and forthright relationships with others and simultaneously acknowledging the difficulty and perils of being completely transparent with all people all the time.

Chapter 6 examines how big liars pull it off. How do people convincingly spew untruths? A growing body of anecdotal and empirical evidence reveals how big liars practice their craft, avoid detection, and get away with their misdeeds. We explain some of our research that has examined the self-reported techniques that people use to tell believable lies. As it turns out, how these liars alter their behavior to seem more believable is the opposite of what most people are looking for when trying to detect if someone is lying to them.

Chapter 7 examines the motivations that drive big liars. We also cut to the core of what leads some to be faithfully honest at all times with all people yet leads others to be just as devoutly deceptive. We address the question of whether big liars simply have no moral compass or whether something unusual in their childhoods set them apart from other people, warping their assessment of right and wrong. It turns out that not all profound liars deceive out of some nefarious attempt to gain an advantage. Compassion and fear are just as likely to drive people away from honesty and into a spiral of lies.

Chapter 8 explores the consequences of extreme lying, both for the big liars and for those who interact with them. Lying can have devastating effects in any domain, from romantic relationships to friends and family or the workplace. We discuss the costs big liars impose on everyone else.

Chapter 9 assesses the state of the field of lie detection. It's not possible to attach every person in our lives to a lie detector, but are there more subtle verbal and behavioral cues that give away liars' deceit? We separate the myths from the reality about lie detection.

Finally, Chapter 10 provides guidance and advice on how people can avoid being duped by big liars. While there is no surefire way to avoid being deceived by others, there are several psychological adjustments that everyone can make that minimize our susceptibility to being duped.

CASES

Throughout this book, we present numerous cases describing individuals who are liars themselves or who have dealt with liars in their lives. We hold compassion, concern, and respect for these people, who were generously willing to share their accounts for our benefit. Unless they wanted to be identified, we have preserved their privacy and confidentiality, withholding their true names and other identifying information. Our aim in sharing these cases is to help the reader better understand extraordinary liars through specific real-world examples.

ACKNOWLEDGMENTS

We thank our families for their endless patience, love, and support during the writing of this book. We also thank Drs. Timothy R. Levine, Kim B. Serota, and Bella M. DePaulo for their insights and inspiration on the topic of big liars. We extend our deep appreciation to the various reviewers who provided helpful feedback and advice on this book. Finally, we thank Emily Ekle, Krissy Jones, Liz Brace, Gail Gottfried, and the rest of the American Psychological Association team for their tremendous support and encouragement.

BIG LIARS

CHAPTER 1

A WORLD AWASH WITH LIARS

Man is not what he thinks he is, he is what he hides.
—André Malraux

In 2009, during President Barack Obama's joint address to Congress, Representative Joe Wilson did not agree with what the president was saying about health care reforms. In front of everyone seated in the Chamber of the House of Representatives and in front of a live television audience of millions, Wilson yelled at the president, "You lie!" The insult echoed through the Chamber and into Americans' living rooms. Had Wilson cast such an aspersion 2 centuries earlier, he would have been risking his own life (Parker, 2009). Earlier in America's history, an accusation that someone was a liar was the central insult leading to most duels (Greenberg, 1990). The prevailing view was that, among men of honor, to have one's honesty and integrity questioned was the gravest of all insults. That form of tarnish on one's reputation was so damaging in social and business matters that one was left with no option other than to strike down the person who had defamed them. If someone accused another of being a liar, the recourse was to defend one's character by dutifully attempting to kill the accuser.

Representative Wilson's accusation did not lead to a duel. Admonished by politicians from both parties, Wilson quickly and publicly apologized for his insult, seeking forgiveness for his impropriety. President Obama noted the offense and accepted Wilson's apology, saying, "I'm a big believer that we all make mistakes. . . . He apologized quickly and without equivocation and I'm appreciative of that." There would be no need for firearms in settling the matter.

In this book, we throw around the label "big liar" without much consideration of honor, reputation, and hurt feelings, and without much fear of being challenged to a duel when we pin the label on some people. These days, claims of truth and falsity tend to be resolved through open debate, and disputes about whether someone is a liar or a straight shooter generally don't devolve into mortal combat. Fortunately, we live in a time in which we can openly consider the facts about lying and liars. We can discuss who the big liars are, and we can examine why they are so dishonest. Lying is now an open topic of scientific inquiry.

When was the last time you told a lie? What was the lie about? Did you tell your boss that you were sick at home when you were actually relaxing poolside? Did you tell your spouse that you liked something more than you really did? Did you say to someone, "It's good to see you too," when it wasn't particularly good to see them? Most people are sporadic liars. Whether they intend to or not, most find themselves occasionally dropping bits of falsity into conversations. More often than not, those little lies are relatively benign and trivial untruths used to spare someone's feelings or to facilitate polite social conversations. Few would be morally outraged if they discovered those white lies. However, other times the lies hold tremendous weight, concealing the most despicable truths. The world is awash in the lies of 8 billion people. With every little falsehood, each of us contributes a few drops to that sea of deception.

While everyone is prone to bend the truth on occasion, some people lay out lies with such frequency that they seem entirely severed from any need or ability to speak the truth or to share genuine versions of themselves with others. Those profuse prevaricators spew lies with complete abandon, often leaving a wake of broken hearts, chafed coworkers, and exasperated friends and family. Other liars are conspicuous because of the gravity of their lies. They tell extremely consequential lies that upend the lives of everyone around them. This book is about lying in general, but it focuses on the big liars—those few people who use lies as one of their principal strategies for navigating life. By telling lies prolifically or by telling enormously consequential lies, they warp our understanding of reality.

If you peruse the news on any given day, you will likely come across stories of people who made headlines because of their lies. Every day, journalists track the veracity of statements by politicians, pointing out each instance in which this congressman twisted the truth or that president told a bald-faced lie. Some statements by politicians are deemed to be gentle varnishings of the truth, while others fall into the "pants on fire" realm. Financial leaders are jailed after being caught red-handed in their fraudulent schemes. Industry titans are dethroned when they are found misleading investors about the bottom line or lying to customers about the effectiveness or safety of their products. Religious leaders are defrocked when they are discovered conning the faithful or weaving untruths to conceal their own sinful escapades. Big liars make great headlines.

Jessica Vega is one example of a little-known person who rose to a certain degree of notoriety because of her big lies. Jessica was a 25-year-old living in New York. She and her boyfriend, Michael, had been together for a while and had a kid together. She had dreams of having a fancy wedding with a nice dress, flowers, and all the rest, but she and Michael couldn't afford it, at least on their own income. She was aware that people were often generous toward people who were dying, so she decided just to tell people she was not long for this world. She claimed that she had been diagnosed with leukemia and that doctors had told her she only had 5 months to live. She produced a forged letter from a doctor confirming that leukemia would soon end her life. She even lied to her boyfriend, convincing him that he would soon be raising their child on his own. She stated that before she died she wanted to have a nice wedding and marry her boyfriend. Plans for a lovely wedding soon got underway. She lied to the owner of a wedding dress shop about her terminal affliction. The owner felt desperate to help and generously gave Jessica a $1,500 dress, a seamstress to take care of any alterations, and some nice shoes. Jessica had shaved her head to make a more convincing case for her leukemia, so someone donated a new wig for her to wear at the wedding. Another person donated a set of wedding rings. Someone else donated a stay in Aruba for the honeymoon. Others donated plane tickets for the flight. Someone else, touched by her story, paid for a wedding photographer. Many came to her aid donating cash. As one person duped by her lies said, "It seemed so genuine. I never questioned it." Finally, the day arrived, and Jessica celebrated the wedding she had always hoped for. However, not long after they wed, her husband Michael started to grow suspicious about her illness. He did a little investigating and found out that the letter from the doctor was a forgery. His wife was not dying and did not have leukemia. As Michael put it, "Jessica lied about everything, and she's not sick. She pulled the wool over everybody's eyes." Jessica was arrested and charged with six felonies. Michael divorced her.

In total, Jessica's lies netted her many thousands of dollars in donations for her wedding. As the prosecutors contended, "By pretending to have a terminal illness, Vega inexcusably took advantage of the community's hearts and minds, and profited off of their generosity," adding that "our office will hold this individual accountable for fleecing the public through lies and deception." In court, Jessica admitted to making it all up. She apologized. She spent some time in jail and was ordered to pay back all her victims (Crimesider Staff, 2012; Ng, 2012). Stories about big liars like Jessica Vega can be found in news stories around the world almost daily.

We need not look to the news to find big liars, though. They are all around us, from the uncle whose every story is a self-aggrandizing exaggeration to the romantic partner who professes love each day but has devoted their heart to another. Everyone probably has stories about big liars we have crossed paths with. Sometimes when we discover a big liar, we can avoid their deceit by simply avoiding them. Other times we are forced to deal with their dishonesty because they are at our workplace, in our social circles, or in our families.

WHAT IS A LIE?

Before we discuss lying in more depth, we first address exactly what a lie is. People get caught up in semantics about what counts as lying and what does not, so it's important to be crystal clear about how we define lying. All untrue statements are not lies. Sometimes people are simply misinformed or mistaken. If someone mistakenly says, "Thomas Jefferson was the second president," though it was actually John Adams, most will consider that a mistake, not a lie. If we consider the distinction between a lie and a mistake, we immediately recognize what distinguishes the two—it is the intention. If someone wanted you to fail your history test, so they intentionally misinformed you that Thomas Jefferson was the second president, they would be lying. Only the intention to mislead separates the mistake from the lie. Most dictionary definitions of lying capture this element of intent, with definitions, such as "to make an untrue statement with intent to deceive" (Merriam-Webster, n.d.). More broadly, people tend to see intent as a central feature of most immoral wrongdoing; otherwise, they treat the incident as a mere accident or oversight (Schein & Gray, 2018). Thus, deception researchers also place intent as a central criterion of lying (Bok, 1978; Buller & Burgoon, 1996; Ekman, 1985; Vrij, 2000).

But things get more complicated. Consider the following situation. Brian's girlfriend, Shannon, asks him what he did last night. Brian says that he stayed at home and watched television, which he actually did. What Brian left out, though, is that he also invited his ex-girlfriend over, and they had sex. Did Brian lie? After all, he said nothing that was untrue. Does omitting some important fact constitute a lie? If so, are we lying when a kid asks how we like their drawing, and we say something like, "I like the way you made the person green," but we don't say, "I think this looks weird and amateurish"? Many people view such attempts to intentionally exclude information with the intent to mislead as *lies of omission*.

What if Shannon asks Brian what he is going to do today? Secretly, Brian has made plans for his ex-girlfriend to come over and have sex again. He tells Shannon, "I'm just going to hang out at home alone." As it turns out, Brian's ex-girlfriend never arrives for their clandestine dalliance. Could we say that Brian lied? Sure, he intended to lie, but what he told Shannon turned out to be true. So, did he lie? By most definitions, he had lied because he believed that what he was saying was untrue when he said it. So, the reality of the world is not as pertinent to defining a lie as the belief and intention of the liar is.

Some philosophers (e.g., Bok, 1978) have argued for a broader definition that dispenses with the criterion that a lie must be a statement that is untrue. They prefer that lies be defined as *statements intended to deceive*, whether those statements are technically true or not. Likewise, using language that is technically true but intentionally misleading would also be viewed as a lie. For instance, if I said, "You should be aware that John drinks at work," you might be concerned about John's alcohol problem. While my statement is technically true (John actually drinks water at work all day long), my language was chosen to erroneously paint John in a negative light. In a real-life example of misleading language, President Clinton contended that he had been honest when he said "there's nothing going on between us" when referring to his sexual affair with Monica

Lewinsky. He argued that the truth or falsity of the statement "depends on what the meaning of the word 'is' is." For the most part, then, the broad definition of lies (statements intended to deceive) seems to capture most examples of what people consider to be lies.

People also deceive with their silence. Imagine that you find a wallet in the gym and you put it in your pocket. A couple of minutes later, someone asks, "Hey has anyone seen a wallet around here?" You remain silent. Have you lied? If intentional silence is used to communicate a deceptive meaning, we view that silence as a type of lie. Silence is just another way we communicate untruths.

Looking at the various definitions of lying, we can see three key common criteria (see Mahon, 2008, for a review). The first is that there must be a communication, usually by speaking words but also via sign language, gestures, the pen, social media posts, smoke signals, silence, and so on. The second criterion is that the communicator must believe that what they are communicating is not the full truth that one would expect in such a situation. The third condition is that the communicator intends for their communication to be misleading. With those criteria in mind, we prefer to define a *lie* as an intentionally misleading communication meant to create untrue beliefs. This definition includes lying as one form of deception, a form that hinges on the intentionally dishonest use of communication, whether wholly untrue, misleading, or omitted. For most practical purposes, we can stick with the shorthand: A lie is a communication intended to deceive.

At its core, a lie is simply an attempt to persuade (Stiff, 1996). People all have goals. They use lies to help achieve those goals. Lying is just one form of social manipulation, and it is a rare form at that. It is useful to think of lying not as a unique dastardly tactic. Instead, it is one of the many tools people use to try to influence others to get what they want in life.

DEFINING BIG LIARS

With lying sufficiently defined, we now consider big liars. We define *big liars* as people who tell big lies or who lie frequently. Some people manage to accomplish both. Our definition has two elements. First, big liars can be defined as people who tell big lies. By *big lies*, we mean lies that are extremely consequential and are likely to produce substantial effects, often disastrous ones. This definition is somewhat idiosyncratic because it hinges on a subjective evaluation of the consequences of a lie. Nonetheless, most people can readily recall someone whose lies caused massive problems. A business owner who finds out that her co-owner has been lying about company profits for years would surely view her betrayer as a big liar. A man who is scammed out of his life savings would similarly identify the perpetrator as a big liar. Likewise, a political leader who uses a lie with calamitous effects would undoubtedly be labeled a big liar by many of their constituents. Big liars who tell massive lies are defined subjectively by the impact their lies have on others. Those subjective outcomes are difficult to calculate scientifically. Instead of using a scientific metric, we tend to identify these big liars based on the level of reputational notoriety they achieve. A second way of defining big liars involves how often a person lies. We can define big liars as people who lie very frequently. These big liars seem to lie with a predictable regularity that far surpasses the dishonesty of an average person. We can identify these big liars simply by finding those people who lie the most; however, we must find a way to measure how often they lie.

MEASURING LYING

A young woman sat at a café enjoying coffee and a good conversation with one of her closest friends. They talked about work, their romantic lives, worries, and plans for the future. They shared and bonded. It was a lovely conversation. When the conversation ended, the young woman took a diary book out of her purse. She jotted down some notes about who her friend was, what they had talked about, and how long the conversation had lasted. She wrote some notes about how many times she had lied to her friend, and she wrote down what she had lied about and why she had lied. This woman was a participant in a large psychological study on lying. She had agreed to take detailed notes after each social interaction or conversation she had. She would track the particulars of each social interaction, especially information about every lie that she told. She would do this for the next week, as would many other people who were participants in the study.

These types of diary studies are common techniques used to assess the prevalence of lying in the world around us (DePaulo et al., 1996; George & Robb, 2008; Hancock et al., 2004). One obvious limitation of self-report techniques is that we can never know how accurate and honest the diary recordings are. After all, why would a researcher trust a liar to provide honest information about their own lying? Most deception scientists are cautious in their analyses and interpretations, taking self-reports about honesty with a grain of salt. As researchers in this field, we (the authors) know that when people are asked to self-report, they generally provide accurate responses, especially when asked via the types of anonymous surveys that we used in our deception studies. For instance, when people answer survey questions and later are asked those same questions again while hooked up to a polygraph machine, their answers tend to be the same (Brigham et al., 1974; Clark & Tifft, 1966). Other studies have also assessed the accuracy of self-reported lying (e.g., Halevy et al., 2014). In those studies, researchers asked people how much they lie. Then, unbeknownst to the participants, the researchers created situations in which they could verify if participants in fact cheated and lied in a game. It turned out that people who reported being big liars actually did lie more frequently in the games. While we can never be absolutely sure that someone is being truthful in our surveys, several lines of research suggest that they generally are.

HOW OFTEN DO PEOPLE LIE?

Pete Rose was a dominant force in American baseball for decades, first as a player and then as manager of the Cincinnati Reds. He had held the all-time hitting record, he was a three-time World Series winner, and he had been selected as an All-Star 17 times. However, he had secrets. In 1989, the commissioner of Major League Baseball announced that Pete Rose was being investigated for serious allegations that were later revealed to be about gambling. Pete was accused of gambling on Major League Baseball games, breaking one of the most serious rules in the league. For the next decade, Pete denied having gambled on baseball to anyone who would listen. He professed his honesty to reporters, fans, baseball officials, and anyone else who would listen. He was asked about the gambling accusations at every turn, and he was always adamant that he had never gambled on Major League Baseball games. His ardent fans believed him and supported him. Finally, after almost a decade and a half of vehement denials, Pete came clean, acknowledging that he had indeed bet on baseball games (Rose, 2004). However, he was clear to note, he had never bet on games involving his own team, the Cincinnati Reds. Pete had lied, consistently, regularly, and effusively for years. Nobody knows how many times he lied, but it was considerable by any measure. Eventually, many baseball fans began to forgive Pete for his deceit, with many arguing that his sins should be forgiven and he should be inducted into the Hall of Fame. Then, 3 years after his initial admission, Pete made another confession. He had, in fact, bet on games involving the Cincinnati Reds. His mountain of lies was a bit taller.

If we want to measure how often people lie, we ultimately have to ask them. There are some laboratory approaches in which researchers bring subjects into a lab, have them play a game or complete a task for money, and then secretly note how many lie to get more money (Ariely, 2012; Halevy et al., 2014). However, how much can a contrived laboratory study tell us about lying in the real world? To understand people's dishonesty in real life, we have to trust their self-reports. That is, we have to ask them how often they lie.

Returning to the lie diary studies we discussed at the beginning of this chapter, we can look at what those studies found. In the 1990s, a couple of studies found that people told about one or two lies per day (DePaulo et al., 1996; Kashy & DePaulo, 1996). A more recent diary study found that people told an average of 1.6 lies per day (Hancock et al., 2004). Another found that, on average, people told slightly less than one lie per day (George & Robb, 2008). So, across the diary studies, researchers found that people told an average of about one to two lies per day. Across the diary studies, people lied in 20% to 33% of their conversations (DePaulo et al., 1996; George & Robb, 2008; Hancock et al., 2004). Based on all those studies, we consider one to two lies per day as a baseline average. Keep in mind that big liars lie much more than average.

Information about lying is also available from several national polls that asked Americans whether or not they lie at all. In the early 1990s, the soon-to-be-famous author James Patterson was working as an advertising executive. He and another market researcher, Peter Kim, carried out a huge nationwide study in which they anonymously surveyed thousands of people. One of the topics they covered was lying. They found that 91% of the Americans they surveyed reported lying regularly. Two thirds reported that they saw nothing wrong with lying, and the majority indicated that they lie to their spouses, friends, and family. If you think that makes Americans seem morally bankrupt, consider the fact that almost one in 10 of the participants said they would gladly murder a stranger for a few million dollars (Patterson & Kim, 1991). A *Reader's Digest* poll found that 99% of readers reported engaging in lying or other forms of dishonesty (Kalish, 2004). In another study, 96% of people admitted that they had lied to avoid work, and the vast majority reported that they had never been caught (Tomaszewski, 2021). It seems that almost all Americans lie.

According to one study, the vast majority of people express a willingness to lie to others (84%; Drouin et al., 2016). In another, about one in five people reported lying every day (J. E. Grant et al., 2019). In other studies, less than half the people said they have lied on a given day, but when asked about lying over a week that number grows to 92%, and over 3 months, it grows to over 99% (Serota & Levine, 2015; Serota et al., 2010, 2021). In our own research, we found that people report an average of 1.4 lies per day, which is very similar to what others have found (Hart et al., 2021; Serota et al., 2010; Verigin et al., 2019). Taken together, these studies suggest that most people lie, and on average they seem to do so a couple of times per day.

OUTLIERS

We have documented the fact that, on average, people seem to lie somewhat regularly. However, it is interesting also to examine those who lie most. Thus, we turn our attention toward those at the extremes. If we take a second look at the diary studies in which people on average lied about one or two times a day, we can examine the patterns of dishonesty a bit more closely (DePaulo et al., 1996). Though the average was about two lies per day, things were a little more nuanced than that. What that means is that not everyone lied once or twice a day; there was quite a bit of variability in deception among those people. Some people certainly did lie exactly two times per day, but others lied much more than that, and others lied less often. We can analyze that variability and identify the most dishonest individuals.

If we look at most traits and characteristics of people, we see that individuals can differ quite a bit from one another. Take income, for example. In 2019, the U.S. Census Bureau calculated that the average household income from wages was about $52,000 (as cited in Wang, 2021); that number provides a fine summary of how households in the country are doing financially. That average value also hides some important details. For instance, it conceals the fact that in 2019, a couple of hundred households each brought in more than $50 million in wages alone. Those extreme values are called *outliers*. The average (also called the mean) can hide the outliers. When I tell you the average human is 5 feet, 5 inches tall (Roser et al., 2013), you know nothing about Sultan Kösen, the tallest living human, who stands at 8 feet, 3 inches tall (Guinness World Records, 2021). Sultan Kösen is an outlier. Knowing the average tells you little about people at the extremes.

What happens if, instead of looking at the average number of lies people tell per day, we look at the details behind that average? Just as with household income and height, we can see substantial variability. Some report lying very little or not at all, and some lie substantially. What interests us is the small handful of people who report lying considerably more than everyone else. Those outliers (or *outliars*) are a major focus of this book.

A detailed analysis of DePaulo et al.'s (1996) data from diary studies on lie frequency revealed that some people lied habitually (Serota et al., 2010). On average, people told about two lies per day, but one person reported telling 46 lies over the course of the week; that works out to about 6.6 lies per day. Serota et al.'s reanalysis showed that a small group of liars (about 9%) told a disproportionately large percentage (26%) of the lies. Additionally, each of those liars told an average of about five lies per day.

In our research, we became interested in the outliers only recently. We wanted to understand the people who lie much more than the average person, so we set out in pursuit of the big liars. Who are the people who practice deception every single day and in most of their social interactions? What separates the big liars from the rest of the populace? How did they become big liars? How does their dishonesty affect their lives and the lives of the people around them? Ultimately, what can we do if these big liars are in our lives?

With lying, we find what, in the world of research and statistics, is called a *positively skewed distribution*. The majority of the people lie very little, but a small segment of the population lies a lot. Household income in the United States follows this positively skewed distribution as well. The top 10% of households bring in more than 30% of the income. If you look at the graph in Figure 1.1, you can see that in 2014 the bulk of households earned under $206,600 per year, but a smaller subset earned substantially more. Those households at the far right side of the graph are the outliers.

We can also see positively skewed distributions in the studies on lying. For instance, we can examine the data from one study in which the researchers recorded 10-minute conversations people had with a stranger and then counted how many times they had lied (R. S. Feldman et al., 2002). On average, people told two lies during their short conversations. However, a reanalysis of the data showed a positive skew—41% of the people told no lies at all, and another 19% told only one lie (Serota et al., 2010). Thus, most people either were completely honest or hardly lied at all, while a small group of participants (26%) told 72% of the lies. The biggest liars passed off 12 lies in only 10 minutes!

The outliers, the people who lie more than everyone else, stand out even more in studies in which researchers measure how many lies people have told in the past 24 hours. In one of those studies (Serota et al., 2010), 60% of people reported that they told no lies at all on the preceding day (see Figure 1.2). Another 15% reported telling only one lie. So, again, most people seemed to be pretty honest.

FIGURE 1.1. Distribution of Household Income 2014

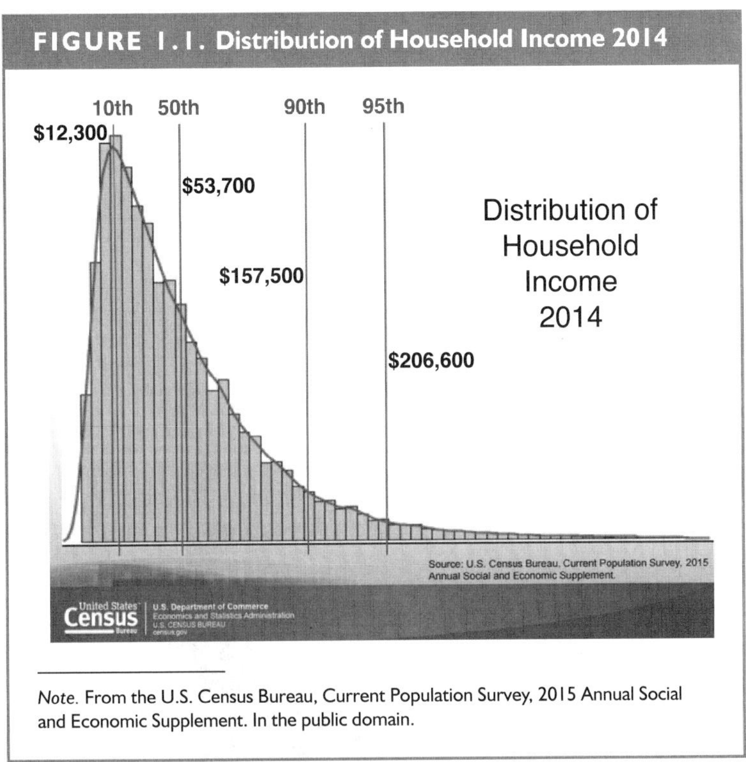

Note. From the U.S. Census Bureau, Current Population Survey, 2015 Annual Social and Economic Supplement. In the public domain.

However, a small group (5%) told 50% of all the lies! What happens if we look for the top 1% of liars in that group? These people are the top of the heap in terms of dishonesty. Those top liars report lying over 20 times per day. The biggest liar in that group reported telling a whopping 53 lies in one day. Talk about big liars!

The positively skewed pattern of lying follows what is known as the *Pareto principle* (Pareto, 1896). Vilfredo Pareto was an Italian economist in the 19th century. Pareto noticed that many distribution patterns follow a type of power law in which roughly 80% of the instances are accounted for by around 20% of the agents.

FIGURE 1.2. Distribution of Lies Told per Day

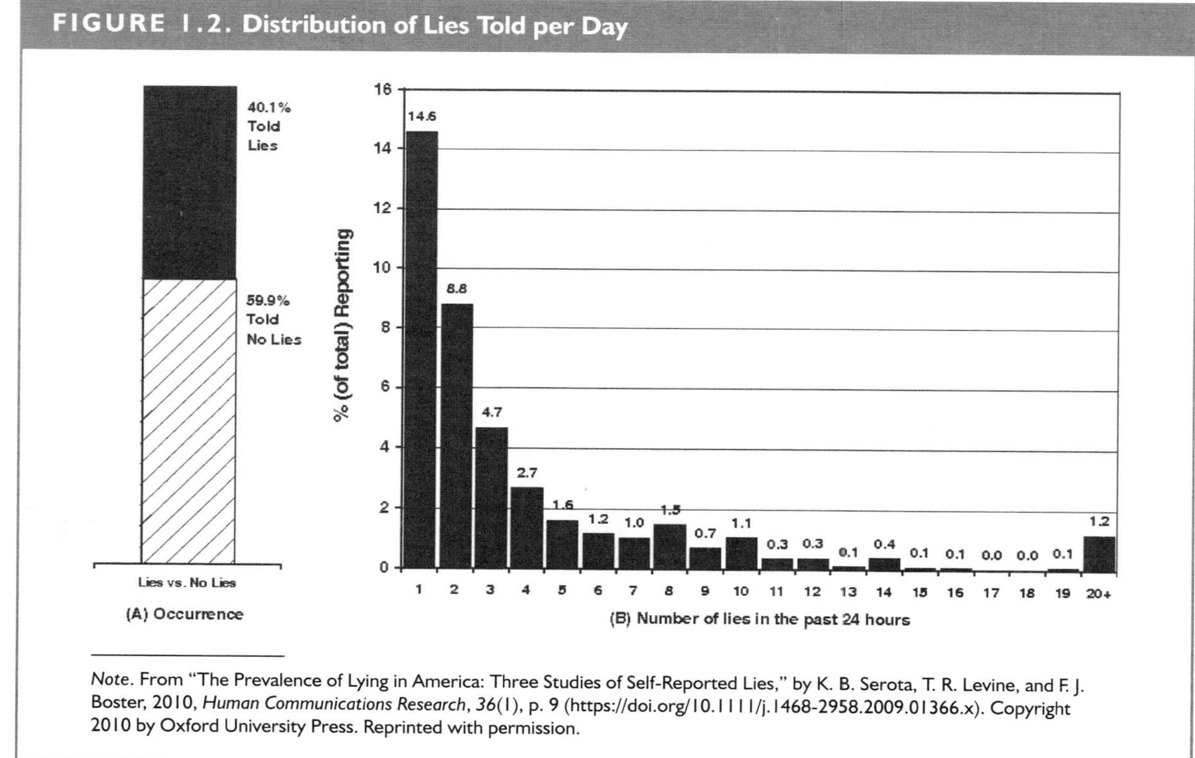

Note. From "The Prevalence of Lying in America: Three Studies of Self-Reported Lies," by K. B. Serota, T. R. Levine, and F. J. Boster, 2010, *Human Communications Research*, *36*(1), p. 9 (https://doi.org/10.1111/j.1468-2958.2009.01366.x). Copyright 2010 by Oxford University Press. Reprinted with permission.

For instance, Pareto noted that 80% of the land in Italy at the time was owned by 20% of the population. Likewise, researchers have found that about 80% of criminal convictions in the United States are tied to just 20% of the population (Caspi et al., 2016). As professors, we have ventured a guess that 20% of the students account for 80% of the cases of people reporting that their dog ate their homework. It looks like deception also tends to follow the Pareto principle, with a handful of people accounting for the bulk of the dishonesty in the world around us.

IDENTIFYING THE BIG LIARS

In our own studies, we too have found a positively skewed distribution of liars. In one study, the participants reported telling an average of 2.4 lies per day, yet one person told 20 lies per day (Hart et al., 2019). Along with measuring lies per day, we have measured the number of lies people tell per week, as lying is more stable over a week than it is over a single day (Serota et al., 2021). In one study, participants reported telling an average of five lies per week, yet a small group lied considerably more; the top 10% of liars told over half of the lies, with one person lying 100 times per week (Hart, Curtis, & Randell, 2023). In a similar study we carried out (Hart et al., 2021), people told an average of 13 lies per week, but a small number of people said that they told over 100 lies per week. This research informs us of an important finding related to lying—a small group of big liars do most of the lying in U.S. society.

Big liars are not unique to any one culture: They have been detected in various cultural groups and around the world. Even among hunter–gatherer tribes, lying is commonplace, and some members of the tribes are recognized as big liars compared with others. For instance, the Hadza are a nomadic group of 300 hunter–gatherers who live around Lake Eyasi in the hinterlands of northern Tanzania. The Hadza men hunt for giraffes and zebras, while the women forage for tubers and berries (Marlowe, 2010). Anthropologists have found that the Hadza can exhibit blatant displays of selfish dishonesty (Apicella, 2018). The Hadza can also readily rank the people in their camp from the most honest to the most dishonest (K. M. Smith & Apicella, 2020). It turns out that the Hadza have big liars too.

This is our jumping-off point. We discuss lying in general, but we also examine the big liars more specifically. We are interested in studying the outliers in the world of dishonesty—people who lie more than everyone else or wreak havoc with their lies. We are after the people who make the average person look like a real Honest Abe. So, how do we separate those who belong to that elite group of prevaricators from those who are just typical, run-of-the-mill fibbers? If you were ever at an amusement park as a kid, you may recall a sign that read, "You must be *THIS* tall to ride," with a line indicating the requisite height. Some evidence suggests that prolific liars tell about five or more lies per day and make up around 5% of the population (Halevy at al., 2014; Serota & Levine, 2015; Serota et al., 2021). In our research, we have also found that the top 5% of liars each tell about five lies per day. Additionally, when we asked people how many lies someone would need to tell per day for their lying to be problematic, the typical response was five. Thus, five or more lies per day or the top 5% are probably good criteria for identifying big liars. While those cutoff scores can help identify big liars who lie frequently, it's important to keep in mind that some big liars tell fewer but significantly more problematic lies. To identify them, we need to look at the substantial mayhem their lies cause. Throughout this book, we work from the definition we presented earlier: Big liars are people who lie excessively or who tell big lies.

TRAITS OF BIG LIARS

If we want to identify and perhaps avoid big liars, it helps to know who to look for. A number of personal traits and situational factors are consistently associated with lying. Not surprisingly, big liars possess more of those features than the average person. In this section, we explain what those features are.

Age

Reminiscing about childhood lies, one person recalled, "My friend said his dad had eggs and beer for breakfast and then peed for 3 hours straight" (Spohr, 2018). Kids are notoriously dishonest, so it might not be surprising that youth is one trait that partly predicts who the big liars will be. The most prolific adult liars in the population tend to be young (Serota & Levine, 2015). This finding is not surprising given that lying peaks in late adolescence and then gradually declines across adulthood (Debey et al., 2015; Gerlach et al., 2019; Glätzle-Rützler & Lergetporer, 2015). In our own studies, we also have found that the biggest liars tend to be several years younger than the rest of our participants (Hart et al., 2021; Hart et al., 2023).

Gender

We have also explored whether gender is associated with the tendency to be a big liar. There are consistent gender differences in a number of behaviors and mental processes, such as aggression, sexuality, cognitive abilities, and mental health. When it comes to lying, there have been conflicting findings, with some studies showing substantial gender differences and others finding none. When those studies are taken together, it appears that men are slightly more dishonest than women—a difference of only 4% (Gerlach et al., 2019). Men and women also tend to tell different types of lies. While men are more inclined than women to tell self-serving lies, women are more apt to tell altruistic lies aimed at making someone else feel better or aimed at strengthening a relationship (DePaulo et al. 1996;

Erat & Gneezy, 2012; R. S. Feldman et al., 2002). When it comes to big liars, the evidence seems pretty clear that men are much more likely than women to be the most prolific liars (Hart et al., 2021; Markowitz, 2021; Serota & Levine, 2015).

Intelligence

Some have argued that intelligence might make someone a more capable liar. Just imagine if Albert Einstein had focused his immense cognitive resources on lying instead of relativity theory. However, no clear link has been observed between big liars and intelligence. Some researchers have found a link between higher intelligence and lying (Sarzyńska et al., 2017), while others have concluded that people with lower cognitive abilities are the ones who tend to lie most often (Littrell et al., 2021). We think that the jury is still out on whether big liars are more intelligent than people who lie less often. Perhaps highly intelligent people are more able to tell convincing lies than those with lower intelligence, but there is no convincing evidence that they take advantage of that ability.

Attitudes About Lying

Another approach to understanding who the big liars are is to look at people's attitudes about lying. If people consider lying to be immoral, we should expect them to be honest. But what if they have no qualms about lying? There is quite a bit of variability in people's attitudes about deceit, with some people seeing lying as very wrong and others viewing it as entirely permissible (Oliveira & Levine, 2008). Not surprisingly, we have found that the biggest liars tend to view lying as more morally acceptable than those who lie less often do (Hart et al., 2019). Most people have a need to see themselves as good and morally dutiful, so they are mostly honest (Ariely, 2012). When people break with their moral principles, they feel guilty. People who are unencumbered by feelings of guilt tend to lie significantly more than those who feel more guilty (Ashton & Lee, 2007, 2009; T. R. Cohen et al., 2012). Paying attention to people's moral attitudes about dishonesty will help you spot big liars.

Religiosity

Somewhat relatedly, we have examined whether religious beliefs and attitudes correspond with a person's tendency to lie a lot. In Christianity, Islam, Judaism, Buddhism, and Hinduism, and most other religious faith systems, dishonesty is discouraged (Zagorin, 1996). If religious adherents recognize honesty as important to their faith systems, it stands to reason that people with stronger religious convictions might be less likely to be big liars.

Some studies found that people with stronger religious beliefs were morally opposed to lying and lied less than people with less strong beliefs, but other studies found no connection between religiosity and dishonesty (Childs, 2013; Kramer & Shariff, 2016; Oliveira & Levine, 2008; Shalvi & Leiser, 2013). To address this controversy, we recently completed a large study in which we measured both religiosity and lying in several different ways (Cox et al., 2022). One clear finding was that the more religious a person was, the more negative was their attitude toward lying. They saw lying as wrong. However, we found that religious people seem to lie as much as nonreligious people do.

Relationship Style

Lying occurs within relationships, including parent and child, romantic, friendships, workplace, and so on, and a person's relationship style is related to their patterns of lying. Relationship styles, sometimes known as *attachment styles*, can be understood by looking at how one person connects or bonds with another (e.g., Ainsworth & Bowlby, 1991). Some people see others as safe, reliable, and warm, so they are comfortable letting down their guard and being vulnerable with others; these people are referred to as *securely attached*. Other people are psychologically independent and are often unresponsive to others or emotionally unavailable. These people have an *avoidant attachment style*. Others worry about abandonment, require reassurance, and are extremely sensitive to the judgments of others; these people have an *anxiously attached* style. People with anxious and avoidant attachment styles tend to lie more in romantic relationships, friendships, and with strangers than do people with secure attachment styles (Cole, 2001; Ennis et al., 2008). People with avoidant and anxious attachment styles use dishonesty to manage and regulate social attachments: People with avoidant styles tend to keep people at a distance, and people with anxious styles try to avoid negative judgment. So, knowing how a person approaches relationships can help you discern who is likely to be a big liar.

Self-Esteem

Commenting in an anonymous online forum about lying, one person wrote,

> I have a problem. It haunts me every day. My entire life is a lie. I've lied to my parents, my significant other, my closest friends, strangers. I made up everything about my life, and I can't go back because those lies ARE my life now. Everyone in my life thinks I'm perfect, but I'm the opposite. I lie about very big things. I lie about my accomplishments the most, however. People think I'm successful; I'm really not. . . . My lies were all about my image. . . . They were just for my own personal ego.

A woman we refer to as Amy began to notice her prolific lying in high school (Whyte, 2017). For instance, she lied to people about her sexual experiences: "I made up everything. I made up the name and everything about this fictitious person, and, yeah, that person actually never existed." Amy explained, "It wasn't the pleasure of telling the lie. It was the pleasure of the fact that I would be noticed because of telling the lie." Eventually Amy was telling 20 to 30 lies per day. "Pretty much everything out of my mouth was a lie," she said. Her lies were driven by her low self-esteem. "The whole purpose behind it was for my own self-satisfaction and to make me feel better about the person I was," she said. "I believed if I lied I would be perceived as someone who was better than who I was."

Big liars often have low self-esteem. People with low self-esteem believe that they lack good qualities and tend to see themselves as failures (Rosenberg, 1965). On the other hand, people with high self-esteem take a more satisfied and positive view of themselves. Like Amy, people with low self-esteem sometimes present an enhanced version of themselves to the world or may conceal their shortcomings to avoid a further decline in how the world might view them (J. E. Grant et al., 2019; Hart et al., 2019).

Dark Traits

Dave was a good-looking man in his 30s who was working on his third marriage. He was a relatively new employee of a fast-growing company and had come to the attention of a psychologist who was hired to help with organizational changes at the company (see Babiak, 1995). Dave's manager noted that he was often disruptive and offensive. While Dave impressed everyone with his intellect and drive, his boss soon noticed that Dave was copying other people's work and turning it in as his own. When confronted, Dave brushed aside the concerns and said that it would have been a waste of his time and talents to reinvent the wheel. Dave concocted lies to avoid meetings, to take advantage of people, to get out of projects he found boring or beneath him, or to shift blame to others. After only a few months on the job, his colleagues realized that Dave was consistently dishonest. They described him as a phony yet felt anxious about calling him out on his lies. When interviewed by the psychologist, Dave came across as superficially charming and egotistical. He fancied himself a key player in the company. He seemed unconcerned about the impression his colleagues had of him and seemed to view them as mere objects. When asked how he managed to get what he wanted at work, Dave said, without emotion, "I lied" (Babiak, 1995, p. 180).

Some people like Dave callously and remorselessly use lies to manipulate and victimize others. Some other more notorious examples are the serial killer Ted Bundy and the fraudster Bernie Madoff. What is it about their personalities that allowed them to casually use deception to take advantage of others? There is a cluster of personality traits, called the *dark triad* of personality traits, that is generally associated with a selfish disposition (Paulhus & Williams, 2002). The first of the dark traits is *Machiavellianism*, which is the tendency to engage in cold, self-interested manipulation of others. People with Machiavellian personalities are opportunistic and have little allegiance to conventional morality. They tend to see others as instruments they can use to achieve their own goals. Next is *narcissism*, which is a grandiose sense of self and a need for admiration, often coupled with a sense of entitlement and a disregard for the needs of others. Narcissists are self-absorbed and are often boastful. It seems like most workplaces have one. Finally, there is *psychopathy*, which is the tendency to engage in antisocial behavior, typically coupled with a lack of empathy or guilt. People high in psychopathy coldly and often impulsively violate the rights of others and frequently engage in criminal behavior. At their core, the dark triad traits share self-centeredness and diminished empathy. All three dark triad traits are correlated with excessive lying and other dishonest behaviors (Flexon et al., 2016; Halevy et al., 2014; Hart et al., 2019; Zvi & Elaad, 2018). If you interact with someone with these dark triad traits, you will likely observe that they use deception and other antisocial practices to get what they want.

Compassion and Empathy

In contrast to people high on the dark triad traits, we might expect empathic and compassionate people to lie very little. However, the relationship between empathic compassion and lying depends on the type of lies we are looking at. Compassion increases altruistic lying (Lupoli et al., 2017)—compassionate people are motivated to reduce harm, and that desire leads them to tell altruistic lies to spare feelings, reduce worry, and so on. For instance, if a compassionate parent noticed their child feeling down about their lack of musical ability, the parent might feel inclined to tell an altruistic lie: "I think you are one of the best musicians I've ever heard!" In contrast, compassion reduces self-serving lies. People who are deeply concerned with others around them are unlikely to use dishonesty to take advantage of those people. Likewise, empathy decreases self-serving lying, but it simultaneously increases altruistic lying (Pierce & Thompson, 2021; Xu et al., 2019).

Histrionicism

Another personality trait, *histrionicism*, is also associated with lying. Histrionic people tend to present themselves in a dramatic, attention-seeking manner (Renner et al., 2008). They often engage in overtly flirtatious or theatrical behavior in social settings. Their dramatic style is often aimed at drawing attention to themselves. They may act excessively emotional, intimate, or provocatively and become frustrated when others do not reassure them that they are the center of attention. We found that people who are high in histrionic traits are much more prone to be big liars (Weaver & Hart, 2022). It might be that dishonesty is just one way these people attempt to draw all attention to themselves.

Personality Traits

In our final analysis of personality traits that are associated with being a big liar, we examine what are referred to as the *Big Five* personality traits (Costa & McCrae, 1992). The Big Five are personality dimensions that are thought to best account for most of the variation in human dispositions. *Openness to experience* is the tendency to be open-minded, curious, and adventurous. *Conscientiousness* is an inclination toward being organized, dependable, and diligent. *Extraversion* is a disposition in which one is sociable, outgoing, and energetic. *Agreeableness* is the propensity to be warm, friendly, helpful, and tactful. Finally, *neuroticism* is the tendency to be emotionally unstable, irritable, and negative. We have found nuanced results, with certain personality traits corresponding to specific types of lies. Openness, conscientiousness, extraversion, and agreeableness were associated with fewer self-serving lies, while neuroticism was associated with more frequent self-serving lies. Higher conscientiousness was associated with telling fewer altruistic lies. Finally, high agreeableness was associated with telling fewer vindictive lies. When considering the Big Five personality traits, each type of lie seems to be associated with a somewhat different personality profile.

On the whole, we think there is good evidence that big liars tend to have a particular set of demographic and personality commonalities. The traits that correspond with higher rates of lying are the ones that should be predictive of being a big liar. If we can be mindful of the people in our lives who possess those traits, and especially if we can notice when people exhibit many of those traits together, we may identify big liars before we fall victim to their lies.

THE SITUATION

While understanding the person and their underlying personality traits can be helpful in understanding the propensity to lie, we should also give serious consideration to the situation. Most of us have probably been in situations in which we felt that lying was our best option for sparing someone's feelings, helping a friend out of a difficult spot, or avoiding some other catastrophic outcome. Even the most honest person might be tempted to lie if the contextual variables were just so. The psychologist Kurt Lewin (1936) offered an equation meant to account for human behavior. It is written as $B = f(PE)$, or behavior (B) is a function (f) of the person (P) and the environment (E). The equation can be understood as an explanatory system for all human behavior. It suggests that we cannot know about a person's tendency to lie simply by knowing their personality dispositions. We must also consider the context in which that person is operating and all the forces that are influencing them. An extremely honest person might start lying in a situation because it would spare someone's life, and an extremely dishonest person would likely stop lying in a situation in which they could easily have whatever they wanted through honest means. As it turns out, people do not lie at random. Rather, they lie when contextual variables motivate them to do so (Hart, 2022; T. R. Levine et al., 2016).

An incentive to lie must be present, either securing a desired consequence or avoiding a negative consequence (Bond et al., 2013; Gerlach et al., 2019; T. R. Levine, 2020). When it comes to lying, the situation may be much more powerful than personal characteristics in predicting when someone lies versus when they tell the truth

(Vedantam, 2018). So, what types of situations tend to be associated with being a big liar? An obvious condition is when people are violating the rules and expectations of others. Whether children behaving disobediently, spouses being unfaithful, or employees embezzling funds, people at risk of being harshly punished tend to lie. People also lie if they worry that the truth will harm others they care about. People lie to spare the feelings of people they care about, such as spouses and friends (DePaulo & Kashy, 1998; R. E. Turner et al., 1975). More broadly, people tend to lie when the truth will cause others to react in ways they want to avoid. However, people do not lie if their dishonesty is sure to be detected and punished. People lie when they feel confident they will get away with their deception (Fellner et al., 2013; Lundquist et al., 2009; Markowitz & Levine, 2021). Interestingly, anonymity or even the sense of anonymity increases lying. In one study, people who were in a darkened room were significantly more likely than those in a well-lit room to lie for a greater financial reward, even though the brightness of the room had no effect on anonymity (Zhong et al., 2010).

Our honesty or dishonesty is also influenced by the people around us. If people see lying as socially sanctioned, they are more apt to lie. For instance, if we see people with whom we identify (referred to as *ingroup members*) lying, we are more inclined to lie. Even seeing someone from the same school or who shares the same birthday lie is enough to influence people to deceive (Ariely, 2012; Gino & Galinsky, 2012). People are also more likely to be frequent liars if they affiliate with frequent liars (Mann et al., 2014). Birds of a feather flock together, even when it comes to dishonesty. Additionally, people in groups become more dishonest than they were as individuals (T. R. Cohen et al., 2009; Kocher et al., 2018). It seems that being in a group allows one to spread blame or moral responsibility for dishonesty to all the other group members, leaving every individual person feeling less culpable.

Looking at lying from a broad cultural level, we can see that dishonesty is imbued in the fabric of some cultures more than others (see J. A. Barnes, 1994, for a review). For instance, one study found that people around the globe are mostly honest, but the citizens of Switzerland, Norway, and the Netherlands were more honest than the people of Peru, Morocco, and China (Cohn et al., 2019). It is unlikely that people from one region are inherently more honest or dishonest than people from another region. It is more likely that some countries simply have social or cultural structures in place that promote or minimize the motivation to be dishonest. A study of people in 23 different countries showed that the amount of dishonesty in each country was correlated with the amount of institutionalized rule-breaking, such as government corruption, election fraud, and tax evasion, that occurred within those countries (Gächter & Schulz, 2016). In countries where rule violations were rampant, people in experimental settings were more likely to lie for financial gain. It seems that people adjust their levels of honesty or deception to the context in which they live. People surrounded by dishonesty will tend to be dishonest themselves.

Another situational feature associated with frequent lying is the presence of moral reminders and moral commitments. Moral reminders and moral commitments can be presented in the form of honor codes that people are asked to sign (Mazar et al., 2008). By signing honor codes (usually at schools or workplaces), people agree not to engage in dishonest behavior. People who sign honor codes lie significantly less than those who do not. In a study on moral reminders, the researchers asked participants to sit in front of a mirror. The idea was that seeing oneself would be a moral reminder, in particular that seeing oneself misbehave would be an unavoidable reminder of one's moral shortcomings. People who were seated in front of a mirror were much more honest than people who were not. However, not all moral reminders seem to be effective. The researchers found that having people reflect on the Ten Commandments from the Bible had no discernible effect on lying (Verschuere et al., 2018).

People's level of moral engagement is not stable, but rather it is high in the morning and then fades through the day. Interestingly, people were much more likely to be honest at the start of the day and increasingly more likely to be dishonest as the afternoon rolls around (Kouchaki & Smith, 2014). A similar effect appears with sleep deprivation—people deprived of sleep lie more (C. M. Barnes et al., 2011). Also, we can cause moral disengagement by wearing people down with a mentally taxing computer task. Once worn down, people lie more (Gino et al., 2011). All this research informs us that big liars may lie more in situations that decrease their moral engagement. Taken another way, we can reduce the odds of people lying to us if we can increase their moral engagement.

Let's consider one last situational variable that influences lying. As we can all attest, interacting with a wonderful person can brighten your day, and interacting with a jerk can ruin your day. Those situational variables are important in determining the honesty or dishonesty of people in social situations. In one clever study, the researchers gave participants false scathing feedback about an essay they had written (Yip & Schweitzer, 2016). Soon thereafter, the upset people were placed in a situation in which they could either lie or tell the truth. The upset people were much more likely to lie. In another study, researchers found the same effect in the opposite direction. People who were made to feel happy and grateful by someone else were much more inclined to be honest afterward than were people who were not (DeSteno et al., 2019). It seems that feeling threatened or attacked leads people to lie more frequently (Tangney et al., 2007; Yip & Schweitzer, 2016).

We hope we have made the case that big liars are not always inherently dishonest people. Rather, big liars seem to be products of both their innate dispositions and the contexts and situations they inhabit. If we want to identify the big liars in our world, we should be mindful of both.

A THEORY OF LYING

Deception researchers have uncovered a copious amount of information about the traits of people who lie frequently and the types of situations in which they are most likely to lie. The information allows us to piece together an understanding of who the big liars are and what factors seem to underlie their dishonesty. Taking all that information together, a theoretical perspective begins to emerge. We can begin to distill the tangle of data and identify a clear set of features that are common among liars. A theory of liars can be crafted.

Liars have similar reasons for lying, namely, the prospect of speaking truthfully seems antagonistic to their goals. Speaking honestly, at least in their assessment, would lead to undesirable outcomes. Honesty impedes the pursuit of goals for people prone to lying. Thus, concealing the truth seems more attractive. Also, liars believe they can get away with their deception. People don't lie if they think they will be caught unless they view the consequences of being caught as relatively minor. Thus, liars assess the risk of lying, which includes the probability of being caught and the consequences of being caught as well as any other negative outcomes that might be produced by the lie. Finally, we can also see that people have, to varying degrees, a need to maintain their self-images; many want to preserve a vision of themselves as honest, good people (Cressey, 1953; Frank, 1987; Mazar et al., 2008). Most will refrain from substantial lying because it violates their moral principles. People who lie more freely are less concerned about morality, or they find it easier to morally justify their dishonesty. From these conclusions, we have formulated a theory of lying, called the *tripartite theory of lying and dishonesty*, that hinges on three criteria (Hart, 2022). The first is the perceived utility of lying.

The Expected Utility of Lying (U)

Utility, a concept from the field of economics, is the satisfaction that is derived from something. People lie when they think lying will produce some satisfying outcome or utility. They behave dishonestly when they spot an opportunity for dishonesty to allow them access to desirable outcomes that honesty would not. When people have violated rules, lying allows them to escape punishment. When they spot an opportunity for nefarious gain, a lie might help them go undetected. The utility of lying might also stem from avoiding the dangers posed by others who are more threatening and powerful. But people also lie for more noble reasons, such as to spare the feelings of a loved one. Still, lies occur when the liar spots an opportunity to get a desirable result that honesty would not produce. For the most part, people tend to lie when the truth will cause others to think, feel, or react in ways they want to avoid.

The Expected External Disutility of Lying (ED)

Disutility, or *negative utility*, is a concept that encompasses the idea that something produces an unsatisfactory outcome. People lie when they expect the disutility of lying to be low. That is, they tend to behave dishonestly when they think their dishonesty will go undetected or when they expect that the consequences of detection are tolerable. People do not lie if their dishonesty is likely to be detected and punished harshly. In short, people consider the bad outcomes that may follow dishonesty.

The Expected Internal Disutility of Lying (ID)

Internal disutility is an intrinsic aversion to something. People can conceptualize a higher moral realm that they perceive as satisfying. People usually behave morally (honestly) to feel the satisfaction of being in that higher moral realm. Likewise, people generally avoid dishonesty because it leads to moral dissatisfaction or a degraded sense of self. When we notice that we are behaving immorally, most of us feel the weight of shame, guilt, and regret. We have a moral aversion to lying per se.

However, people have a remarkable capacity to ethically justify their dishonesty. They manage to convince themselves that they are lying for the greater good ("My lie will prevent many other bad things from happening"). They devalue the target of their dishonesty ("That person doesn't deserve the truth because they have always been a jerk to me"). They use counterfactuals to rationalize their lying ("If others were in this situation, they would do the same thing"). Also, people will engage in a form of moral accounting to justify their dishonesty ("I was honest all week, so a little lie right now isn't that bad").

Taken together, the tripartite theory of lying and dishonesty (see Figure 1.3) predicts when people will lie and when they will refrain from lying. Essentially, if we can understand when people see a utility in lying, when they perceive external disutility, and when they expect to feel internal disutilities, we can predict the circumstances in which people will be dishonest. For example, imagine a mother who cannot afford the expensive medical treatment for her severely ill child. Now imagine that if she lied on a form about having medical insurance, the doctor would deliver the treatment. We can see how that mother might see a strong utility in lying. Now further imagine that she knows that doctor is very sympathetic and would likely not report her to the police should the lie be discovered. In that case,

FIGURE 1.3. Tripartite Theory of Lying and Dishonesty

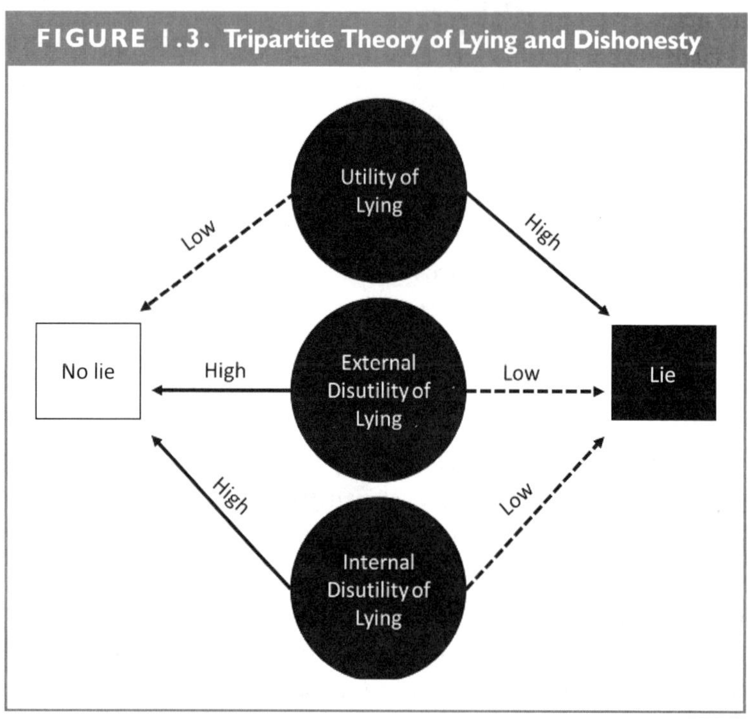

the mother might rightly perceive a low external disutility of lying. Suppose even further that the doctor normalized lying by saying to the mother, "I know a lot of people who can't afford this treatment simply lie on the insurance form, and I think that is not a bad thing to do," as he winks at her and hands her a pen. We might surmise that the mother would now view the lie as morally permissible. The tripartite theory of lying and dishonesty tells us that mothers in this situation would be much more likely to lie than they would if the child were less ill, the consequences of being caught lying were harsh, and the doctor discussed the importance of absolute honesty. The theory lets us know who tends to be honest and who tends to lie.

THE THEORY OF BIG LIARS

The tripartite theory of lying and dishonesty addresses situations in which we might expect people to lie. However, it also predicts who is likely to be a big liar. Big liars are simply people who meet the three criteria regularly. That is, big liars are people who consistently see a utility or an upside to lying, consistently view the probability and consequences of being caught as tolerable, and consistently view their lying as morally or ethically permissible. Using this theoretical perspective, we can break down the three elements of being a big liar.

The first criterion is that big liars see some advantage to lying. They consistently calculate that others will respond in undesirable ways if they are honest. So, who are these big liars? For starters, they are people who are regularly doing bad things and don't want to be caught and punished. A thief is likely to lie regularly to cover their tracks. A spy will need to lie frequently for the same reasons. A kid with difficult-to-please parents is likely to lie to conceal violations of rules. Importantly, people with things to hide are not always bad people. Gay children growing up in intolerant homes may lie to conceal their sexual identities from parents who might treat them harshly. People with a high need for approval may lie to receive the approval they desire from others. People who feel unworthy may lie to seem less deficient. Someone who worries they are boring may lie to seem more interesting. A lazy person may lie to seem more productive. People with low self-esteem may lie considerably. Big liars can also be people who constantly worry that their honesty will harm others. They may lie often because they don't want to hurt people's feelings, or perhaps they want to boost someone's ego when that person appears fragile. In all cases, liars lie to avoid unwanted outcomes.

According to the second criterion, big liars consistently view the risk of being caught as tolerable. Risk is a function of both probability and consequences. Any time someone lies, there is a probability that their lie will be detected and there will be consequences if they are caught. Big liars regularly compute the probability of being caught as acceptable or they assess the consequences of being detected as acceptable (at least compared to the consequences of being honest). Big liars believe they have a workable lie that can reasonably substitute for the truth. Who are these people? Certainly, people who are confident in their ability to get away with lies. People who feel well-equipped for deception are likely to lie more. Big liars will also believe the consequences of detection are tolerable. They could simply underestimate the negative outcomes of being caught in a lie. They are also likely to believe that lying is tolerated by others. We have seen, for example, in certain cultures lying is more tolerated than in others. They may also be more willing to tolerate risk. Risk-averse people are probably less inclined to gamble by telling a lie. Additionally, we might expect people with a short-term focus to lie more than people with a long-term focus do. Lying is often more attractive than honesty in the moment, but if the lie were to be discovered days later, the consequences could be enormous. Finally, people who are less likely to suffer severe consequences if their lies were discovered might lie more frequently. Those with nothing to lose may be more apt to lie.

The third criterion is that big liars will view their lying as a morally or ethically permissible alternative to honesty. We might expect to see big liars emerging from subcultures in which lying is tolerated or viewed as morally permissible. People who don't consider the morality of their behavior are likely to lie more often. Psychopaths and Machiavellian types who have lax moral systems should be expected to lie more. People who do not value cooperation and group harmony should view lying as more acceptable. Also, people who believe others are lying to them or otherwise treating them unfairly should be more inclined to lie reciprocally. In this vein, we expect that people who feel oppressed or morally violated will lie frequently to their oppressors.

Additionally, we can expect that big liars will justify their behaviors morally and ethically via belief systems, such as *just-world beliefs* (i.e., people get what they deserve) or by blaming the victims (i.e., people are victimized because they somehow bring about their own exploitation). Researchers have found that people who are prone to guilt lie less than people who are unencumbered by those feelings. We expect big liars to view their lies as being relatively harmless and therefore justifiable. Similarly, we expect people with lower levels of empathy to tell more antisocial lies and people higher in empathy to be more inclined to tell altruistic lies.

This theory of liars provides a convenient way of organizing ideas about when and why people are dishonest. We refer to it as we move through this book discussing big liars. Lying is driven by external incentives, such as the desire to secure gains that could not be had through honesty, and by internal incentives, such as the desire to view oneself as a morally upstanding person. We find that big liars are heavily incentivized to depart from the truth and to use deception to achieve their goals.

CONCLUSION

We have introduced definitions of lying and of big liars. We have offered a detailed depiction of the frequency of lying, showing that most people are honest most of the time but big liars are statistical outliers who lie considerably more than the rest. We characterized the traits and characteristics of big liars as well as the contexts and situations in which they are most likely to lie. Finally, we offered a theory of big liars that considers their incentives and allows us to accurately predict who will be the big liars in our lives. We think that big liars are a distinguishable group of people whose prolific and consequential lying can be predicted from a cluster of individual and situational variables.

In the chapters that follow, we examine examples of the various big liars in our world. We explore how they lie and how their lies affect the people around them. But first we consider the development of big liars. Why do most people develop into fairly honest individuals, whereas some become big liars?

CHAPTER 2

FROM BABY FIBBERS TO ADULT DECEIVERS

> *My 6-year-old told his acting teacher his parents were dead and he's home-schooled. All lies. Is this a thing?*
>
> —A question posted on a parenting forum

By the time the FBI tracked down 17-year-old Graham Ivan Clark, his arrest was perhaps the only plausible capstone of his long history of childhood lies (Popper et al., 2020). The 30 felony charges against him, including organized fraud over $50,000, were just some more consequences of young Graham's years-long habit of using deception to take advantage of people who entered his sphere of influence. At age 10, Graham became very involved in online collaborative video games. In that gaming world, he developed a reputation for using deceit to scam other players out of money. He offered to sell other players accessories for their online gaming characters, but then he disappeared with the cash without delivering the goods. He also offered to sell other players cool usernames that he claimed to own, only to slyly vanish once he received payment. The gamers were left wondering why they had fallen for the scam. While Graham's double-dealing shenanigans may sound like child's play, the fruits of his lies enriched him. Graham boasted that his online gaming scams were netting him thousands of dollars each month.

By his mid-teens, Graham had moved into the world of computer hacking. Even in that shadowy world with its fair share of nefarious actors, young Graham was known as a cheat. He was eventually banned from an online hacker forum for agreeing to pay people for various services, only to later renege on the deal.

As his lies and schemes continued through his mid-teens, Graham developed a special interest in the cryptocurrency Bitcoin. In 2019, 16-year-old Graham was allegedly involved in an incident in which hackers made off with almost a million dollars of Bitcoin from the account of an unsuspecting investor. He is then alleged to have tried to extort even more Bitcoin from his hapless victim. Graham's lying had become the engine behind a lucrative operation. Though unemployed, he managed to afford his own waterfront apartment, a BMW, and a jewel-encrusted Rolex watch. Graham's earlier schemes had flown under the radar of law enforcement, but his nearly million-dollar Bitcoin heist drew their attention. The U.S. Secret Service zeroed in on him and recovered much of what was stolen, returning the Bitcoin to its rightful owner. Interestingly enough, the authorities did not charge Graham because he was a minor.

The brush with law enforcement had only a brief effect on him, if any. Just weeks after the run-in with the Secret Service, he began his boldest con job yet. At only 17 years old, Graham Clark set his hacker sights on Twitter. He hatched a plan in which he would steal the accounts of well-known public figures and then use those accounts to scam people out of Bitcoin. The heart of this scam rested on a simple lie. Graham contacted a Twitter employee and convinced that person that he was a coworker in the information technology department. He convinced the Twitter employee to provide login information that he was then able to use to access Twitter's computer systems (Al Jazeera, 2020).

Once he had infiltrated Twitter's computer systems, Graham took control of accounts owned by high-profile people, such as Joe Biden, Barack Obama, Elon Musk, Mike Bloomberg, Amazon founder Jeff Bezos, Bill Gates (the founder of Microsoft), and Kim Kardashian. With all other pieces of the scam in place, Graham executed the final element: He sent out tweets from the accounts that he had hijacked. Thus, the tweets appeared to be coming directly from Obama, Musk, and the other high-profile people. Although each tweet was tailored to sound like it was coming from a real account, they all had the same theme—getting people to send Bitcoin to an anonymous account owned by Graham. Consider an example of the tweet sent from the billionaire Bill Gates's Twitter account: "Everyone is asking me to give back, and now is the time. I am doubling all payments sent to my BTC (*Bitcoin*) address for the next 30 minutes. You send $1000, I send you back $2000." Wow! What a generous offer Mr. Gates was making. Over the next few hours, many dupes fell prey to the scam, sending about $120,000 in Bitcoin to Graham's account before Twitter was able to shut down the operation.

Two weeks later, Graham Clark was in court, charged along with his two accomplices with a string of felonies. According to prosecutors, Graham was the mastermind of this scam. Despite his young age, prosecutors charged him as an adult, and the judge set his bail at $725,000. Part of the reason his bail was so high was that Graham was worth more than $3 million, not including his haul from the Twitter scam. The teenager had used his constant lies to net a small fortune before his Twitter scam led to his downfall. Graham was eventually sentenced to 3 years in jail.

BEGINNINGS

Reflecting on Graham and other kids like him, one wonders how they develop into big liars. Is there a specific event that sets them off on a path of chronic lying, or are they simply destined to lie prolifically? Perhaps dishonesty is coded in their genes and baked into their basic nature at birth. Could it be that all kids start off as liars, but most transition into honest adults, with a small handful carrying on with deception? When do children move from being sweet purveyors of the truth to scheming little prevaricators? In this chapter, we examine when and why kids wade into the world of deception.

Infants are not born into the world with the capacity to lie. Even after they learn to speak, most children remain quite honest for some time. However, at a certain point in early cognitive development, children start to develop into proficient deceivers. The onset of lying is tied to the development of new cognitive abilities, such as empathy, perspective taking, and realizing that others can hold different beliefs. Early childhood environments begin to shape the degree to which one tells lies. In this chapter, we first explore how and why kids begin to lie and will then explore why some depart on more deceitful trajectories and become big liars. Then we examine the factors that lead to kids becoming big liars, and we explore some psychological disorders that may underlie many cases of prolific lying.

The study of the development of lying began with Charles Darwin in the early 1840s. Darwin made systematic observations of his son Erasmus's development, including his reflexes, emotions, morality, cognitive processes, and language. He also described the first instance in which he witnessed young Erasmus lying at age 2 years, 8 months:

> I met him coming out of the same room, and he was eyeing his pinafore which he had carefully rolled up; and again his manner was so odd that I determined to see what was within his pinafore, notwithstanding that he said there was nothing and repeatedly commanded me to "go away," and I found it stained with pickle-juice; so that here was carefully planned deceit. (Darwin, 1877, p. 292)

Modern studies that examine the development of lying are ingenious examples of entrapment (Lewis et al., 1989). Researchers bring a child into a lab room and seat them. Then, on a table behind the child, the researcher unpacks a toy but instructs the child not to turn around and look at it. The researcher then says that they have to leave the room for a minute, but they remind the child not to turn around and look at the toy. Ignoring the instructions of the adult, the children typically turn around and catch a glimpse of the toy. Unbeknownst to the young research subject, the whole episode is video recorded so that the researcher can have objective confirmation of what the child does in their absence. When the researcher finally returns, they ask the child, "Did you peek?" At this point, the child must decide whether to come clean about their rule violation or to conceal their misdeed with a lie.

WHEN THE LYING BEGINS

Kids don't enter the world lying, though it is an ability that emerges early in their development. Their first forays into deception are often clumsy and transparent. In one study using the aforementioned "don't peek at the toy" paradigm, the toy that was used was a purple dinosaur from the television show *Barney*. When one child was asked if she peeked, she lied and said, "No." She then said, "I didn't peek at it. I touched it, and it felt purple. So, I think it is Barney" (K. Lee, 2013, p. 93). Only about 30% of 2-year-olds lie in laboratory studies, but more than 50% of 3-year-olds lie. By age 4, over 70% lie, and at age 5 and beyond, the percentage who lie levels off at slightly more than 80%. As they gain more experience lying, they cover their lies in sophisticated ways. Young kids accurately mimic the behaviors of people who tell the truth. For instance, when lying, they deliberately make eye contact while lying, just as honest kids do while telling the truth (Talwar & Lee, 2002a). So, kids start lying at age 2, and by age 5, most seem to have the hang of it. However, like adults, not all children lie at the same rate. Some are fairly honest, while others are big liars (Hall, 1890; Healy & Healy, 1915).

Because big liars emerge in childhood, we should look at why they make their first forays into lying; we can see that they start lying for the same reason that most adults lie: Lying serves their self-interests (Ding et al., 2018). As kids are exposed to more and more situations in which a lie would help them get what they want, they soon learn that lying works. In one study, researchers played with young children a game in which a treat could be earned, but the only way to win was to lie (Ding et al., 2018). They played this game several times over 10 days. On the first day of play, the kids only lied on 12% of the trials. However, by the 10th day of the study, the kids lied 84% of the time. It seemed that repeated exposure to opportunities to lie for gains was key to the emergence of lying in young kids. To put this finding in terms of the tripartite theory of lying and dishonesty, we can say that kids recognize that lying has some utility. Their first lies tend to be fibs told to avoid the consequences of some misdeed. But also like adults, not all lies that young kids tell are aimed at avoiding negative consequences or procuring ill-gotten gains. Kids also tell lies to spare people's feelings (Talwar et al., 2007). The art of deceptively massaging the truth to protect the egos of others is firmly in place by the time most kids reach age 7. By that age, children have learned the social conventions of deception. They have learned that when someone serves up a meal that is less than stellar, one should conceal the hurtful truth that the meal was subpar, and say something supportive like, "That was great. I like it!" In fact, kids who don't learn that form of dishonest tact are often considered immature or rude.

Kids who tell self-serving lies for personal gain or to avoid punishment also tend to tell prosocial lies to be polite or helpful (Talwar et al., 2019). As kids get older, they tend to tell more prosocial lies and fewer selfish lies. Interestingly, children are consistent in their practice of lying over time. Kids who tend to be big liars at age 3 still tend to be big liars at age 6 (Talwar et al., 2019). However, there are several trajectories of lying across childhood. Some children tell mostly selfish lies when they are young but shift to more prosocial lying when they are older. Some tell no prosocial lies when young but do when older. However, some kids tell selfish lies when young and then continue to tell them as they get older. Are these children the budding big liars? This pattern of persistent selfish lying may be evidence that once big liars find that deception works for them, they stay with that strategy.

In one anonymous online forum, a father wrote,

> My daughter is only 9! She lies about everything! Big ones small ones, it's all the same to her. . . . She'd steal my soda and I'd ask her. She'd say no and I'd find the bottle in her room. It's not just when she steals stuff it's also when she wants to play with friends. She'll ask if she can go play in the club house and I'll say yes and she decides to go to her friend's house. Or ask if she washed her hair or brushed her teeth and hair. She responds yeah. Even if her hair is still ratty. I'm at a loss . . . I've tried everything.

Also from an anonymous online forum, another man wrote of his 12-year-old daughter,

> She constantly lies. . . . She has been claiming she was in a gang, stabbed someone, was pregnant, was from Sweden. . . . We live in a rural area, there are no gangs here and she isn't from Sweden. She most certainly hasn't stabbed anyone. She created 15 different email accounts all with different identities on different chat apps. Each of her alter personalities has bad habits, like drugs, violence, stealing or criminal behavior. I am confused and don't know what to do.

Kids learn to lie early, and they soon learn to lie proficiently. Their proclivity for dishonesty seems to peak during late adolescence and then begins a slow decline across adulthood (L. A. Jensen et al., 2004; T. R. Levine et al., 2013). While adults lie, on average, 1.65 times per day, teenagers lie, on average, 4.1 times per day. In fact, 95% of teenagers report lying on any given day. Though most teens lie on most days, the pattern of lying in teenagers is similar to that of adults—a small subset of the population accounts for a disproportionate share of the lies that are told. In one study, just 10% of teenagers accounted for a third of the lies that were told. The biggest liars told as many as 17 lies in one day (T. R. Levine et al., 2013). The vast majority of teenagers say that they lie to their parents, but they tell lies to their friends just as often. If we look at the topics of their lies, they seem to lie the most about their friends, followed by money, parties, alcohol and drugs, dating, and sex (L. A. Jensen et al., 2004). Teenage boys tend to lie about money, alcohol, and drugs more than girls do, but boys and girls do not differ regarding how much they lie about other topics.

Given how often children lie to their parents, you might wonder if parents can accurately detect those lies. In lab studies, parents detected that their child was lying only about 41% of the time. It was easiest to detect their lies when the children were young (53% accuracy), but by the time kids got close to age 11, parents correctly detected lies only about 27% of the time (Talwar et al., 2015). Like adults, most kids can lie capably and believably.

THINKING AND LYING

Why don't kids lie as soon as they can speak? Why does it take them around 3 years to get the hang of it, and why do they get better and better at lying as they age? It seems that lying is like many other behaviors. Certain cognitive abilities underlie the complex task of deception, and those cognitive systems aren't fully developed at birth. It takes time for the systems that handle lying to develop. Once they are developed, children start lying. Those cognitive systems continue to mature through childhood, and accordingly, the capacity to weave believable lies advances in tandem. Once a person moves from adolescence into adulthood, all cognitive faculties are fully formed, and the machinery of lying is wholly forged. The person has become an entirely capable liar and has the psychological hardware to be a big liar.

As easy as lying may seem, it is actually a very complex task for a child to pull off. First, they must be able to represent the minds of others and understand that other minds can hold other knowledge and beliefs. They must understand that other minds can possess accurate representations of the world, but those other minds can also hold inaccurate information. The kids must come to the powerful realization that they can promote false beliefs in others. In essence, they can control others by manipulating information and beliefs. To lie, a child must possess the executive function capacity to remember and track truthful information about the world. They also must be able to generate believable false information. This ability to contrive false narratives involves the creative construction of alternative realities. They must then be able to keep track of that untruthful information. They must also be able to inhibit truthful responses. They must be able to appear innocent and honest, which means that they need to know what they typically look like when being honest. They must be able to perform all of those mental and behavioral tasks, often with no forewarning and with the need for an immediate response. With that level of sophisticated analysis, creative production, memory, and strategic planning, it is no wonder that it takes years for children to tell their first lie. It is also no wonder that it takes several more years for them to tell the calculating dishonest tales that would fool the most suspicious interrogator.

If we uncover the hardware of the mind, we discover some essential components of the machinery of deception. Perhaps foremost, to be a successful liar, a child must have language. As children get older, they use increasingly complex styles of language to mislead others (Hu et al., 2020). They also begin to understand the minds of others. This ability to make accurate attributions of others' mental states is called *theory of mind* (Premack & Woodruff, 1978). Children develop the ability to use the sparse cues from others' behavior and context to infer their plans, intentions, goals, and feelings. Theory of mind is crucial for deceiving others. To effectively fool people in sophisticated ways, big liars need to be able to see things from their target's perspective, and to do that, they need to be able to get inside the heads of others. Interestingly, if you take kids who do not yet lie and you train them to see things from another's perspective, they start telling lies (Ding et al., 2015). Perspective taking seems key to the emergence of big liars.

Ironically, another developmental key for lying is empathy. When a friend asks if their new haircut looks unflattering, we don't dare tell them that it does, even if we believe the haircut is awful. We can feel their uneasiness, anxiety, or uncertainty, so we feel compelled to allay those feelings with a supportive lie. Very young children often don't display this empathic warmth. With no hesitation at all, a child will look someone in the eye and say, "Your breath stinks!" People are not born with the gift of empathy, but fortunately, it is a faculty that develops early in life. Children who have developed an empathic understanding of others tend to conceal hurtful truths with lies and other forms of deception (Nagar et al., 2020). Big liars are successful because they have learned early how people feel.

Other sets of cognitive skills linked to the emergence of lying are referred to as *executive functions* (Alloway et al., 2015; Ding et al., 2018; Lewis, 2015; Talwar & Lee, 2008). Executive functioning includes processes, such as attention, cognitive flexibility, working memory, and decision making. Complex lying relies on all these cognitive operations. One must notice the opportunity to lie, concoct a false narrative that does not conflict with known facts, generate a believable counternarrative, and then remember that lie going forward. Imagination and creativity are critical too (Harris, 2000). For kids to tell convincing lies, they must be able to mold a new and believable reality—one that does not actually exist (Byrne, 2005). Big liars are not born into the world with the capacity to deceive others. A great many mental processes must develop and mature before they can convince others of something that is untrue.

TRAJECTORIES

So, what determines which kids largely refrain from lying as they move into adulthood and which ones go on to be big liars? Recent research suggests that children have different lying trajectories. Some of them chart a course in which they are mostly honest; some swerve into a pattern of dishonesty for a bit but ultimately return to a fairly honest routine. Others, however, depart on a lasting trajectory of prolific lying. We have begun to understand the combination of factors that shapes those trajectories and lead to the emergence of big liars. All psychological patterns have their roots in a complex interplay between the genes we inherit from our biological parents and the myriad experiences we have with other people and the world around us, which we refer to as the *environment*. Patterns of dishonesty are no exception. The trajectory of big liars begins early in life. The development of big liars hinges on the complex interactions between a person's underlying genetic predispositions and biology and the environmental factors of the social worlds that they inhabit.

GENES

When it comes to genetic predispositions toward lying, there is no big-liar gene. Like all complicated psychological traits, the tendency to be dishonest is influenced by a complex constellation of genes.

Multiple genes influencing a single trait is referred to as a *polygenetic effect*. Multiple genes come together to shape one's tendencies toward sincerity or deceitfulness. Rather than a single gene that either causes one to be a liar or causes one to be truthful, each person carries a whole host of genes that each incrementally pushes them toward a habit of integrity or a penchant for the lie (Ahern et al., 1982; Eaves et al., 1999; Loewen et al., 2013; Shen et al., 2016; P. A. Young et al., 1980). As a consequence of this polygenetic effect, honesty and dishonesty exist along a continuum rather than as discrete categories. For this reason, it is artificial to have distinct categories, such as "normal liar" and "big liar." We all exist to some degree on the lying spectrum. Some lie very little, and some lie a lot. Nature has no cutoff point that marks one as belonging to the honest camp or the liar camp. But to be sure, some people have inherited more genes that predispose dishonesty than others have. For most people, their collection of genes leads them to be fairly average or typical in their innate impulses toward deception. Others, however, inherited the full menu of genes that might incline them toward double-dealing. These unlucky winners of the genetic lottery may find that lying comes much more easily, and manipulating others feels as natural as breathing. No genetic test currently highlights who is likely to be dishonest and who is not, but with rapid advances, such as genome-wide association tests, that day may not be far off (Duncan et al., 2019). The best evidence suggests that people's genes account for about 30% of the variability in dishonesty in the population, meaning that whether someone is a big liar or not may depend more on their environment than their biology (Loewen et al., 2013).

THE ENVIRONMENT

The genes that children carry influence their psychology in important ways, but children do not develop in a vacuum. Big liars are also shaped by the environments they occupy. From the moment of conception and throughout childhood, the world exerts forces on them and those forces affect development. Those forces include teratogenic factors, such as prenatal alcohol and lead exposure; local environmental conditions, such as disease prevalence and weather; nutritional variables, such as water availability and caloric sufficiency; and many others. The world kids live in influences who they will become. One factor that greatly influences how honest kids will be is the social world in which they operate. From birth onward, children are taught, cajoled, punished, encouraged, and led by a host of characters, starting with parents and close family members and then broadening to friends, teachers, and figures from their community, and finally by the wider society in which they mature. Each of these social entities bends the development of a child's character, even their affinity for honesty.

Kids who are likely to become big liars have home lives that influence them in that direction. Specifically, parents can have a powerful influence on their children's honesty or dishonesty. Most cultures share a pervasive social norm that parents attempt to instill in their children: One should not lie. Early on, kids make their first fumbling attempts to deceive. They adamantly deny having drawn on the furniture, even though they are still clutching the pen. What parents do next will alter the course of their young child's journey into the world of deception. Some parents might fly into a fit of rage, some may dole out cool-headed punishment, others may laugh at the absurdity of the lie, while others may attempt to have a nice conversation about morality, trust, and the importance of honesty.

Punitive environments seem to be fertile grounds for cultivating big liars. When kids perceive that their mistakes and rule violations will be punished harshly, they tend to lie (Talwar et al., 2015; Talwar & Lee, 2011). If adults make clear that kids will not be punished for their transgressions as long as they are honest, kids tend to be honest. However, if adults ask kids to be honest but also indicate that transgressions will be punished, kids tend to lie. In line with the tripartite theory of lying and dishonesty, if a kid believes that their misdeeds will be met with punishment rather than understanding, that child is likely to consider lying as an option.

This pattern can be seen in an example. Two groups of children attend separate schools in West Africa (Talwar & Lee, 2011). One school takes a nonpunitive approach to child misbehavior and does not use any form of corporal punishment. The other school is much more punitive. Order is maintained through the regular use of corporal punishment, such as slapping children, pinching them, and hitting them with sticks. Even minor offenses, such as getting a math problem wrong, can sometimes earn a slap on the head. As you probably expect, children in the punitive environment are much more likely to lie. People tend to lie when they believe honesty will bring about undesired consequences. In punitive environments, lying offers a utility that would not be there in less punitive environments.

Big liars also adopt their dishonest patterns by imitating the behavior of dishonest people around them (Engarhos et al., 2020; Hays & Carver, 2014). Kids are very adept at learning by watching others (Bandura et al., 1961). This social learning is how kids acquire language, learn how to eat, and figure out the rules of humor. Every parent who has heard their child use the F-word for the first time knows the peril of inadvertently modeling inappropriate behavior in front of a kid. One way that parents can lead their children down the path to becoming big liars is to model lying themselves (Santos et al., 2017). When parents lie a lot, their kids also tend to lie a lot. It seems that being immersed in an environment of deception shapes kids' morals and behaviors. Additionally, people who are reared by parents who lied considerably have poorer social outcomes in adulthood than do those raised in a more honest environment. If kids are reared in an environment where dishonesty abounds, they will adopt the propensity to tell lies.

Almost all parents tell their kids that lying is wrong. However, some parents have more permissive attitudes about lying than others. Some parents tell their children that while lying is inappropriate, it is necessary in some circumstances (Lavoie et al., 2017). Children raised by these more permissive parents are significantly more likely to tell lies. On the other hand, parents who instill the rule that lying is always wrong are more likely to have kids who adhere to honesty. Kids are taught behavioral norms by their caregivers. They are also indoctrinated into moral norms at an early age. If that moral instruction allows for lying, then kids will tend to lie (Setoh et al., 2020). The theory of dishonesty posits that moral discomfort is one thing that inhibits lying. When lying is viewed as morally or ethically permissible, there is little reason to be honest all the time.

It is not just the parents who influence kids to lie (Nagar et al., 2019). Children mimic their brothers' and sisters' behaviors. By watching their sibling lie and manipulate, kids learn to do the same (O'Connor & Evans, 2018). Having both younger or older siblings appears to increase the odds that a child will lie.

When considering the effects of the environment, behavioral geneticists draw a distinction between those aspects of childhood environments that siblings in a home share and those that they do not share. For instance, all siblings in a home will typically have identical access to the same types of food, television, computers, and books in the home, and roof over their heads. Scientists refer to this as the *shared environment*. However, kids in the same home experience some aspects of the environment quite differently; for instance, parents do not treat each child the same way. They may treat boys differently than girls. They may treat older kids differently than younger ones. They treat first-born kids differently than later-born ones. Also, while siblings may attend the same school, they have different teachers who push them in different ways. The children likely belong to different social clubs and sports teams, with experiences that are quite unique. Geneticists refer to this amalgam of differences as the *nonshared environment* (Plomin, 2011).

Modern behavioral genetics studies suggest that, in a surprise twist, the nonshared environment exerts a much greater influence on kids than the shared environments. One of the most powerful forces in the nonshared environment is the friend group that a kid surrounds themselves with. Peers are instrumental in a kid's tendency toward being big liars. Parents often attempt to steer their children away from bad influences, such as misbehaving friends. This redirection is for good reason. Parents surmise that kids who affiliate with liars tend to become liars themselves. One fascinating consideration is that a child's genes may, to a certain extent, steer them toward selecting mischievous friends (Plomin, 2011).

The interaction between genes and the environment can be complicated and challenging to understand fully. Genes seem to drive one toward certain nonshared environmental experiences (Charroin et al., 2021). Dishonest kids, as it turns out, tend to choose dishonest friends, and they are further influenced by those friends to lie. Interestingly, kids who, by nature, tend to be honest are not influenced to lie by peers, even when they have chosen dishonest friends. Only kids who tend to be dishonest on their own are influenced to lie by their peers.

DEVELOPMENTAL DISORDERS AND LYING

Lying is commonplace among children, but some children are certainly bigger liars than others. Much of the variability in dishonesty is likely attributable to natural variation, just as kids also tend to vary in height, weight, and intelligence. However, some cases of excessive lying in children may stem from psychological disorders. We address psychological disorders associated with lying in much more detail in Chapter 3, but here we mention some that are especially relevant to childhood.

One such disorder, albeit fairly rare in children, is *factitious disorder*. Children with factitious disorder deceive others to appear physically or mentally ill, sometimes by actually making themselves ill or by injuring themselves. These feigned illnesses and injuries aren't your typical examples of a kid acting sick to skip school or concocting an injury to avoid chores (M. D. Feldman, 2006; Jaghab et al., 2006). In one case, a 12-year-old boy who had sickle cell disease was admitted to a pediatric hospital complaining of hip pain (Jaghab et al., 2006). The boy, who had very challenging life circumstances, lived with his grandmother. He never saw his father, and his mother was in and out of jail. While in the hospital, the child received much-needed attention from the doctors and staff. His hospital stay was reportedly the first time he had received such good care in his life. He was treated with fluid and painkillers and eventually sent home. He soon returned to the hospital with other complaints. The hospital visits became regular. On one visit, it was chest pains, on another, it was vomiting, and on yet another, it was abdominal pain. Every medical test came back negative, yet his visits to the hospital continued. During that year, he was hospitalized nine times. The following year, he was admitted 13 times, staying in the hospital for a total of 6 months. The medical staff became suspicious that his illnesses were fabrications, so they ordered a psychiatric evaluation. The child was uncooperative with the psychiatrist, so the evaluation could not be completed. The following year, he came to the hospital 19 times, again spending a total of 6 months as a patient. Again, no biological cause for his complaints was ever discovered. The following year, he was admitted 14 times, and the staff began to detect evidence of his deception. They discovered that the boy was intentionally scratching and putting dirt on his IV sites to cause infections and that he was intentionally dehydrating himself. They later caught him adding blood to his urine and injecting himself with contaminants. These invasive tactics are not uncommon among kids with factitious disorders. In other cases, children have used heating pads to fake fevers, inserted stones into their urethras to feign kidney stones, beat themselves to cause bruising, injected air under their skin to cause dermatitis, painted their skin, and injected themselves with all manner of contaminants, including milk, eggs, and feces. Ultimately, the hospital staff confronted this boy about his hospitalizations. They made it clear that they were aware that he was surreptitiously causing all his medical problems. They indicated that his illness was psychiatric rather than physical. The young man left the hospital, never to return. He was later reported to have sought admission to other hospitals, apparently searching for the attention and care that nobody else was providing him.

A more prevalent disorder of childhood that also has excessive lying as a chief symptom is *conduct disorder*. Conduct disorder is characterized by a repeated and persistent pattern of disregard for the rights of others and a blatant disregard for social norms. In other words, the child or adolescent engages in antisocial behavior. Conduct disorder is diagnosed in childhood, and if the person is still behaving in the same manner when they reach adulthood, they receive the diagnosis of antisocial personality disorder (American Psychiatric Association, 2013).

Kids with conduct disorder generally have little empathy, moral sense, or conscience. They exhibit cruelty to others, they are inclined to be destructive, they flaunt the rules, and they disregard authority. They lack remorse for their antisocial behavior, and they lie a lot (Hinshaw & Lee, 2003). Many children with conduct disorder, especially children diagnosed by age 10, exhibit a lifelong, persistent pattern of antisocial behavior, including excessive lying, that results in a consistent pattern of difficulties in school, on the job, and in relationships. Certainly, many children with conduct disorder do not go on to become big liars in adulthood, but it is possible that many adults we would classify as the biggest liars started as kids with conduct disorder.

Conduct disorder goes well beyond lying, though. Some kids with this disorder torture and kill animals, set fires, bully other kids, and vandalize property. They create mayhem and don't seem to care if anyone gets hurt along the way. This problem is much bigger than simply lying a lot. But, as with most people who violate rules, laws, and norms, these kids use deception to avoid detection, to callously manipulate others, to bully and harm others, and to create mayhem for their own enjoyment. Kids with conduct disorder are typically big liars, but lying is simply one tool they use in their endless misadventures.

Some researchers have suggested that kids with conduct disorder might warrant special attention from health care workers. Kids who have callous and unemotional traits may be budding psychopaths (Kahn, 2012; Raine, 2013). Researchers have argued that kids whose psychopathic tendencies can be identified before age 5 years sometimes go on to become prolific cheaters and liars later in life, manipulating others with a complete disregard for the pain and suffering that they cause (Caspi et al., 1996). A recent study confirmed that individuals who start life as fledgling psychopaths disproportionately become criminalistic manipulators and perpetrators later in life (DeLisi et al., 2020).

THIS LYING IS A PROBLEM

Regarding her 9-year-old, one mother wrote,

> We are having issues with my oldest with lying . . . all the time . . . about everything and not just little fibs but blatant lies, things I have no idea why he would even think to lie about. When I say everything I mean I could catch him in the middle of doing something he's not supposed to be doing and he will fight to the death that he wasn't doing it, knowing full well he was caught and that I saw him. But the very idea of owning up to the truth

> appears to be a concept that is unknown to him. He lies when he doesn't even have a reason to lie. This issue has been ongoing for quite some time now. My husband and I have done everything you could think of to curb this behavior, from losing electronics, chores, groundings, spending more time with him, sitting down and calmly talking to him about the importance of telling the truth, being honest and taking responsibility for his actions and understanding there are consequences for our actions good and bad. I have told him so many times that the truth may get him in a little trouble but not nearly as much as lying will. I have read countless articles, adjusted my own behavior to try and help, I ask him why he feels the need to lie, he just says he doesn't know. But no matter how calmly I address the problem or how upset we get with him . . . the behavior doesn't change. It's like a second nature to him. Compulsive.

Excessive lying in children was first discussed by the American psychologist G. Stanley Hall (1890). Hall studied lying in a group of 300 school-aged children. He examined what they lied about, who they told lies to, and so on. He noted that approximately 7% of the kids in his study engaged in what he called pathological lying. He observed that some of those kids would take on fraudulent personas and engage in other manner of deception, often in an attempt to gain attention. He noted that some of those pathological liars would carry out very sophisticated cons and lies. He was intrigued because while many of the kids initially lied for attention, thrills, or material gains, some of them seemed to get lost in their lying, repeatedly telling lies with no obvious motive or incentive. Hall questioned whether these youngsters would go on to become the adult imposters and big liars in our world. Pathological lying in adults is covered more in Chapter 3.

In 1915, the Healys, a husband-and-wife team, studied 1,000 repeated juvenile offenders (Healy & Healy, 1915). They found that for about 18% of the youths they observed, lying was an "excessive and a notorious characteristic of the individual" (p. 5). They concluded that pathological lying is a condition that starts early in life. The Healys also noted hints of optimism: "That some of our cases have more or less recovered from a strongly marked and prolonged inclination to falsify is a fact of great importance for treatment and prognosis" (p. 7).

In one case study, the Healys described their experience working with a teenage girl, Hazel (Healy & Healy, 1915). Hazel first came to the attention of mental health professionals as a result of her attempt to raise money to bury her dead brother. Hazel arrived at a social center and told the tragic story of how her brother, an army soldier, had suffered and eventually passed away at a nearby hospital. Her story, from a medical standpoint, was detailed and quite believable. Hazel went on to describe how she had been trained as a nurse and so understood the gruesome details of her sibling's illness and death. A social worker insisted on going back to the hospital with Hazel to help make funeral arrangements. At the hospital, the staff insisted that no person matching the identification or description of Hazel's brother had died there or had even been a patient there.

Hazel was brought to mental health professionals for evaluation. For several days, she recounted to them the details of her life. She claimed that she had grown up in several small towns and had graduated high school in Des Moines, Iowa. She had one year of nursing training and had worked as a nurse in Cincinnati and then in Chicago. She had also spent time on several army posts, as her only family was brothers who were in the army. She also had had a stint in San Francisco. She was entirely believable. A detective eventually got involved to try to track down any of her family members. Despite Hazel's claims that both her mother and father were dead, the detective found her mother living across town in Chicago. When her mother was brought in to see her daughter, Hazel was asked what she would say if someone told her that her mother was waiting in the next room. In a very convincing display of sincerity and surprise, Hazel offered, "She would have to rise out of her grave to be there."

With the help of her mother, the authorities were able to discern that Hazel's accounts had been almost entirely fictitious. She was born in Chicago and had never left. She had a notable habit of lying since she was very young; for example, she came home from school telling her family about having been chased by a horse in the streets of Chicago. She dropped out of school in the eighth grade, had never received training as a nurse, and had never nursed anyone. She had six brothers and sisters. She had frequently run away from home—lying about her age, living under an assumed name, and claiming to be married. The lies about her marriage included very detailed letters written to her mother about her married life with her fictional husband, Jack.

The goals of Hazel's falsifications remained inscrutable to the treatment team that worked with her. As is the case with many pathological liars, her lies seemed to have no discernable purpose at all. Interestingly, after a few years' work with a treatment team and her family, Hazel stopped lying so much and went on to lead a fairly normal life. Other researchers have confirmed that pathological lying tends to emerge in adolescence (B. H. King & Ford, 1988).

Taken together, the evidence suggests that several psychiatric disorders of childhood manifest in excessive lying. For many of these cases, lying is just one feature of the disorder. Furthermore, for most children who express these disordered patterns, the habitual lying diminishes as they grow into adulthood. Thus, being a big liar in childhood is not a sure indication that one will be a big liar in adulthood. As we noted earlier, lying in childhood has many trajectories, with only some individuals adopting a pattern of persistent lying across the lifespan.

PROMOTING HONESTY IN KIDS

Is there some way to nip dishonesty in the bud and prevent darling little liars from growing up into big liars? Are there interventions or adjustments that can be made to prevent a steady escalation of lying? The evidence is not entirely clear, but some research findings offer hope. Several tactics can facilitate the development of attitudes that seem to be negatively correlated with lying. For instance, parents who cultivate negative attitudes about lying in their children will surely notice a decrease in deceptive behavior. After all, there is a strong negative correlation between how a person views lying and that person's tendency to tell lies.

Researchers at the Harvard Graduate School of Education (2018) created a set of recommendations for increasing honesty in children. First, try to encourage honesty with children. Encouraging honesty includes discussing how and why honesty is important. It involves talking about how dishonesty can harm a relationship by fracturing trust. It also involves conversations about trust and how to build trust in a relationship. Encouraging honesty in children, they argued, also means that parents must share with children that complete honesty is not always tenable. Parents can acknowledge that when kids receive a gift they do not like, they can't exactly tell the truth. In certain situations, they must shade the truth or delicately use white lies to avoid hurting people they care about.

Another strategy they suggest is modeling honesty. Young children don't invent their behavioral repertoires out of whole cloth. They begin by imitating the behavior of the adults around them. If adults hope to see honest behavior from the kids in their lives, they need to show them how it's done. Adults have to be sure-footed guides down the path of veracity. Even adults find it hard to be honest always. When parents slip up, they should own it. Parents should acknowledge that they have failed to be completely honest, express regrets, and discuss how they should have behaved. Adults should also praise honesty when kids tell the truth in difficult situations. Let kids know that being honest is very hard sometimes. Parents can let kids know that they are proud of them for telling it like it is.

As kids get older, they start to develop their own moral compasses, deciding for themselves whether honesty is the best policy. Young kids tend to hold rigid moral positions in which lying is categorically wrong. As those kids reach about 10 years old, they start to adopt a nuanced perspective about lying. They begin to consider the morality of dishonesty from a consequentialist position, engaging in moral reasoning based on the outcomes that a lie produces. They begin to see that all lies are not equally reprehensible. They assess lies told to protect the feelings of others as more morally acceptable than selfish lies. They think and feel about lying in a more adult manner. Though we may not be able to raise offspring who are 100% honest all the time, nor should we want to, we can model, inspire, and support authenticity and honesty. Through acceptance and caring, we can cultivate an environment in which kids can learn on their own that honesty and being genuine generally lead to a life much more pleasant than that of being a big liar.

CONCLUSION

No single trigger in a person's early years propels that person to become a big liar. Similarly, no single clue from childhood distinguishes kids who will become big liars as adults from those who will not. It seems that almost all kids lie. They test-drive lying as a strategy for getting what they want. It's a natural developmental milestone. Eventually, most kids adopt the moral and cultural norms of their home and society more broadly, becoming fairly honest people. Youngsters tend to learn that lying is often not worth the risk, or they remain honest because they want to be good people. The negative outcomes of getting caught in a lie, including punishment, social rejection, loss of social capital, and fractured relationships, teach kids that honesty is, in fact, the best policy. Some kids don't get that message, though. In line with the tripartite theory of lying and dishonesty, some children come to see lying as morally acceptable. Likewise, some fail to see the risks of being dishonest. Some take to lying like fish to water and never look back, entering adulthood well trained in the deceptive arts and prepared to use guile to get their way at every turn. Evidence suggests that the environment in which a kid is raised can influence their tendency to lie. Kids raised in cultures that tend to use dishonesty more tend to be more dishonest themselves (Hendy et al., 2021; T. R. Levine et al., 2016). At the family level, kids who see their parents lie tend to be liars themselves. The fact that lying parents often produce lying children could be viewed as evidence of a genetic link to lying, but we also know that parents can produce a brood of children that contains both the most observant truthtellers and also conspicuous prevaricators. Evidence is clear that both environmental and biological or genetic factors give rise to the big liars in the world.

The way that kids are socialized at home and in school can dramatically affect the degree to which they adopt a habit of honesty or veer into a pattern of repeated deception. All kids fib. They learn to lie and then hone that craft throughout adolescence. Attempting to entirely eradicate lying from their children's behavioral repertoires is a challenging venture. While kids will almost certainly tell lies, parents can help to shape their children into people who appreciate the value of honesty and sincerity. Parents may not be able to stop kids from lying entirely, but they can usually reduce the frequency of lying and influence the types of lies the children tell.

We can conclude that, even among children, some lie more than others. Some are big liars. Children who are big liars often turn toward more honest patterns in adulthood, but some continue on the big liar trajectory into adulthood. In the next chapter, we examine the variety of ways that excessive lying manifests itself in adulthood, from people who simply enjoy spinning tall tales to people who are diagnosable as pathological liars.

CHAPTER 3

PATHOLOGICAL LIARS AND OTHERS WHO LIE EXCESSIVELY

I have a higher and grander standard of principle than George Washington. He could not lie; I can, but won't.

—Mark Twain

Many years back, there was a courageous and adventurous man who experienced several extraordinary occurrences. On one occasion he had arrived at an island to accompany a hunting group. On his excursion, he had fearfully encountered a lion, which rushed toward him after he fired a shot toward it. The lion leaped to maul the man, who fell to the ground. After realizing he had not been eaten by the beast, the man looked up to see that the lion had jumped into the open mouth of a crocodile. Rushing to his feet, the man drew his sword, cut off the lion's head, and suffocated the crocodile with the lion's head. This dramatic story is one of many about the adventures of Baron Munchausen (Raspe, 1785).

Is there a difference between telling tall tales and fibbing? In this chapter, we turn our attention to examining differences between fiction and lies. We focus on how to more keenly discern whether someone may be a big liar, and we detail some specifics of pathological lying as well as lying found in other psychological disorders.

Would the Baron be described as a big liar? Munchausen was not considered a liar by his peers. Rather, he was considered an honest man who simply loved to entertain others by telling absurd and hilarious stories. Good stories are appealing, especially if they capture the mind with visual imagery, plausible happenings, and some rare twist in the plot. Audiences can be enticed by ordinary characters in extraordinary circumstances. The depiction of incredible events is one of the reasons that we are entertained by movies and fictional stories. That attraction to amazing tales also may contribute to our propensity to be duped by others. However, a person who tells numerous fictional stories is not necessarily a big liar. The definition of lying and deceit involves an intent to deceive "without forewarning" (Vrij, 2008, p. 15). People generally have an awareness and an expectation of deceit prior to watching movies, reading fiction, and being entertained by magicians. Therefore, fictional stories and tall tales do not qualify as deception, as both the speakers and the listeners are in a consensual relationship in which the exchange of untruthful information is agreed upon. Even though fiction is not intended to be deceptive, it can promote misinformation and faulty beliefs (Lewandowsky et al., 2012; Schreier, 2009).

While fiction itself is not a form of lying, a big liar could tell numerous lies through exaggerated stories. One of our relatives would often boast about extraordinary encounters. This person boasted about seeing a 95-pound chicken. He often told this story to family members. In addition to the big bird tale, he told a whopper about being on a jet inside the eye of a hurricane (this was untrue). His claims were not presented as fiction meant to entertain but were instead blatant lies or exaggerations likely told to beckon attention. A mere storyteller may receive attention too, but the difference with storytelling is that both parties are in prior agreement that the information is not true. The storyteller forewarns or at least implies to the audience that the events did not actually happen. The context in which a person tells elaborate stories can be the key difference between a good storyteller and a big liar.

BIG FISH OR BIG LIAR?

There is a fine line between telling a good story and telling a lie. Where that line is drawn, the listener experiences tension—wanting to believe stories, myths, and exaggerated claims and simultaneously seeking and knowing the truth. One theme of the book *Big Fish* (Wallace, 2003), which became a movie, is the dilemma between the appeal of fact and that of fiction. The story focuses on the tension between a son who desperately wants to know the truth about his father and his father's desire to recount his life in the form of exaggerated mythical tales (Canavan, 2011).

In one vein, telling a story about catching a fish bigger than it actually was can captivate and impress an audience. The bigger the catch, the more extraordinary the fisher. A parent's exaggeration of events can impress on children a sense of grandeur and high regard for the parent. Additionally, an embellished story attracts more attention than a mundane and predictable one does. A 7-pound largemouth bass seems more exhilarating and unique than a 1-pound fish. However, embellishment has a cost. A discovery of fabrication can lead to distrust or disappointment. Learning that the catch was one pound instead of seven can be disappointing and may change the future trust in the person who claimed to catch a big fish. People generally want the truth, but they also love to be entertained. They may enjoy an untruthful story that harmlessly entertains them, but they typically react negatively to untrue accounts when their goal is to understand the facts of the world around them. The line between stories and lies can be blurry and requires discerning intent and forewarning, knowing ahead of time that the person is telling you a story rather than trying to convince you of a belief they hold. Thus, our attraction to unusual and novel claims may contribute to our being duped when we attend to the stories of big liars.

WORLD'S BIGGEST LIAR

Every year in November, The World's Biggest Liar Competition is held in Cumbria, United Kingdom (The World's Biggest Liar, 2020). The event is based on a 19th-century local, Will Ritson, who is famous for telling many tall tales. One of his claims was that "turnips . . . were so big that after the dalesfolk had 'quarried' into them for their Sunday lunch, they could be used as sheds for the Herdwick Sheep from the fells" (The World's Biggest Liar, 2020, para. 4). Thus began a tradition of inviting all big liars, except lawyers and politicians, to flock to the United Kingdom to tell their tall tales. Though people compete for the title The World's Biggest Liar, it may be more appropriate to call them convincing and engaging storytellers rather than liars.

LABELING A BIG LIAR

When you think about a liar, what comes to mind? Whereas people usually have positive feelings toward storytellers, we tend to think quite negatively of liars—likely that they are cold, malicious, and selfish. Big liars especially tend to be shunned and loathed. In Biblical accounts of lying, God hates a lying tongue while the Devil is labeled as a big liar, the father of lies, and the deceiver of the whole world. Outside of religious texts, lying was deserving of death according to the Code of Hammurabi (L. W. King, 2008). Moral stories, such as "The Boy Who Cried Wolf," communicate that lying is bad and liars will not be believed, leading to their death by hungry wolves.

When we think about liars, we tend to think of others who lie, not ourselves. However, we know that the vast majority of people admit to lying at least once a week, and typically more than that. Why, then, do we attach the "liar" label to others but not to ourselves?

In one study, we found that if another person tells a lie, we are inclined to label that person a liar, but when we tell the same lie, we are much less likely to see ourselves as liars (Curtis, 2021b). Essentially, we attribute our own dishonesty to situational exigencies, whereas we attribute others' dishonesty to their dispositions. If you lie, it is because you are a liar. If I lie, it is because something or someone forced me to lie. Thus, we may be likely to label others who tell many lies as big liars.

BIG WHOPPER

Recall that a big liar can be someone who tells numerous lies or someone who tells a single influential whopper. In 2009, a father reported that his 6-year-old boy, Falcon Heene, had floated off in a large homemade helium balloon (History.com Editors, 2011). The oversized balloon was located floating outside of Fort Collins, Colorado. As the balloon approached Denver International Airport, planes had to be rerouted. The police were called, and National Guard helicopters were deployed to look for the balloon and the boy. Finally, after an hour-long flight, the balloon landed. Upon discovering that young Falcon was not inside the balloon, searchers began to look along the balloon's path, worrying that the child had fallen out during the flight. Hours later, the boy was discovered hiding in the family's attic, perfectly safe. The whole thing, the police determined, had been a hoax. Prosecutors argued that the big lie had been part of a scheme by the family to secure a reality television show. Instead, the father was convicted of a felony. In this case, the family told one big lie, which was discovered later through confession. The parents were branded big liars in the court of public opinion. This story shows that some big liars acquire a reputation for being a big liar by telling a single consequential lie.

GENERAL OR NICHE BIG LIARS

A 20-year-old university student had sought psychological services at his university mental health clinic (Grzegorek, 2011). Over numerous sessions, the student discussed his mental health problems with the dutiful therapist. At the final session, the patient began smiling and revealed that he had been fabricating his mental health complaints. Almost all the information he had shared with the therapist was false and intentionally misleading. The therapist was angry and confused and asked the patient why he would seek counseling services and lie about everything. The patient told the therapist that he wanted to see if he could successfully deceive someone who was supposedly a master of human behavior. This person told many lies aimed at one goal, to foster a specific impression of psychological distress. Having contrived all false details and telling numerous lies, this person could be considered a big liar. However, there is no evidence that he told excessive lies in the other domains of his life. It seems that he may have lied extensively only in the therapist's office.

Some people may lie pervasively in all situations, but others might only lie in a niche situation. Jonnel Perkins was a banker in Philadelphia. She was accused of embezzling more than $200,000 from the account of a customer who had died and then lying about it. Perkins's dishonesty seemed to be confined largely to her workplace. After her lies were discovered, she was arrested, and she eventually pled guilty. Some people, like Perkins, have siloed their excessive dishonesty into particular facets of their lives, such as their romantic relationships, friendships, or, like Perkins, their work lives.

People who tend to tell numerous lies in one context are different from the typical big liars who lie frequently to many people across situations. We might call the former "niche big liars" and the latter "general big liars." Perhaps general big liars are dispositionally inclined to lie and do so across contexts. Niche big liars, on the other hand, are perhaps dispositionally honest, but a specific type of context tempts them to lie. Niche big liars may lie only to their spouses, and even then perhaps only about one topic, yet they lie often in that niche.

BIG LIARS VERSUS PATHOLOGICAL LIARS

At the age of 22, Lorraine was incarcerated at a forensic psychiatric unit for an assessment of "criminal responsibility for three arson-related offenses, two counts of public mischief (false reports), three counts of making false statements, two counts of fabricating evidence, and one count of perjury" (Birch et al., 2006, p. 307). Lorraine claimed that she would spontaneously make up stories and was good at conning people. At various points in time, she reported to the police that her coworker, her best friend, and her fiancé's ex-wife had each sent her death threats. She indicated that her best friend had stalked her, abducted her, and continued to make death threats even after being imprisoned. Last, Lorraine reported that her fiancé's 3-year-old son had set two fires—one in Lorraine's mother's apartment and the other in her own apartment. In the forensic assessment, Lorraine confessed that her accusations were false (Birch et al., 2006). Lorraine would seem to be a big liar, as she certainly told many lies across situations.

While Lorraine told an excessive number of lies to different people, some other features distinguish her lies as pathological. Before we discuss aspects of pathological lying, it is important to note that it has been referred to by other names, such as "compulsive lying," "habitual lying," and "morbid lying." We see all of these terms as referring to the same phenomenon—pathological lying. Our work has investigated the difference between pathological liars and big liars. Recall that most people are fairly honest while a small subset of people tells numerous lies. These are the big liars. But are they pathological liars? We suggest that pathological liars are different in important ways from big liars.

To understand what makes pathological lying different from normal lying, it is necessary to discuss what makes a behavior pathological. Psychopathology is not a specific behavior but rather a set of criteria applied to human behaviors. When categorizing a person's thoughts, behaviors, and feelings as abnormal or pathological, researchers and clinicians note four distinct features of their behavior: (a) atypicality—the behavior is statistically infrequent in the population, occurs with unusual frequency, or violates social norms; (b) maladjustment—the behavior impairs functioning; (c) suffering—the behavior causes emotional distress to the person; and (d) risk or danger—the behavior creates risks of harm or loss for themselves or others. For example, let's examine handwashing. Most people wash their hands daily. However, some people wash their hands hundreds of times per day, every day. Excessive handwashing is sometimes seen in people with obsessive-compulsive disorder, a disorder in which individuals experience intrusive thoughts (obsessions), such as of germs or contamination, and engage in excessive behavior (compulsions), such as excessive handwashing. This behavior meets the four criteria of psychopathology. Handwashing occurs much more than normal, so it is atypical. It often interferes with work or socializing, so it is maladaptive. People engaging in this behavior are often extremely upset and distressed that they cannot stop washing their hands, so they are suffering. The constant handwashing often leads to skin ulcerations and infections, so their behavior presents a risk or danger. Taken together, excessive handwashing meets the criteria for psychopathology.

We applied the same four criteria to lying behavior to help differentiate between normative lying and pathological lying (Curtis & Hart, 2020b). We set out to determine if people who tell numerous lies are merely prolific liars or if a subset of these individuals exhibit features of psychopathology and so could be considered pathological liars. In a large study involving hundreds of subjects, we found that pathological liars were a distinct group. Unlike other big liars, pathological liars told numerous lies that often impaired their social relationships, caused them distress, and put them or others at risk of harm or danger. Additionally, pathological liars began telling lies excessively in adolescence, had problematic lying for more than 6 months, and lied compulsively.

Consider whether Lorraine, from the previously discussed case, meets the criteria of pathological lying. She certainly lied much more than a typical person does. Her lies also led to impaired social functioning. The lies Lorraine told "caused severe disruption and distress in her own life and in the lives of many other people" (Birch et al., 2006, p. 314). Furthermore, her lies certainly put others in danger, leading to the imprisonment of her best friend, the arrest of her fiancé's ex-wife, and apartment fires. Additionally, Lorraine had engaged in pathological lying for more than 6 years, with an onset at age 16. Lorraine seems to be a clear case of a pathological liar. Our position is that pathological liars are a subset of big liars. All pathological liars are big liars, but not all big liars are pathological liars.

Though case studies, such as Lorraine's, have documented the existence of pathological lying for more than a century, pathological lying is not recognized as a formal psychological disorder. Pathological lying is absent from the two major tools used to classify psychological disorders, American Psychiatric Association's (2013) *Diagnostic and Statistical Manual of Mental Disorders* (5th ed.; *DSM-5*) and World Health Organization's (2019) *International Statistical Classification of Diseases and Related Health Problems* (11th ed.; *ICD-11*). One reason that pathological lying is not recognized as a distinct diagnosis is that features of lying have traditionally been viewed as symptoms of other psychological disorders.

LYING AND PSYCHOLOGICAL DISORDERS

Imagine you see a man on the side of the street talking to someone who isn't there. You approach him and ask if he needs help. He tells you that he's trying to silence a voice that's telling him that others are after him. However, you don't hear any voices. Is the man lying to you? It can sometimes be difficult to tell when someone is lying because some psychological disorders can cause someone to seem like they're lying when they're not. In other cases, excessive lying can be a symptom of another psychological disorder. Understanding lying or presumed lying across various psychological disorders can help identify who is a big liar and who is not.

Delusion or Lie: The Deliberate Difference

One gentleman whom we observed had told people that he was a Vietnam War veteran and had seen intense combat, leading to the development of posttraumatic stress disorder. However, he was far too young to have served during the war. Was he lying? The answer depends. Recall that a lie has to be intentional: A communicator tries to make someone else believe something that the communicator does not believe to be true. Thus, if the man knew that he had not served in the war but stated that he had served in the war, then he would be lying. However, if the man actually believed that he served in Vietnam, even though he hadn't, then he would not be lying. He would be delusional. Someone who is delusional is not intending to make another believe something that they believe is untrue. A person suffering from delusions is communicating to others what they actually believe. Delusions are manifestations of mental illness, such as those under the schizophrenia spectrum and other psychotic disorders (American Psychiatric Association,

2013). The false beliefs can encompass a wide variety of content, from a belief that the FBI has secretly bugged one's house to monitor conversations to a belief that microscopic bugs are crawling on one's skin or even inside one's body.

It is important to differentiate between delusions and lies when attempting to identify big liars because we may assume someone is lying when they are not. Consider the case of a 25-year-old married woman we call Jane (Dua & Grover, 2019). Three months after her marriage, a pregnancy test revealed that Jane was pregnant. However, Jane did not believe she was pregnant and told others that her increasing abdominal distention was due to eating too much. In her final months of pregnancy, Jane claimed that she did not feel any fetal movement. After giving birth to her baby girl, she accepted her child and began to feed her; however, within a week, she stopped caring for the child and stated that she did not give birth to her daughter (Dua & Grover, 2019). Another case involved Mr. X, a 38-year-old single man without children (Lebelo & Grobler, 2020). He arrived at the emergency room after having been found in a gas station restroom with a copious amount of blood loss from his scrotum. He indicated that he cut his scrotum open to remove his testicles "before his 'tormentors' could do so" (Lebelo & Grobler, 2020, p. 1). Mr. X had delusions of persecution, believing that some people were listening to his thoughts and were going to take out his testicles for a ritualistic practice.

In both cases, the patients were not merely fabricating tales to dupe others. The patients truly held their patently false beliefs. Both patients held their beliefs so strongly that they ended up in danger, in one case neglecting perinatal and postnatal care and in the other causing physical mutilation. Understanding psychological disorders helps us view people's outrageous claim appropriately. These people had mental illnesses. They were not big liars.

Antisocial Personality Disorder

Big liars who lie without remorse or with reckless disregard for others are especially difficult to interact with. This pattern of lying can be a symptom or a feature of *antisocial personality disorder* (ASPD; American Psychiatric Association, 2013). People with ASPD typically use deception "to gain personal profit or pleasure (e.g., to obtain money, sex, or power)" (American Psychiatric Association, 2013, p. 660). While lying is one of the diagnostic criteria, it is not required for a person to receive the diagnosis of ASPD.

ASPD is largely, as the name insinuates, a disorder of personality characterized by an individual having a blatant disregard for others and defying authority and the law. Charles Manson is often discussed as an individual who displayed signs of ASPD. Manson actively defied authority and his behavior led to incarceration. This disorder is not very common, as it has been documented in about 0.2% to 3.3% of the U.S. population, with most cases involving men, people with substance abuse problems, or people experiencing legal problems (American Psychiatric Association, 2013). Individuals with ASPD often lie excessively, fitting our description of big liars. Relationships with big liars who have symptoms of this disorder can be challenging. In addition to their excessive lies, they often show impulsivity, aggression, a disregard for the safety of others, irresponsibility, and a lack of remorse.

Psychopathy

Psychopathy is a psychological construct that is typically associated with ASPD (Hare, 1996). People identified as psychopaths are bold and manipulative people who have little empathy for others, shallow emotions, callousness, detachment, and a lack of remorse. They are pretty awful to be around. Hare noted, "most psychopaths . . .

meet the criteria for ASPD, but most individuals with ASPD are not psychopaths" (p. 2). In fact, while 50% to 80% of people in prison meet the diagnostic criteria for ASPD, only about 15% to 25% meet the criteria for psychopathy (Patrick, 2007). A key characteristic of psychopathy is deception (Gillard, 2018), and one of the criteria used to assess psychopathy is pathological lying (Hare, 1991). Very little research has addressed the frequency and the success of lies told by psychopaths, with some research indicating that psychopaths cannot beat a polygraph test any better than individuals who do not exhibit psychopathy (Gillard, 2018; Lykken, 1978; Raskin & Hare, 1978).

In some cases, big liars may be people who have psychopathic features. One of the most well-known serial killers, Ted Bundy, told numerous lies. He lied to many people over the years to avoid getting caught for the murders he committed. Even after he was arrested, he lied to law-enforcement officers, judges, jury members, and other interviewers, denying any involvement in the murders. Another serial murderer was Clifford Olson, who lived in Canada and was known as a gruesome criminal who killed several boys and girls. He was also known to lie at every turn (Hare et al., 1989). Many newspaper articles and reporters indicated that he was a prolific liar and cautioned that people should not believe anything that Olson said because he lied so frequently (Hare et al., 1989).

While Bundy and Olson embodied the image of a dark, cold, callous, and unremorseful big liar and murderer, they certainly do not represent all big liars or even all psychopaths. Hare and colleagues (1989) stated, "not all serial killers are psychopaths" (p. 30). Additionally, telling excessive lies does not necessarily mean that one is a psychopath, as most pathological liars express distress and remorse for telling their lies (Curtis & Hart, 2020). Bundy and Olson reflected a specific subset of big liars—those who are psychopaths and serial killers.

Factitious Disorder

Another psychological disorder, discussed also in Chapter 2, is *factitious disorder*. This disorder is characterized by lying about one's health. The prevalence is unknown but estimated to be around 1%. Factitious disorder involves assuming a sick role for attention, achieved by lying about symptoms or actually inducing them (American Psychiatric Association, 2013; Ferrara et al., 2013). When most people get sick, they get attention from their family, friends, or medical staff. Thus, the attention gained for a small subset of individuals reinforces lying about being sick. Recall the character referenced at the beginning of the chapter, Baron Munchausen. Factitious disorder was originally termed Munchausen's syndrome, based on the Baron's fantastic tales (Asher, 1951; J. Turner & Reid, 2002).

An unemployed 30-year-old single woman named Kim lived with her parents (Hagglund, 2009). She was being considered for a spinal cord stimulator implantation because she had a history of chronic pain. She sought psychiatric services and would frequently share somatic complaints, including asthma, sprained limbs, carpal tunnel syndrome, nausea, vomiting, rectal bleeding, ear infections, a weakened immune system, and chronic pain, among other complaints. Kim noted in her medical history that she had had 16 tooth extractions, surgical removal of a cyst, endometriosis, and other medical procedures. Even though Kim had normal laboratory tests, she still indicated that she was ill. Kim's case reflects factitious disorder. She lied excessively about her symptoms and medical history to assume a sick role.

In rare cases of factitious disorder, people may lie about symptoms or illnesses of other people or may actually induce symptoms in someone else. These cases are referred to as *factitious disorder imposed on another* (American Psychiatric Association, 2013). Factitious disorder imposed on another often involves a parent making a child ill or lying about a child's symptoms to attract attention and compassion. The prevalence rate of factitious disorder imposed on another is unknown because in many cases it may remain undetected. Unfortunately, some cases end in death. For example, in 2014, a 5-year-old boy, Garnett, died from sodium poisoning after his mother, Lacey Spears, put sodium in his stomach tube (McCoy, 2015). Spears was convicted of second-degree murder in 2015 (Higgins, 2015; McCoy, 2015). Through a closer look, several of Spears's lies were uncovered. She had created a blog to document her life and the various struggles she faced as a result of her son's health concerns and her husband's death. However, a review of her past revealed that she had told others that she was the mother of someone else's child, she was deceptive about her son's biological father, and she had reported several unfounded health concerns about Garnett (S. Cohen & Kramer, 2014).

A famous case of factitious disorder imposed on another involved DeeDee and Gypsy Rose Blanchard (Rosenbaum et al., 2019). The life and events of DeeDee and Gypsy were made into an HBO documentary and dramatized in the series called *The Act* (Antosca et al., 2019). From the time that Gypsy was a baby, her mother had claimed that she had several illnesses, including sleep apnea, leukemia, and muscular dystrophy (Kettler, 2020). Thus, Gypsy was confined to a wheelchair, had a feeding tube, and had a bald head (Kettler, 2020; Rosenbaum et al., 2019). DeeDee gained attention and made several Make-A-Wish trips with Gypsy to Disney theme parks (Rosenbaum et al., 2019). However, Gypsy "could walk, didn't need a feeding tube, and did not have cancer. Her head was bald only because her mother shaved off her hair" (Kettler, 2020, p. 4). DeeDee also lied about Gypsy's age and changed information on her birth certificate so that Gypsy would appear to be younger than she actually was (Kettler, 2020). Gypsy eventually met a man online, Nicholas Godejohn, and asked him to kill her mother so that they could be together, and he did so in June 2015 (Kettler, 2020).

Malingering

In some cases, people lie about sickness for some external motivation. Have you ever called your boss pretending to be sick in order to avoid working? *Malingering* individuals lie about physical or psychological symptoms or induce these symptoms for some external reason (American Psychiatric Association, 2013). Unlike factitious disorder, in which the motivation is to assume a sick role, malingering is motivated primarily by some tangible gain or the avoidance of some negative consequence. For example, people may engage in malingering to seek medications, get financial compensation, avoid military duty, or mitigate criminal charges.

Consider the case of a 23-year-old man who presented with blunt trauma to his right hand (Swiergosz et al., 2017). The man reported that an electric motor rolled on his right hand and forearm while he was working. He did not have any fractures and did not need surgery or sutures. The man reported pain for 15 months and was diagnosed with reflex sympathetic dystrophy. After receiving several different treatments across several months, he claimed that only the last treatment was effective for pain reduction. Around 15 months after the injury, the patient presented for an evaluation that was required for a workers' compensation litigation procedure. The evaluation revealed no signs or symptoms normally associated with a debilitating injury, such as sensitivity, atrophy, or bone changes. Subsequently, a private investigator captured the man on video fishing with the hand that he falsely claimed to be immobile.

Another case involved Joey, a 9-year-old boy who had a moderate traumatic brain injury from a motorcycle accident (Marasa, 2018). He indicated that he had "spastic quadriparesis, dysarthria, and cognitive impairment" when he was hospitalized (p. 7). Two years later, Joey's mother filed a lawsuit against the motorcycle company and was initially awarded $4.5 million. Years later, after various hospitalizations, Joey boasted about his ability to evade legal charges and avoid being homeless through hospital admissions. A neuropsychological evaluation found that Joey was malingering and that he displayed symptoms of ASPD.

In both of these cases, the individuals lied about symptoms for financial gain, to avoid work, and to avoid criminal charges. Malingering involves a specific type of lying and for a specific reason, for an external incentive. The deception is about physical or psychological symptoms (American Psychiatric Association, 2013). Some big liars are deceptive about their health for tangible gains.

Other Personality Disorders

Some additional personality disorders are associated with being a big liar. Though lying is not a central feature of most other personality disorders, some scholars have suggested that lying may be involved in narcissistic personality disorder, histrionic personality disorder, and borderline personality disorder (e.g., Dike et al., 2005; Garlipp, 2017).

Narcissistic personality disorder involves a consistent pattern of grandiosity, a lack of empathy, and a need for admiration (American Psychiatric Association, 2013). People with narcissistic personality disorder may also be exploitative of others. Thus, in being exploitative of others, they may lie by exaggerating features of themselves to gain approval of others (Dike et al., 2005). This lying behavior may be the reason that some believe excessive lying is a symptom of narcissistic personality disorder (Garlipp, 2017).

Histrionic personality disorder presents as a pattern of excessive emotions and desire for the attention of others (American Psychiatric Association, 2013). People with histrionic personality disorder "feel unappreciated when they are not the center of attention" (p. 667). While lying is not a criterion for diagnosis of the disorder, people with this personality disorder may lie through self-dramatization or by exaggerating features of themselves to gain the attention of others (American Psychiatric Association, 2013; Dike et al., 2005). However, some individuals with histrionic personality disorder may be presumed to be faking emotions when they are not because their emotions fluctuate quickly (American Psychiatric Association, 2013).

Borderline personality disorder has also been associated with excessive lying or pathological lying (Dike et al., 2005; Snyder, 1986). Dike and colleagues (2005) stated that the "core characteristics of [borderline personality] disorder foster falsification" (p. 345). Borderline personality disorder involves a pattern of impulsivity as well as instability in relationships, sense of self, and emotions (American Psychiatric Association, 2013). Because individuals with this disorder show patterns of instability, self-destructive behavior, and changing views of themselves, it appears that they readily lie (Dike et al., 2005), although lying is not a diagnostic criterion for borderline personality disorder.

CONCLUSION

When we think of big liars, we may think of the most notorious cases like Ted Bundy. Bundy was a big liar who had a psychological disorder and was a serial killer, so he is an exception rather than an accurate representation of the typical big liar. While some big liars may have a psychological disorder, the majority likely do not. Generally speaking, people with psychological disorders are not more likely than other people to lie or be big liars. However, some people—the pathological liars—may tell lies that are unusually excessive, impair their functioning, cause distress, or pose a danger to themselves or others. Their excessive lies cause significant problems in their lives (Curtis & Hart, 2020b). Most pathological liars show remorse and feel guilty about telling their excessive lies. People with psychopathy or ASPD, on the other hand, also lie in excess, but they feel no such remorse. Their lies adversely affect others and often result in their incarceration. Several other psychological disorders can also have lying as a feature; thus, excessive lying can sometimes be a symptom of a larger problem rather than a solitary trait or feature of a person.

Big liars are all around us. Though some big liars may be prone to dishonesty because they have psychological disorders, most are mentally healthy people who simply lie a lot (Curtis & Hart, 2020b; Serota et al., 2010; Serota & Levine, 2015). Some of these otherwise healthy big liars use manipulation, deceit, and cons to fulfill their needs, make money, or climb corporate ladders. In Chapter 4, we discuss some of the big liars all around us, including scammers, fraudsters, and con artists. We also examine big liars across several professional fields, including sales, advertising, politics, and the law.

CHAPTER 4

BIG LIARS ALL AROUND US

Clinton lied. A man might forget where he parks or where he lives, but he never forgets oral sex, no matter how bad it is.
—Barbara Bush

Lying is a pervasive aspect of human nature and can be seen across a wide range of professions and situations. From the smooth-talking salesperson making false promises to close a deal, to the con artists and scammers who use elaborate schemes to defraud unsuspecting victims, to the politicians who twist the truth for personal gain, big liars abound. In this chapter, we explore people who gain notoriety for their falsehoods as well as the people in whom we place our trust but who ultimately repay that trust with dishonesty.

Anna Sorokin was born in Russia in 1991, and her family moved to Germany when she was 16 (Berman et al., 2021). After moving to London for school and then moving to Paris for work, Anna finally moved to New York City at age 21. She didn't know anyone when she arrived in New York, but she quickly made friends. Perhaps it's somehow easier to make friends when you are rich. Anna's new friends learned that she was living off a trust fund worth about $80 million and was an heiress to her father's fortune; he was an extremely wealthy oil magnate. That all made sense, as Anna stayed at swanky hotels in Manhattan, spent afternoons at high-end spas, took luxurious vacations, and could regularly be spotted eating at the most expensive and trendy restaurants. Anna did not work, but she was attempting to set up an art foundation with her wealth.

The one problem with Anna's escapades was that it was all a fraud. She was actually from a family of modest means and had almost no money of her own. She had been able to convince her wealthy New York friends and acquaintances to pay for her expenses. In some cases, she used the tried and true "Oops, I left my wallet at home" trick with her new friends. In one case, she invited a friend to come along on an all-expenses-paid luxury trip to Morocco. When her credit card was mysteriously declined and she was unable to pay for the trip, she convinced her friend to cover the $62,000 bill until she could get the credit card issue resolved. Using forged documents, she took out several loans at banks worth tens of thousands of dollars. She even attempted to secure a $22 million loan against her inheritance. She chartered a private jet for $35,000 and never paid the bill. The New York district attorney concluded that in just 10 months Anna scammed the New York crowd out of at least $275,000 (District Attorney of New York, 2017). Anna, confident she could beat the legal case against her, opted to go to trial instead of being deported. She lost her case and was sentenced to prison at Rikers Island.

SCAMMERS

Anna was a scammer and a big liar, clear as day. She used her powers of manipulation and persuasion to extract from others the things that she wanted. She deftly employed an array of psychological tools from her exploitation toolbox. She had goals that depended on twisting others to her designs. If you think about it for a moment, it's clear that Anna's behavior was not all that dissimilar from the strategies and tactics that all people use from time to time. We all have agendas. To get where we want to be, we have all needed to occasionally persuade others. Sometimes we have to convince a friend to go to a movie with us. Other times we have to persuade a boss that we deserve a raise. And at other times we might try to convince a police officer not to write the speeding ticket. When buying a car, we haggle over the price, attempting to get the seller to drop a few hundred dollars from the asking price. We are minds in a world of other minds, and each of us employs psychological tricks and levers to influence the minds of everyone else. We are each trying to bend others slightly more to our will so that we can achieve whatever kinds of successful outcomes we value. Certainly, Anna was extreme in the tactics she used to get her way. She was willing to use ploys that most of us would deem unethical. She was perfectly willing to harm others to get what she wanted. In the end, like Anna, we all bend the truth to manipulate others. We exaggerate, we withhold information, we conceal our true intentions, we feign emotions, and we otherwise shape narratives in self-interested ways to get where we want to go. Like Anna, we sell ideas to others.

In the marketplace, we can conceptualize selling as the use of pressure and persuasion tactics to facilitate immediate self-interested economic exchanges. But selling doesn't occur only in commercial exchanges. People sell ideas, beliefs, ideologies, cultural habits, religious faiths, political causes, and behavioral preferences. In our complex social world, many people benefit in some shape or form when they successfully sell an idea to you. Deception is but one strategy used to sell. We all do it, and people do it to us. Who, on a first date, has not attempted to accentuate their positives and sweep their negatives under the rug? We all sell ideas, including ideas about who we are, and sometimes we use deception to help make that happen. The reality is that some forms of deceptive marketing are socially sanctioned. If, at the end of a first date, someone asks their companion if they would like to come up to their apartment to listen to some music, most people understand and accept the sexual innuendo. *Innuendos* are subtle deceptions that offer plausible deniability. Both parties understand that the person is likely interested in sex, yet neither has to openly acknowledge the topic. Innuendos are deceptive tactics that allow people to politely ask, accept, or decline offers without having to expressly put anything on the line. In fact, in these types of cases, most people would see honesty ("Hey, do you want to come up so we can have sex?") as a crude and clumsy gesture that would likely cut the evening short.

We can also view impression management as a deceptive sales tactic (Goffman, 1956). We carefully curate the version of ourselves that others are allowed to see. We hide things about ourselves. Think of things you might do at home alone that you would not do if your boss, preacher, or fitness instructor were watching. We all, even if only subtly, use deception to manipulate others' impressions of us. Scammers like Anna Sorokin differ only in degree.

Anna was not the first person to tell big lies about having rich relatives. In 1897, Canadian-born Cassie Chadwick "accidentally" let a lawyer see a $2 million (about $65 million in 2023 dollars) promissory note she had from the industrial titan, Andrew Carnegie (Abbott, 2012). In confidence, she told the lawyer that she was Carnegie's illegitimate daughter and that he was leaving her substantially more upon his death. The lawyer promised to keep her secret, but he did not. Instead, he shared the information with bankers who soon came to Ms. Chadwick, offering her loans and other financial services. Over the next 5 years, she accepted and spent millions from the banks. Eventually, the fraud was discovered, and she died serving her prison term. As it turned out, her big lies had gone on for most of her life and had resulted in the dissolution of three marriages and several prior arrests and imprisonments.

Some big liars leave a wake of destruction, bankrupting some, destroying relationships for others, and wasting the time and efforts of still others. There is a special category for big liars who use their deception to defraud people after first gaining their trust. We call them *scammers*, *swindlers*, or *con artists*. Whatever name we choose, at their core, these people are big liars.

STAGES OF A SCAM

Cassie Chadwick and Anna Sorokin were con artists. The psychologist Maria Konnikova (2016) has studied all sorts of con artists with the careful focus of an entomologist studying butterflies. She interviewed the scammers, their victims, and people who merely observed the scams from the sidelines. She observed that cons, though wildly different in their aims and their subject matter, typically follow a similar script. At their base level, all swindlers use deception to manipulate how we see the world around us. By distorting our perceptions of reality, they convince us to give them what they want. We surrender the goods willingly.

Scams have several stages, but they are all simply psychological manipulations aimed at encouraging dupes to hand over their assets voluntarily. The first stage is the "put up," which involves the scammer identifying their mark. Con artists have become very good at identifying just the right person who is likely to fall victim to the con. As it turns out, no particular type of person will definitely fall victim to cons. Rather, we are all vulnerable to certain *situations*. We might want something a little too much, or we might feel vulnerable and ignorant enough that we rely a little too much on advice from someone else (E. H. Smith, 1923). So what leaves us most vulnerable to scams? It is usually some degree of need, greed, or compassion. Scammers learn to identify people in situations that leave them vulnerable to greed, need, or compassion.

The next stage is "the play." In this stage, the scammer befriends the mark and seduces them by using their psychological vulnerabilities against them. We all at times have deep psychological needs, such as the need for love and affection, the need for people to see us as we truly are, or the need to affiliate with people we admire. When we need too much, we start to take chances to get what we want. A large number of scams rely on emotional needs, such as the need for love and belongingness, to be the driving force. The forces motivate victims to ignore the red flags that even the best scammers present. Considerable evidence suggests that the need for belongingness and the need for emotional connection weigh heavily on people, and when they are deficient, people often experience psychological problems (Baumeister & Leary, 1995; Leigh-Hunt et al., 2017). This ache for connection leaves people vulnerable to scammers. One study that examined over 580 different scams found that the scammers typically used emotional pleas, signals of trust, and behavioral commitments to entice their victims (Fischer et al., 2013).

Another psychological feature that sets people up to be victimized is greed. Cons often rely on the greed of the victim to be the fuel for their own undoing. Scams often promise opportunities to get rich quickly. People are so tempted by the prospect of easy riches that they become less discerning, seeing only what they wish to be true. Psychologists refer to this cognitive error as *confirmation bias*. We tend to notice the evidence that supports what we want to be true, and we simultaneously fail to notice or discount the evidence that runs contrary to our cherished hopes and beliefs.

Compassion is another Achilles' heel that leaves people vulnerable. Seeing a person who is supposedly in peril and could be rescued with a little help from a stranger is compelling. Most people feel a strong urge to alleviate suffering in others. Scammers use little tricks of psychology to hook their marks. Fraudsters use our sense of compassion and charity to open up our hearts and wallets. After natural disasters, fraudulent charities pop up to take advantage of those whose heartstrings are pulled by the helpless. Scammers solicit donations, and we compassionate people risk being duped.

In "the play," scammers use subtle techniques, such as asking a mark to hold their wallet for them or sharing embarrassing information about themselves. The fact that the scammer seems so willing to make themselves vulnerable leads the mark to trust them and to form an emotional connection with them. They use their persuasive techniques to get marks to like them, to love them, and to trust them. Most people have been conditioned to trust and to be helpful. Scammers capitalize on those tendencies within us.

With the confidence of their marks secured, con artists then move to the next stage called "the rope." The rope is where the scammer first pitches the ploy to their mark. "Hey, I have inherited 10 million dollars from my aunt, but I'm behind on my taxes so I can't legally claim my inheritance." Or perhaps, "I have fallen in love with you and really want to be with you, but I'm stuck overseas and am unable to cash my paychecks right now." In this stage, the con artist capitalizes on greed, need, or compassion.

In the next stage of the con, "the tale," the swindler convinces the victim with the bait. "If you can help me, I'll split the money with you." Easy money! Or "If you can send me money for an airline ticket, I'll fly out to see you next week and we can be together. I'll just pay you back when I arrive." Or maybe, "If you could just loan me a small amount, together we can save my child's life with the medication she needs." The scammer creates a scenario in which your dilemma or theirs could supposedly be resolved with a small gesture. Many people seeking simply to show a bit of compassion and goodwill step up and fall into the scammer's trap. Often the ask is quite small, to not scare off the mark. For example, "The bank won't allow me to access this enormous inheritance until I pay off some back taxes. If you can loan me $100 to pay off a person I know at the bank, they'll release several thousand dollars to me. I can pay you back $250 tomorrow."

The tale sets the stage for the next stage in the scam, "the convincer." After the victim loans the $100, the con artist actually does pay them back $250. This payback convinces the mark that the risk they took was a great decision. The success convinces them that they have a surefire way of getting easy money. They may also convince themselves that they are a truly generous person for helping out the person in need. Not all scams are financial. In romance scams, the convincer could be a profession of love or intimacy, such as "When I saw how generous you were with me, it made me think that I want to be with you forever."

With the mark fully convinced of the con artist's legitimacy, the fraudster moves in for the kill, often referred to as "the send" stage. They might say something like, "My friend at the bank says that if we can pay her $10,000 by Friday, they can release the remaining $10 million to us. If you can lend me the $10,000, I can pay you back $50,000 on Saturday, just like we did last time." They may even add a little extra pressure: "If you are unable, I am pretty sure that one of my other friends will be happy to help. Let me know ASAP so I can include you."

Once the mark has been fleeced of their savings, the scammer will often cover their tracks and prevent the victim from reporting the crime: "Oh my gosh! My friend at the bank has just been arrested for helping us out, and now the FBI is trying to figure out who we are. I'm not sure how we'll get our money back. We should probably lie low for a while." Often the fear of arrest is not necessary to keep a victim silent. The shame and embarrassment of being duped so easily is enough to keep many victims quiet.

The big liars who carry out cons and scams are motivated by greed. They want your money, and they want it for free. Honesty does not typically cause people to part with their wealth, so the con artists lie. Reflecting on the tripartite theory of lying and dishonesty, we can see that scammers recognize that honesty will not lead to desirable responses. People will not hand over their money simply because a scammer wants it; thus, scammers see a utility in lying. They also believe they can get away with the lie. Scammers often lie for a living. They are good at it, and they know it. Additionally, they can morally justify their lying. Scammers often believe that they deserve the wealth that others have. They view their victims as part of an unfair system that has held them down. They convince themselves that other people would do the same things, if they were also smart and resourceful. Frank William Abagnale Jr., the serial con artist portrayed in the movie *Catch Me if You Can* (Spielberg, 2002) claimed, "As long as I didn't hurt anyone, people never considered me a real criminal, my victims were big corporations. I was a kid ripping off the establishment" (Strickler, 2002)—despite reports from his victims that they had been grievously harmed by his lies. Konnikova (2016), who studied dozens of con artists, claimed that they feel a narcissistic, inflated sense of self. They believe that they are more special than the rest of us and are therefore entitled to take what they want. They feel that they deserve your money more than you do (Pazzanese, 2019). Though not all big liars are con artists, all con artists are big liars. They use the tool of lying to take whatever they want.

PONZI SCHEMES

Bernie Madoff was an American financier who managed to defraud his victims of $64 billion (Graybow, 2009). He convinced eager investors that if they deposited their money with him, he could earn fantastic returns for them—consistently more than any other investment house on Wall Street. However, those fantastic financial returns were all based on a foundation of lies. Madoff was running a Ponzi scheme, the largest such scam in American history. A Ponzi scheme works by paying off earlier investors with the money from subsequent investors. The supposed high returns paid to the original investors serve as great marketing for the operation. The early investors eagerly boast to others about how rich they are becoming because of the genius investment manager. This enthusiastic praise leads many more investors to deposit their money, perpetuating the scheme. Many investors, wowed by how rich they are becoming, reinvest their earnings, further supporting the Ponzi operation. Bernie Madoff carried on his scam year after year, investor after investor. However, a Ponzi scheme can only continue if a constant supply of new investors bring in more money. After all, the new dupes are the only source of income. With Madoff's Ponzi scheme, people started to withdraw their investments faster than new investors were contributing. Madoff tried quickly to recruit new investors, but his luck had run out. The operation ran too low on funds and collapsed.

The Ponzi scheme, like all Ponzi schemes, collapsed under the weight of the lies. All along, Bernie Madoff had lied to the Securities and Exchange Commission, avoiding any detection or prosecution by the federal authorities. He also lied to his family members, who helped run the company but had no idea of the Ponzi scheme, which he kept siloed away from all but a select handful of people. In fact, Madoff was never actually caught. He turned himself in once he realized he would no longer be able to fool his investors. He finally confessed to his two sons who worked for him, letting them know that the whole multibillion-dollar company was "all just one big lie" (Appelbaum et al., 2008).

How was Madoff able to keep his scheme going for what federal authorities estimated to be about 30 years? He lied. He lied every day. He lied to investors, to the feds, and to his family. But there is more to it than simply lying. If a simple lie could allow someone to swindle billions of dollars, it would happen much more frequently. His success as a big liar can probably be attributed to a few things. First, Madoff had credibility. Before starting the Ponzi scheme, he had previously been a successful legitimate investor. He was also on the board of directors for the Securities Industry Association, a role that lent him even more credibility. Madoff also made use of identity affinity in his con. We all feel a special affinity for people who belong to our circles, whether they are family members, friends from our childhood, people who also attended our college, or even people who root for the same sports teams as we do. We have a special liking or affinity for our ingroup. Madoff was a Jewish man, and he used his ingroup affinity in the Jewish community to his advantage. More than any other tactic, though, Madoff relied on the greed of his victims. This is not to suggest that his victims were at fault. Like every other investor, they wanted to maximize their earnings. Sometimes greed can blind people to warning signs.

In the end, Madoff's scheme victimized a range of people, from fabulously wealthy Hollywood celebrities, such as Steven Spielberg, to fairly anonymous retirees who had entrusted Madoff with all they had (Pak, 2021). One victim was the Nobel Peace Prize winner and Holocaust survivor, Elie Wiesel. Madoff scammed him out of his entire life savings and another $15 million from a nonprofit organization Wiesel had set up to combat injustice and intolerance in the world. All told, Madoff swindled over 30,000 victims.

Research makes clear the enormous financial and psychological toll that scammers exact on society (European Commission, 2020; Gee & Button, 2019). Recent estimates are that worldwide losses due to fraud exceed $5 trillion. The core element of all these costly frauds is a lie. But not all big liars in the world are career criminals. For some, their occupation involves lying.

SALESPEOPLE AND ADVERTISING

Marketing and advertising practices seem to date back several thousand years (Eckhardt & Bengtsson, 2010). No doubt, across those many centuries, marketers acting as lay psychologists realized the ease with which they could use misleading advertisements to bend the feeble-minded population of consumers to their advantage. One of the first advertising scientists was a professor of psychology at Northwestern University, Dr. Walter Dill Scott. Scott (1903) remarked, "Man has been called the reasoning animal but he could with greater truthfulness be called the creature of suggestion" (p. 59). He recognized that rather than using powers of reason to assess the veracity of advertisers' claims, people react emotionally to advertisements, whether they are truthful or not. Advertisers use tricks, such as bait-and switch schemes, embellished pictures or descriptions, false claims about quality or effectiveness, and hidden charges. Those lies leave consumers challenged to discern the truth of any marketing claim.

In the United States, the Federal Trade Commission (FTC, 2021) finally enacted the truth-in-advertising laws, reining in the outright lies that advertisers had been using. Still, advertisers push big lies to encourage us to buy their products. In 2016, the FTC charged Volkswagen for marketing and selling their vehicles with supposed "clean diesel" engines (FTC, 2016). That lie concealed the fact that Volkswagen was actually selling cars that produced illegally high levels of pollution. In many cases, false claims are made about the health benefits of products. In some cases, vaguely meaningful words, such as "natural" and "organic," are used to convey a sense of wholesomeness and health. But on occasion, the claims slip into full untruths, such as when the Dannon food company suggested, without evidence, that their Activia yogurt boosted the immune system. The FTC (2010) charged them with false advertising and also charged Kellogg for making the same false claim about Rice Krispies cereal (S. Young, 2010). While it may be harder to get away with being a big liar in advertising these days, it seems that advertisers continue to push the limits.

Advertising and marketing can be viewed as a tool for sales, so one might expect to find big liars involved in the sales force of some organizations. Sales is a form of negotiation. If I want to buy something, and you want to sell that thing, we can negotiate the terms of the exchange. In many cases, this process is collaborative—we have a shared goal of completing the exchange in a manner that ensures both parties are satisfied with the terms. In other cases, the sales negotiation is adversarial—each side uses every weapon in its arsenal to gain an advantage over the other party (Shonk, 2021). Adversarial approaches often utilize tools for deceiving the other party. "An act of betraying," "a contrivance, fiction, etc.," "a planned deception, hoax, take-in"—these are a few elements of the definition of the word *sell* in the *Oxford English Dictionary*. There are horror stories of overt deception in the name of closing a deal. In a legal case in Texas, a car dealership was sued because, among other things, the sales staff hid a deaf and mute customer's keys so that the customer could not leave until buying a vehicle (*George Grubbs Enterprises, Inc. v. Bien*, 1994). The court determined that the sales team had systematically used deception and other forms of psychological manipulation to maximize their profit.

Lying by salespeople is not universally viewed as a bad trait. Researchers at Johns Hopkins University and the University of Chicago Booth School of Business studied how liars are perceived in the workplace (Gunia & Levine, 2019). Their principal finding was that people tend to view lying as a marker of competence in jobs that necessitate selling, such as salesperson or advertiser, but much less so if the person's job does not involve sales (e.g., chemist, librarian). Furthermore, they were actually more inclined to hire liars for jobs in sales. Thus, being a big liar, or at least a competent liar, seems to be viewed as an asset in sales fields.

It is important to note that consumers also lie to salespeople (Anthony & Cowley, 2012; Papachristodoulou, 2019). They lie to negotiate the best deal they can get. Some customers lie to get refunds and exchanges when one is not warranted. They misrepresent their ability to pay full price, they make erroneous claims to qualify for discounts, they lie about their level of interest in a product, and they lie about their ability to get a better deal elsewhere. They scheme and lie to place themselves in a better financial position. Perhaps, then, it should not be surprising that salespeople, too, use deception as a tool in these sparring matches over price and availability. Haggling is a negotiation over contested ground. Perhaps it is a context that turns people into big liars.

CORPORATE LIARS

Elizabeth Holmes was a brilliant and ambitious chemical engineering student at Stanford University with the public relations talents of a career marketing professional. Before the age of 20, she had mapped a plan to start a blood-testing company that was destined to change the medical landscape. When a person goes to the doctor for blood tests, a medical technician inserts a needle into the arm and draws out several vials of blood. Those vials are typically then shipped off to a lab, while the patient and doctor wait for the results. Holmes had a design to create a miniaturized blood-testing unit that could offer inexpensive and immediate blood testing with a single drop of blood. No more need for needles, vials, and labs. Just a finger prick of blood and a few minutes of processing would generate all the results.

Holmes dropped out of Stanford and founded a company, Theranos. She quickly raised cash from venture capitalists and private investors. In a few short years, Theranos was valued at $9 billion, and Holmes was showered with accolades from the likes of Barack Obama, Joe Biden, and Bill Clinton. In early 2014, not yet 30 years old, Holmes was worth $4 billion (Pflanzer, 2019).

The blood-testing machine, dubbed Edison, was rapidly progressing, according to Holmes. Soon, the Safeway grocery store chain and Walgreens pharmacy chains had partnered with Theranos and were pouring millions of dollars into retrofitting their pharmacy locations to use the Theranos device. But alas, all was not as it seemed. The chief financial officer of Theranos was terminated for questioning the reliability of the company's products and the honesty of its management team. Theranos was accused of pushing products to market before the technology was viable, and some said that Theranos was fabricating test results. An article in *The Wall Street Journal* skewered Theranos and Holmes (Carreyrou, 2015). The article shined a spotlight on the many shortcomings of the Theranos technology and the questionable claims made by Holmes and other executives. Contracts were canceled, investigations were initiated, and investors grew wary.

Holmes, as it turned out, was a big liar. She had been deceiving investors about the technological progress her company had made. She claimed that the Edison machine could work magic, but the reality was that it could do very little of what Holmes claimed. The company imploded. By 2016, Holmes's fortune had evaporated. In 2018, Theranos ceased to exist. The U.S. Securities and Exchange Commission charged Holmes and Theranos with "massive fraud." She was convicted of defrauding investors and sentenced to more than 11 years in prison. Additionally, she will likely owe over $100 million in restitution to the people she defrauded.

Corporate organizational expert Ron Carucci was interested in why leaders at some companies like Theranos seem to behave as if deception is a core value, while other business leaders are notably honest. Through his consulting company, he conducted research based on thousands of interviews carried out over years of work with companies large and small. What he found was that corrupt individuals don't seem to be at the heart of duplicitous companies. Instead, organizational factors lead people in some companies to be dishonest (Carucci, 2019). He found that companies with deceptive practices tend to lack strategic clarity. That is, what the company actually does is not congruent with its stated mission. An inconsistent company's employees notice the disconnect and seem to disregard all the stated values of the company, including honesty and integrity. Carucci also found that dishonest companies tend to have employees who perceive their company as unfair. They believe that no matter what they do, they will not be given proper credit for their work, so they lie to get ahead. The most dishonest companies also tend to have poor governance. Meetings are seen as a waste of time. The true decisions are based on rumors and gossip rather than facts and clearheaded management. Finally, he found that when people or small groups are isolated or siloed in an organization, they run amok with dishonesty. Small groups within the organizations begin to compete with each other. They use lies to get ahead. It turns out that collaboration and transparency within companies maintain honesty.

University of Oregon professor David Markowitz and his colleagues (2021) may have identified another important clue to why some organizations are populated with big liars and others are not. The researchers examined the codes of conduct at 190 Fortune 500 companies. They were curious about whether the manner in which the codes of conduct were written had any discernible downstream effects on ethical and honest behavior at the companies. They conducted a detailed linguistic analysis, studying the types of words and phrases that were used in each code of conduct. What they found was intriguing. Most companies have policies that cover ethical territory around honesty, fairness, loyalty, respect, and so on. However, the researchers found that not all companies clearly communicate expectations around those values. They determined that many companies use very straightforward, direct, and clear language. However, others were a bit more vague, confusing, abstract, or complicated in their wording. Using this obfuscated language results in what the researchers called a *deception spiral*. When people read a muddled code of conduct, they perceived the company to be low in trustworthiness, low in morality, and low in warmth. You can imagine that an employee at one of these companies might not sense that their employer actually cares about virtuous behavior.

The deception spiral continues further. The researchers found that people who read unclear codes of conduct were significantly more likely to engage in various forms of cheating than were people who read a clear and direct set of values and expectations (Markowitz et al., 2021). So, the way a code of conduct is worded can actually lead people to behave dishonestly.

In the final arc of the deception spiral, the researchers examined ethical violations at the Fortune 500 companies in their study (Markowitz et al., 2021). Ethical violations included fraud, rules violations, and other infractions. The results indicated that companies that had obfuscated codes of conduct were significantly more likely to have ethical violations than were companies with clearly written ones. It seems that the message coming from the top of the organization translates into attitudes held by the employees, which drives honest or dishonest behavior, leading to broad patterns of unethical behavior at the companies. Companies, it seems, can also be big liars, and whether they are or not hinges on the structure and culture of the company.

Founded in the mid-1980s, Enron was an energy supplier and trading company that made innovative moves into e-commerce. Under the leadership of Kenneth Lay and Jeffrey Skilling, Enron became a powerhouse during the 1990s and early 2000s. Year after year, Enron was posting massive earnings that almost defied belief. At its peak, the company was valued at $70 billion. The phenomenal success of Enron hinged on a little trick. Its officers lied. While the company was suffering massive losses, executives would create partner companies and then transfer the massive losses to those companies. Billions of dollars of red ink were essentially swept under the rug. Arthur Anderson, one of the biggest and most reputable accounting companies, vouched for Enron's bookkeeping, conspiring to help Enron carry out one of the most massive frauds in corporate history (National Public Radio, n.d.; Thomas, 2002). The leader of Enron pressured lower level executives to conceal debt, meet Wall Street expectations, and generally obscure what was really happening at Enron via several accounting tricks, intentional smoke screens, and distorted messaging about profits (McLean & Elkind, 2003). Enron convinced investors and regulators that their earnings had grown in 4 years from $13 billion to more than $100 billion, a remarkable 750% growth.

People started to question why Enron was so secretive with its balance sheets. Investors got spooked. The Securities and Exchange Commission started an investigation. In late 2000, Enron shares were trading at $90. A little over a year later, those same shares fetched only a few cents. Enron had collapsed. Investors experienced massive losses. Lower level employees of Enron, ignorant of the fraud, had their retirement accounts tied up in company stock. Their life savings vanished. It was the largest accounting fraud in U.S. history at the time. A year later, however, another company, WorldCom, engaged in similar accounting fraud and beat that record.

LAW ENFORCEMENT

A 2020 Gallup poll suggested that confidence in the police had fallen to a record low, with fewer than half of Americans expressing faith in law enforcement (Brenan, 2020b). While widespread news coverage of the killing of George Floyd and other instances of apparent police misconduct definitely contributed to this decline, relatively low trust in police is persistent and may be tied to dishonesty amongst the ranks.

Throughout history, anecdotal rumors, claims, and even documented examples of law enforcement officers lying and otherwise behaving dishonestly have appeared regularly. There have even been many systemic examinations of police dishonesty in large cities in the United States. For instance, in 1994, the New York City mayor, David Dinkins, appointed the City of New York Commission to Investigate Allegations of Police Corruption and the Anti-Corruption Procedures of the Police Department, commonly known as the Mollen Commission, to investigate the nature and extent of police misconduct. The commission concluded that a culture of lax attitudes toward corruption had led to pervasive corruption, criminality, and lawlessness among the officers of the NYPD. Deception and a blind eye to rule violations had shaped the department into a den of lies. A widespread tolerance of lies to protect their own was also documented in police departments in Chicago (Morell & Smith, 2020), Los Angeles (Rector et al., 2020), and other major cities. Police were viewed by many citizens as big liars.

But not all lying by the police is illegal. In fact, many of the big liars in police departments are fully supported by the legal system, and the lies themselves are endorsed as legitimate practices. In 1969, the U.S. Supreme Court heard the case of *Frazier v. Cupp*. Martin Frazier had been drinking at a bar with his cousin. Police later found that another patron of the bar had been murdered. The police picked up Frazier and his cousin and separated them for questioning. The investigators lied to Frazier, falsely telling him that his cousin had already confessed and implicated Frazier in the murder. Frazier denied the accusation but ultimately confessed to the murder. At trial, Frazier's attorneys argued that the deception by the police should invalidate any confession that Frazier later offered. The Supreme Court ruled otherwise, finding that the deception by the police did not render the confession inadmissible.

Since then, courts have seen this case as an affirmation of the legality of interrogation tactics that involve outright lying by the police. In various cases, police officers have elicited confessions by lying to suspects about the evidence against them. For instance, officers have falsely claimed that a dead suspect is still alive, that fingerprints link the suspect to the crime, that satellite imagery showed the suspect committing the crime, and that DNA evidence was undeniable (Najdowski & Bonventre, 2014). While these deceptive techniques may help police gain confessions from guilty suspects, they also increase the odds that innocent people will falsely confess to crimes.

The Reid technique is one of the most widely used police interrogation techniques in the United States (Sanow, 2011). It was developed in the 1950s by John Reid, a psychologist who had been a Chicago police officer. The technique is used to generate an emotional roller-coaster for the suspect in an interrogation. In turn, the interrogators apply extreme pressure to confess by convincing the suspect that there is no escape and then shifting to an empathic, helpful, and understanding stance to create an alliance with the suspect. The Reid technique proposes several deceptive strategies, including demonstrating false empathy for the suspect's plight, falsely telling the suspect the criminal act seems morally justified, and falsely offering a reason or rationale that would explain why it might have been reasonable to commit the crime. One criticism of the Reid technique is that it leads to false confessions. Principally, the suspects feel so utterly convinced that they have no way out of their predicament that they falsely confess to the crime in hope of receiving a more lenient sentence.

In Germany and England, where such lying by police is not standard practice, law enforcement officials are able to maintain high rates of confessions and also have low rates of false confessions (Craven, 2020). These findings call into question the validity of claims that dishonesty is necessary for police to protect the public effectively.

Some courts in the United States are beginning to view deceptive tactics by police interrogators as overly coercive. For instance, in Illinois, an appellate court overturned the murder conviction of an 18-year-old. In that case, police interrogators deceptively told the suspect that they had incontrovertible evidence that he had fired the gun. They convinced the suspect that in the face of such undeniable evidence, things would go much easier for him if he confessed to the shooting. He offered a confession and was convicted. The appeals court subsequently determined that the suspect falsely confessed to the crime, largely because he believed the lies his interrogators had fabricated (M. Cohen & Kuang, 2018). In 2021, Illinois passed a law barring investigators from lying to minors during questioning, although they are still allowed to lie to adult suspects (Taylor, 2021). In several other states, politicians have introduced bills that would dramatically limit the use of deception in interrogations (Quiroz, 2021).

LIARS IN THE PULPIT

Andy Traub (2017) described the case of the pastor at his church. He found his pastor funny, engaging, and sincere. But he was a big liar too. A few keen members of the congregation noticed that the preacher's sermons were similar to sermons given by other preachers. They did some deep research and came to an unsettling conclusion. Their pastor had stolen almost every single word of every sermon he had delivered for the past 5 years. He stole the titles, the artwork, his interpretations, his jokes, his stories about his childhood, and so on. Everything he said in every sermon was stolen from others and presented as if it were his own. This man at the altar was a big liar. It turns out that some big liars seem motivated by pure laziness.

Other big liars in the pulpit lie for financial gain. The prominent televangelist Jim Bakker served years in prison after being convicted of numerous counts of fraud and conspiracy (Effron et al., 2019). He lied to his followers, telling them that the money they donated would be used to help needy people overseas. He lied to others, telling them that their contributions were invested in a hotel. In reality, he used the funds to support a lavish lifestyle and to pay off a woman who he allegedly drugged and raped.

Other prominent men of the cloth also turned to big lies to conceal bad behavior, such as sexual escapades. Ted Haggard was an evangelical preacher who headed a 14,000-member congregation (Harris, 2010). He preached against homosexuality but later was accused of a same-sex affair and the use of illicit drugs. He denied all the accusations to his followers. Eventually, a voicemail revealed him asking his male lover to secure him some methamphetamine. He continued to lie for a while before finally coming clean to his flock.

Still others lie simply to create an impressive story about themselves. Pennsylvania pastor Jim Moats spent years convincing his flock that he had served as a Navy SEAL in Vietnam (Daily Mail, 2011). He would impress his parishioners with stories of harrowing military escapades. He seemed to borrow storylines from Hollywood movies, including being assigned to kitchen dishwashing duty because of his bad attitude (from the movie *Under Siege* with Steven Seagal; A. Davis, 1992), or the time he was waterboarded as part of his interrogation-resistance training (from the movie *G.I. Jane* with Demi Moore; Scott, 1997). He would walk around town wearing the golden trident emblem of the real Navy SEALs (he bought it at a surplus store). His lies were eventually uncovered by a real Navy SEAL, and Moats admitted to being a big liar.

Other widely covered instances of institutional big liars in the Catholic Church revolved around widespread instances of child sexual abuse. In 2019, Cardinal Theodore McCarrick was found guilty of sexual harassment and sexual abuse of minors and adults. He was subsequently dismissed from the Catholic priesthood. Numerous accusations had been made against McCarrick, but he had dismissed them all. He was regarded by some experts as a pathological liar. As revolting and disconcerting as McCarrick's misdeeds were, there is compelling evidence that church leaders conspired to lie and cover up his crimes (Rocca & Lovett, 2020).

DOCTORS LYING

People in the helping professions are less likely to be judged as big liars. Nursing tends to be consistently rated as the most honest and ethical profession by the public even though some nurses lie (Gallup, 2020; Teasdale & Kent, 1995). Physicians and psychologists tend to fall into the same boat of lying to patients, but their occupations are generally not thought of as lying professions (Curtis & Hart, 2015; Palmieri & Stern, 2009). These helping professions may be regarded as honest specifically because these professionals are helping others, even if at the cost of lying.

In one study, more than half of the doctors surveyed admitted to sometimes describing a patient's prognosis more optimistically than the facts would support (Iezzoni et al., 2012). They also indicated that they would conceal financial relationships they had with drug providers and would conceal instances of malpractice. Overall, though, most doctors reported being quite honest most of the time. About 90% indicated that they had been honest with all patients during the preceding year.

In 2014, the Mental Health Foundation convened a large panel of professionals, researchers, caregivers, and other experts to explore the topic of lying to people with dementia. After an extensive 18-month survey, analysis, and exploration, the panel concluded that many caregivers, professionals, and staff who work with dementia patients regularly use lies and other forms of deception to support the well-being of their patients (Mental Health Foundation, 2016). The panel concluded that it would be best to move away from "never lie" philosophies and instead consider using "untruth" interactions that would minimize distress in their patients. They argued that a kind and compassionate effort to help patients make sense of their own reality was ultimately what was most important, rather than having caregivers impose the truth on patients. That is, they endorsed compassionate dishonesty.

Ryan (2004) argued that as doctors in our culture take on a paternalistic role, leading patients through waters with which they may be largely unfamiliar, they don't usually lie. Instead, they exercise an economy with the truth in their cautious attempts to protect their patients from the pain of deeply unpleasant truths. Rather than doling out the brutal facts of the situation, doctors often conspire with their patients to find the best version of the truth, one that conveys the closest approximation of the truth that the patient can tolerate. Through this shared construction of reality, doctors and patients coauthor palatable narratives of pain, survival, and death. These positive spins need not and often do not necessarily entail outright lying. After all, "You have a great chance of pulling through" is simply a matter of optimistic perspective when describing someone who has a 90% chance of dying soon.

Some doctors are big liars out of a sense of kindness, warmth, and compassion. However, not all physicians are benevolent deceivers. Dr. Farid Fata was an oncologist who owned one of the largest oncology practices in the state of Michigan (Schecter et al., 2015). Several years after he opened his practice, other medical staff began to express concern about his treatment of patients. Fata appeared to be using cancer treatments that were overly aggressive and maybe unnecessary. When authorities looked into some of Fata's medical practices, they found no evidence of wrongdoing. As years went by, more and more patients and colleagues worried that Fata was using nonstandard approaches to treating patients and occasionally misdiagnosing patients.

At one point, Fata was out of the country, and one of his newly diagnosed cancer patients broke her leg. She was treated by one of

Fata's colleagues. That physician was shocked when he reviewed the patient's bloodwork. She had no sign at all of having cancer. Suspicious, the doctor began reviewing the charts of many other patients of Fata. What he discovered was alarming: Fata was diagnosing patients with cancer when there was no indication they were ill. He was then placing them on expensive chemotherapy treatments that they did not need, sometimes for years. The FBI finally stepped in, quickly determining that Fata was lying to patients about their diagnoses and fraudulently billing them and their insurance companies for the treatments. One of the patients, Robert Sobieray, discussed the harm he had endured. The doctor had concocted a false diagnosis for Sobieray, telling him that he had a rare type of blood cancer that would require extensive and expensive chemotherapy and radiation treatments. Those treatments took their toll. Sobieray's body twitched uncontrollably, and his teeth fell out. He eventually learned that his suffering was all the result of big lies. A final tally showed that Fata had lied to at least 553 people, convincing them they had cancer and needed treatment. He had defrauded patients and insurance companies of at least $34 million. He admitted that his lies were all told out of pure greed.

While some doctors may be big liars, others have taken lying one step further. Ayse Ozkiraz's parents wanted their daughter to study medicine and be a doctor (Kaya, 2022). They were overjoyed when Ayse announced that she had scored very well on the medical entrance exams and had been admitted to medical school. Eventually, she graduated and was working as a general practitioner at a state hospital. She found she was interested in surgery, so she began to work with a doctor in the pediatric surgery unit. She conducted examinations and was even allowed to participate in surgeries, stitching up patients at the end of their surgical procedures. But, alas, Ayse Ozkiraz was not a doctor at all. When she failed to pass her medical school entrance exams, she pretended to go to medical school anyway.

She lived in dorms and hung out with medical students, but she never stepped foot in a medical school classroom. She forged her diploma and lied about her qualifications. She was an entire fraud. After she was arrested for her lies, she admitted that she had done it all because she didn't want to let her family down.

LYING LAWYERS

Lawyers are often viewed as less honest and less ethical than most other professions (Gallup, 2020). The classic story *To Kill a Mockingbird* (H. Lee, 1960) depicted Atticus Finch, a lawyer who was forthright and honest. Unlike physicians, lawyers are saddled with the widely held stereotype that they are all liars and schemers (T. L. Davis, 2016). Interestingly, though attorneys are viewed as significantly less honest than doctors, they are viewed as no less professional. It seems that being dishonest is seen as part of the occupational landscape in the law. The occasional bending of the truth is aimed at benevolently helping their clients, much like medical professionals using deception to help their patients.

According to the American Bar Association (2019), "a lawyer shall not knowingly make a false statement of material fact or law to a third person." That is, a lawyer should not lie. Do they? Bruce Green, the director of Fordham Law School's Louis Stein Center for Law and Ethics, argued that while outright lying is unethical, that ethical demand is in tension with the ethical obligation to zealously defend and serve one's client to the greatest degree possible (American Bar Association, 2018). This delicate balancing act may rule out an outright lie by an attorney, but it leaves space for other forms of deception, such as concealment, exaggeration, misdirection, and withholding. Just like the noble doctor, the lawyers, to be effective, cannot lay all facts on the table, as many of those facts are bound to be problematic for their clients. They also do not tell outright lies without remorse. Rather, lawyers accept the challenge of generating economical versions of the truth. They tell the best version of the truth that they can.

Some go much further than that, though. Attorney Michael Avenatti was sentenced to 14 years in prison and ordered to pay back millions in restitution to his victims. Over several years, Avenatti had represented several clients for whom he had secured million-dollar settlements. The only problem was that he kept the settlements for himself. He embezzled a multimillion-dollar settlement from one client but promptly used the money to buy himself a private jet. He dishonestly claimed that the money was being wrongly withheld by the opposing attorneys. With other clients he did the same thing, stealing money and then lying to cover his tracks.

POLITICS

We hope not to shock you when we tell you that politicians sometimes lie. Early American presidents were regarded as pillars of integrity. In fact, people have mythically quoted George Washington as saying that he could not tell a lie when confronted about cutting down a cherry tree. Abraham Lincoln's uprightness led to him being given the nickname Honest Abe. Somewhere along the history timetable, American presidents and politicians traded the badge of honesty for a big liar trophy. A recent Gallup poll (2020) found that politicians are viewed as some of the least honest and ethical professionals.

Accusations of being a big liar have tended to take the forefront in recent presidential elections, with candidates challenging the integrity of the opposing candidate by explicitly calling the other a liar. In the 2016 presidential election, Donald Trump accused Hillary Clinton of lying via covering up emails, and Clinton accused Trump of lying about taxes. Similarly, in the 2020 election, President Trump accused Joe Biden of lying about his role in his son's business, and Biden accused Trump of lying about the coronavirus threat. Mudslinging by way of the term *liar* is not a surprising strategy for presidential candidates because perceived honesty is important for the job. One poll found that Americans consider a candidate's honesty to be the single most important factor in choosing a president, ranking it as more important than positions on the issues and questions of leadership, experience, and intelligence (Fournier & Tompson, 2007). Ironically, politicians who are opposed to lying tend to have lower reelection rates (Janezic & Gallego, 2020). Thus, lying tends to be reinforced in politics.

Lying is pervasive in politics (Macqueen, 2017). In the United States, history portrays a parade of big liars at the top of the government. One can ponder about who is the bigger liar, the one who tells a single lie that launches the country headlong into a trillion-dollar war that cost hundreds of thousands of lives or the liar who drips a steady stream of lies of less consequence. Robert Kennedy once said that Vice President (soon to be President) Lyndon Johnson "lies all the time. I'm telling you, he just lies continually about everything. He lies even when he doesn't have to lie" (Shesol, 1997, p. 109). This statement was spoken of someone within his own administration, not a rival party. In his book *Lying in State*, Alterman (2020) documented the long history of presidential deception, from Johnson's lies about the Vietnam War, to Nixon's prevarication about Watergate, to Reagan's untruths about the Iran–Contra affair in which weapons were secretly sold (even though there was an arms embargo) to the sworn enemy of the United States, Iran, to fund a secret war in Nicaragua (even though Congress had forbidden such assistance). George H. W. Bush told lies about Kuwaiti babies being tossed from incubators by Iraqi soldiers to garner support for a U.S. invasion. Bill Clinton lied repeatedly about his extramarital affairs. George W. Bush spread lies about Iraq possessing weapons of mass destruction, drawing America into one of its longest and most costly wars.

Barack Obama told lies aimed at hyping his agendas, downplaying his administration's shortcomings, and making disingenuous accusations about his rivals. For instance, he claimed, "We signed into law the biggest middle-class tax cut in history," despite the fact that many historical tax cuts had been considerably larger.

No discussion of political big liars would be complete, however, without noting the remarkable capacity for deception of President Trump. He began his term with a lie. Despite the fact that it had rained throughout his inaugural address, he asserted, "And the truth is, it stopped immediately, and then became sunny . . . and I walked off, and it poured after I left. It poured."

The Washington Post kept a running count of every false or misleading statement Trump made while in office (Kessler et al., 2021). By the time his presidency ended, Trump had racked up an eye-popping 30,573 false or misleading claims. That amounts to an average of 21 lies for every day he was in office. Almost half of those lies were told during his final year in office. On a single day, he lied 189 times. Many commentators and historians have noted that, while all presidents have been documented liars, Trump was entirely unprecedented in how frequent and carefree he was with deception. For comparison, one analysis examined only blatant falsehoods and lies, not including misleading statements. They found that Trump told about 124 lies in his first year in office. By comparison, *The Washington Post* documented that Obama told about two each year during his 8 years in office. Trump began his presidency with boisterous lies about the size of his inaugural crowd, and he left office spreading the big lie that he had, in fact, actually won the election.

Despite Trump's transparent lies, a Gallup poll late in his presidency found that over a third of U.S. adults still found Trump to be honest and trustworthy (Brenan, 2020a). Could it be that they believed his lies? People tend to believe stories if they believe the person sharing the story is trustworthy, regardless of the reliability of the person who produced the story (American Press Institute, 2017). Research has shown that when people evaluate the veracity of stories online, they place more credibility on someone they trust than they do on a credible media outlet. So, if a trusted politician makes a false statement and a news outlet suggests it is a false claim, people may tend to place more belief in the politician they trust than the news source pointing out the lie.

But why do people continue to support and follow politicians even after clear and compelling evidence indicates that those politicians are lying? It appears that most people fall victim to tribalism, selective perception, cognitive dissonance, motivated reasoning, and other bugs in our cognitive hardware. We often arrive at our conclusions via our visceral feelings, not the facts we are presented with. Tribalism is pervasive (Packer, 2018). We all have groups we belong to, whether they be sports teams we support, colleges from which we are alums, states in which we live, and so on. These are "our people," and everyone else is "the other." We prefer to affiliate with our tribe, we cut them slack when they make mistakes, we offer them preferential treatment, and we see them as better people.

Tribalism even causes people to look the other way when people from their group lie. In one survey, 96% of people, both Republicans and Democrats, said they see honesty as "absolutely essential" or "very important" in political leaders (Heimlich, 2008). However, 55% of Republicans surveyed said that they would vote in 2020 for a presidential candidate who they believed would lie to cover up the truth (Dallas, 2018). That's up from 12% of Republicans who said the same in 2015. Democrats tolerate lying too. When Bill Clinton was caught lying about his sexual involvement with Monica Lewinsky, his approval ratings among his party remained largely unchanged (Desilver, 2019).

The reason that politicians are allowed by their supporters to get away with bald-faced lies is rooted in *coalitional psychology*

(Tooby, 2017). *Coalitions* are groups of people who share an abstract identity in common. Coalitions can form around geographic proximity, phenotypic similarity, common experiences, similar belief systems, or common goals. As a cohesive group, coalitions act in unison, bound together in a shared identity, to achieve common goals and defend common interests. Tooby, an anthropologist, argued that humans are identity-crazed. People readily identify as coalitional members, whether the coalition be based on a religious, social, political, nationalistic, or other grouping. Coalitional membership allows members to amplify their power when they come into conflict with nonmembers. Imagine how a bar fight might play out if one of the combatants happens to have his rugby team with him. Coalitional members rally to the cause, supporting and defending each other and the ideological value structures that tether them together.

But how do coalitions know for sure that a member will actually stand with them when called upon to fight? One way, Tooby (2017) argued, is to demonstrate loyalty by endorsing shared beliefs that are unique to the coalitions. In religions, for example, members unanimously endorse beliefs, such as that wine is transformed into blood, unseen angels hover above, rats are reincarnated people, faith will protect one from poisonous snake bites, or that by committing suicide one's eternal soul can be rescued by alien gods in a spaceship hidden behind a comet's tail. Likewise, Tooby argued, political tribes bond together around shared beliefs, and the more absurd the beliefs that coalitions rally around, the more certain the coalition can be that each member is a "true" member.

This process may explain Republicans' reactions to some of Trump's lies. When people who were once considered to have solid Republican credentials began to question the lies, such as the idea that the election was stolen from him, other members of the coalition saw them as traitors who deserved to be expelled from the group, or worse. Undeniable facts, rational arguments, and logic and reason did not matter. When coalitional members questioned the sacred dogma of the coalition, they showed that they could no longer be counted on. On the other hand, party members who were willing to repeat obvious falsehoods, even in the face of clearly contradictory evidence, were seen as true believers worthy of continued coalition membership.

According to this theory, the more preposterous the lie people are willing to parrot, the more certain others can be of their devotion to the coalition. In this sense, a person saying that they believe a lie may not indicate their actual belief at all. Rather, the repetition of the lie merely signals the group a person sides with.

Embracing lies is not solely an issue in Trumpian or conservative corners. The coalitional signals in some liberal coalitions include assertions, such as that men and women have no innate differences and that hurtful words are literal violence, among others. These spurious claims are used for social cohesion. One such form of signaling is referred to as telling *blue lies*. Most people find lying to be morally objectionable. However, some lies are viewed as acceptable because they somehow serve the greater good of the group or tribe, binding the tribe together in a set of beliefs that, despite being factually untrue, signal a dedication to the group. In this sense, they are seen as prosocial and thus morally justified (J. A. Smith, 2017). Whether it is Trump's suggesting that Obama was not born in the United States or Hillary Clinton's asserting that investigations into her husband's financial and sexual misconduct were part of a vast right-wing conspiracy, the lie is accepted by the loyal members of the coalition. Challenging the lie is seen as an overt act of disloyalty.

Lies by politicians are exacerbated by their propagation across social media. Researchers found that during the final months of the 2016 U.S. presidential campaign, citizens were significantly more likely to read the top 20 fake news stories about the campaign (e.g., "Pope Francis Shocks World, Endorses Donald Trump") than the top 20 most popular real news stories about the campaign (T. B. Lee, 2016). This finding is all the more concerning when one considers other research showing that most social media users are unable to discern real news stories from fake ones (Donald, 2016). Big liars seem to succeed in politics because the electorate often doesn't recognize the deception, and even when they do, they don't seem to mind.

CONCLUSION

Societies are built on trust. To accomplish anything in a cooperative way, people must believe that others speak honestly. When big liars inhabit our worlds, it becomes challenging to know who can be trusted and who cannot. That breakdown of trust makes life itself difficult, as we must expend attention, effort, and energy trying to discern whether we should believe someone. And when we let down our guard, the big liars in the various spheres of society pounce, taking advantage of our gullibility.

Whether in the world of business, politics, religion, or any other sphere of life, widespread lying does not usually come naturally. Rather, the acceptance of deception as a normal mode of operating is slowly developed over time. Lying perhaps feels uncomfortable and unethical at first, but with more and more exposure, people start to lose sight of the objectionable feelings about deception they once had. This habituation to dishonesty has been referred to as *normalization of lying* (Jenkins & Delbridge, 2017). If lying is common enough within a social environment, it becomes woven into the fabric of society. Slowly, what was once rare and condemned becomes familiar and forgivable. Lying becomes a sign of loyalty. Lying is rewarded. The harms caused by the lies are denied or minimized. Eventually, pervasive lying becomes the cultural norm. We look and find that the big liars are all around us.

This chapter covered the big liars that we encounter in broad societal contexts. Fortunately, these are not people with whom we typically have personal encounters on a regular basis. In Chapter 5, we examine the big liars with whom people are more apt to have intimate connections, including friends, family, and romantic partners. These are the people who, when they are big liars, are most capable of affecting us directly.

CHAPTER 5

LYING TO LOVERS AND OTHERS IN OUR LIVES

The worst part about being lied to is knowing you weren't worth the truth.

—Jean-Paul Sartre

In 2021, Chelsea Curnutt had a pretty nice life (Britzky, 2021; Sicard, 2021). She was living in Virginia, where her fiancé was stationed in the army. There were inconveniences, such as the fact that her fiancé, Lieutenant Colonel Richard Mansir, had to deploy overseas and the fact that he was required to live on the army base while Chelsea had to stay in town in an apartment he rented for her. But she was in love, soon to be married, and pregnant with their first child. Things took a turn one day when she called her fiancé to tell him that she was having contractions. He asked her not to bother him while he was at work and then ignored her numerous texts and phone calls that followed. In desperation, she called his office staff, who said that he was away on leave. Frantic, she called his ex-wife to see if she knew of his whereabouts. What she heard must have left her dumbfounded. This wasn't Mansir's ex-wife. It was his current wife. They were still very much married after 18 years, although she was currently living in a different location with their three children. A little more digging uncovered that Mansir was actually living on base with yet another woman with whom he was engaged. It turned out that, while married, he had been in serious long-term relationships with six women over 5 years. He had told each woman that he was divorced and that one of his children had died. He explained his long absences by saying that he was going away on overseas deployments. One woman to whom he had been engaged several years earlier said, "He's got this playbook. . . . He tells these lies about his dead children, about his [posttraumatic stress disorder], his deployments, and all the horrible things he's had to do. He creates all these imaginary traumas to cloak his lies in." In fact, he had not deployed since 2014. He faked deployment papers to go be with another woman. Mansir managed all of his transgressions by lying a lot; each lie required several other lies to support it. Mansir was a big liar who left an enormous wake of heartache, strife, and shattered lives.

In this chapter, we present examples of people like Lieutenant Colonel Mansir—big liars whose dishonesty contaminates their close relationships. All close relationships can be undermined by excessive liars, including people we meet on first dates, our romantic partners, friends, and family. We discuss the factors related to lying in close relationships as well as the consequences of being in a relationship with those big liars.

LYING IN RELATIONSHIPS

Dishonesty is common across contexts and various types of relationships, so it should perhaps not be surprising that it is also prevalent in romantic relationships. People say "I love you" or "I want you" when they really don't (O'Sullivan, 2008). Some say they are not interested or not desirous of someone when they actually are. For instance, many people maintain different-sex friendships at least partly because of the prospect of having sex (Bleske-Rechek & Buss, 2001). People deceive their romantic partners in all manner of other ways. They deny being angry when they are fuming (O'Sullivan, 2008). They put on a brave face when they are terrified. They act interested when they are bored. They feign enthusiasm about plans that sound horrible. They offer supportive words, even when they are sure those words are untrue. In one study that examined dishonesty in romantic relationships, the researchers found that outright lying was the form of dishonesty that people used most (45%), followed by exaggerations, half-truths, diversionary responses, and secrets (Guthrie & Kunkel, 2013). Over one week, people reported deceiving their partners an average of five times. The most dishonest people did so 11 times. The reasons they gave for their dishonesty included relational maintenance (e.g., reducing confrontation and restoring harmony), being supportive and protecting the feelings of their partner, balancing the needs of the partner versus their own (e.g., independence vs. togetherness), trying to control a partner's behavior, and maintaining a previous lie. Only 3% reported using no deception over the week. Commitments of enduring love do not necessarily come with commitments of total honesty.

Deception researcher Bella DePaulo (2018) reported that married people tell their spouses small white lies in one of every 10 conversations. Nonmarried people tell white lies in one out of three conversations with their partners. DePaulo (2018) argued that people are willing to tell white lies to their loved ones because when faced with the choice of either being frank and speaking a painful truth (e.g., "No, I did not really like that meal you prepared") or telling a kinder, gentler white lie, people often see the lie as the right thing to do. Bigger, more serious lies tend to be rare; however, they are more likely to be told to close relationship partners than to anyone else. DePaulo (2009) found that 40% of the biggest lies were told to romantic partners. In a study of college students, 92% reported lying to their sexual partners (Knox et al., 1993). The most common lies were about the number of past partners (they underreported), but participants also lied to spare their partners' feelings. For example, they lied a lot about how much they enjoyed the sexual experience with their partner, they falsely said complimentary things about their sexual partners, and they often exaggerated the depth of their feelings toward the person. In another study, DePaulo and Kashy

(1998) found that people lie to their unmarried romantic partners in approximately one of every three interactions, which is more than they lie to their friends. Again, with spouses, people were considerably more honest, lying in only one out of 10 conversations.

Williams (2001) examined lying in college students, finding that people were mostly honest with their sexual partners, and they tended to be most honest if they were in a close relationship, as opposed to in a casual one. The participants reported that they mostly told lies to protect their sexual partners' feelings, rather than for self-serving reasons. Metts (1989) compared married and nonmarried couples. For all couples, the most common reason for lying was to avoid hurting their partners' feelings. Dating couples tended to use complete fabrications, whereas married couples tended to lie by omission. Married couples told lies aimed at boosting their partner's self-esteem or preventing embarrassment, but dating couples were more likely to lie to protect their resources, avoid termination of the relationship, or avoid stress.

The tripartite theory of lying and dishonesty contends that big liars are people who consistently believe others will respond undesirably if they are honest. We can see that sometimes lovers tell lies because they worry the truth would reveal relationship-ending details of one's bad behavior. Lies are also told to hide embarrassing details, such as information about one's sexual history. But people also tell lies to avoid hurting the feelings of people they are in relationships with. In all cases, lying has perceived utility. In her study examining people's willingness to tell lies in relationships, O'Sullivan (2008) was clear about who the biggest liars were: They tended to be men. She asked men and women how willing they would be to lie to a romantic partner about various topics. For each of the 14 topics, men were more willing to lie than women. The topics included

- lying about how much money they make or have
- lying about birth control

- lying about having a sexually transmitted disease
- lying about how impressed they are by their partner's sexual anatomy or performance
- lying about future plans, such as marriage
- exaggerating how attractive or intelligent they think their romantic partner is
- saying they are in love when they are not
- lying about how impressed they are by their partner's body or figure
- lying about the time they spend with their friends
- lying about their virginity
- lying about things in their past that their partner would not approve of
- telling a lie to spare their partner's feelings
- lying about flirting with or being interested in other people
- telling a lie to avoid having their partner get angry with them

Interestingly, O'Sullivan did not ask about willingness to lie to conceal infidelities, but the trend in her data suggests a strong possibility that men would express more willingness than women to do so.

When one considers lies told in relationships, lies covering up infidelity often leap to mind. Every year since 1972, the National Science Foundation's General Social Survey has asked Americans about their sexual infidelities (see Parker-Pope, 2008). For any given year, around 12% of men report having sex with someone other than their spouse. The rate is 7% for women. The lifetime incidence rates seem to be around 28% for men and 15% for women. In most studies of infidelity, men report much higher rates of infidelity than women do. This difference appears to be driven largely by differences in sexual interest and sexually permissive attitudes. Treas and Giesen (2000) found that when comparing men and women who held an equivalent interest in sex and had similar (permissive or stringent) attitudes toward sex, the differences in infidelity disappeared. Lies support infidelity. Given that men are much more likely to engage in infidelity, one can logically conclude that the big liars in that realm will tend to be men.

Unfaithful big liars can come in more than one form. Some research has shown that people who are unfaithful once are more inclined to stray again (Knopp et al., 2017). That is, big liars sometimes repeatedly initiate new romantic flings and then lie to cover up each new dalliance. However, other big liars cultivate a single affair and lie for years to conceal it. They concoct such deep and pervasive lies that the very fabric of the supposed bond with their primary partner is a fraud.

For 50 years, Jean Ann Cone and her husband, Douglas Cone, lived the good life in Tampa, Florida (Chachere, 2003). They were multimillionaires, as Douglas owned a successful road construction company. Jean Ann drove a Rolls Royce and sat on the board of the exclusive private school where they sent their three kids. They even had a building at the school named after them. The couple was noted to be very fond of each other and were very much a part of the Tampa social scene. Douglas often had to travel for work, so he was away most weekends. Eventually, it came to light that Douglas wasn't actually at work on the weekends. He was living with his second family 15 miles down the road. For almost 30 years, Douglas Cone (under his alias, Douglas Carlson) had shared a family life with Hillary Carlson. This family had striking similarities to Douglas's first family. He and his "wife," Hillary, were also very affluent. Hillary drove a Rolls Royce. Douglas and Hillary had two children who went to the same elite school as his other set of kids. Hillary and Douglas "Carlson" even had an athletics field at the school named after them. While many assume that Hillary knew of Douglas's original family, their two kids did not. Douglas explained his absence during the week as due to his highly sensitive government job. Douglas's big lies continued for nearly 3 decades, but there is no evidence that he had a reputation as a big liar. Recall that some big liars seem to have a specific facet of their lives that serve as the basis for their frequent lying; we describe them as a "niche big liar" (see also Chapter 3). As Douglas Cone's story illustrates, one dirty secret can require a bounty of lies to conceal.

LYING TO ATTRACT MATES

Lying seems to be present from the very start of relationships, as many people use deception initially to attract romantic partners. Humans do not form romantic relationships randomly. We are selective. We search through a sea of prospects, hoping we find a person who seems likely to satisfy all our wants and needs. Is the person kind enough, physically attractive enough, affluent enough, serious enough, or funny enough? Do they have the right kind of education, religious and political beliefs, or job prospects? Are they loyal, brave, and earnest? Do they like the same type of music, foods, and vacations? Do they want the same things, such as a long-term relationship, marriage, and kids? We search around looking for that person who seems to fit the bill, or at least comes reasonably close to it.

It perhaps is no surprise that men and women do not tend to look for the same traits in potential mates, although there is considerable overlap. Men and women each report an interest in romantic partners who seem kind, healthy, and intelligent. However, across cultures, men and women place other priorities differently (Buss, 1989; Walter et al., 2020). Women, more than men, tend to prefer someone who has good financial potential, who is ambitious and industrious, and who has high social status. Men, on the other hand, tend to prioritize mates who are young and physically attractive.

We expect that the revelation that people are often not entirely honest in the dating marketplace is not surprising. If people believe prospective mates are looking for a particular set of attributes, they can cultivate and offer those attributes. For instance, if a man finds that the women he meets want a partner with a good job, he can go out and try to secure a good job. However, another possible route to attracting a mate is simply to pretend to have the traits that they believe potential mates looking for. Based on his substantial body of research examining sex differences in mate attraction in heterosexual relationships, Buss (1994a, 1994b) argued that women tend to deceive about sex and men tend to deceive about commitment. He contended that women who are looking for men as mates tend to use the prospect of sexual access to entice them. Sometimes they use sex as a lure to bring men into committed relationships. Other times, he argued, women use the promise of sexual access to persuade men to buy expensive dinners, vacations, or other tangible rewards. Men looking to meet women, on the other hand, are more likely to fake an interest in a committed relationship or to feign feelings of affection that they don't actually have in order to gain sexual access.

Thousands of dating sites are now online. These dating websites promise to use sophisticated scientific algorithms to help people identify and connect with ideal dating partners. Many people use the sites because they can quickly and efficiently find potential romantic partners without face-to-face encounters. On dating sites, men and women tend to lie at approximately equal rates (Markowitz & Hancock, 2018). Of every 20 messages sent on those sites, about three are deceptive. The deceptive messages tend to occur most frequently at the beginning of a connection between two people and then decrease as the conversation progresses. The lies are mostly about impression management (i.e., trying to seem more desirable) and availability. Research suggests that men and women tend to tell different lies for the purpose of impression management. For instance, men tend to overstate their height, whereas women tend to understate their weight. Additionally, when men post profile photos, they tend to select photos that display wealth and status (e.g., an expensive car), whereas women tend to select photos of their younger selves (Hancock & Toma, 2009; Toma et al., 2008).

Big liars in the dating realm tend to have dark-triad personality traits (Jonason et al., 2014). They are high in *Machiavellianism*, meaning that they are comfortable manipulating prospective mates for their own purposes. They also tend to be high in *narcissism*, indicating that their sense of entitlement and preoccupation with their own needs leads them to use dishonesty to get what they want from romantic relationships. Finally, they are high in *psychopathy*, suggesting that their bold antisocial orientation coupled with a lack of empathy and remorse leads them to use dishonesty and other treacherous tactics with romantic interests. A woman named Susanna described dating a person with dark-triad traits this way:

> He said, "You are everything to me, my soulmate. You complete me. I desperately love and need you." It was the worst Hallmark drivel mixed with truth and LIES. It was all about HIS needs. . . . It was ALWAYS about HIS needs and keeping everyone else off balance to serve him. Complete parasite. They take pleasure in "winning" and conning people more than anything.

LYING ABOUT SEX

People lie as a way to gain sexual access. In one study, 34% of the college men who participated reported that they had lied to obtain sex, and 60% of the women reported that people had lied to them to gain sexual access (Cochran & Mays,1990). The college students in that study also reported that they lie about their sexual histories; 42% of the women and 4% of the men indicated that they had understated the number of sexual partners they had.

Beyond lying to achieve a first sexual encounter, people continue to lie in the context of their sex lives. For instance, in one study, more than half the women reported that they fake orgasms (Wiederman,

1997). Men are also inclined to feign their levels of passion and enjoyment during sex, although it may be challenging for them to successfully fake orgasms. The motivation to feign sexual excitement is generally aimed at pleasing one's sexual partner or seeming sexy oneself (O'Sullivan, 2008).

We examined the deception and lies that occur within the bedroom (Hart, 2017). In the first part of the study, we asked 151 men and women to describe one situation in which they had deceived a past or current partner in regard to sex. The people listed dozens of different types of deceptive acts, including cheating, faking orgasms, and claiming to be a virgin. Next, we took those several dozen categories of sexual dishonesty and created a survey. We then asked 330 men and women to indicate whether they had engaged in each form of sexual deception. It turned out that, on average, people said that they had lied about eight of the sex-related topics. However, a few big liars admitted to lying about as many as 34 of the topics.

The list of the top 15 lies that women reported telling their partners in the context of their sex lives along with the percentage who reported telling each type of lie is as follows:

- faked orgasm or satisfaction during sex: 73%
- overexaggeration of pleasure during sex: 69%
- deceived about enthusiasm to have sex: 65%
- lied about being too tired or sick for sex: 58%
- denied having sexual feelings for someone else: 43%
- lied about how much they enjoyed or were satisfied with their sex life: 42%
- lied about having interest in sex: 39%
- lied about how sexually attractive they found their partner to be: 36%
- lied about the amount of sexual experience they had: 34%
- lied about the type of sexual activity that they preferred: 32%

- lied about number of past sexual partners: 32%
- deceived them about having cheated on them: 30%
- lied about their sex drive: 30%
- lied and said their partner was good in bed: 27%
- lied about seeing the relationship getting more serious in the future: 24%

For men, the top 15 were

- deceived about enthusiasm to have sex: 51%
- faked orgasm or satisfaction during sex: 42%
- lied about use of pornography: 38%
- overexaggeration of pleasure during sex: 37%
- denied having sexual feelings for someone else: 34%
- lied about how sexually attractive they found their partner to be: 34%
- lied about being too tired or sick for sex: 33%
- lied about seeing the relationship getting more serious in the future: 32%
- lied about overall relationship satisfaction in order to have sex: 32%
- lied about number of past sexual partners: 31%
- lied about the amount of sexual experience they had: 30%
- lied about the type of sexual activity that they preferred: 28%
- lied about how much they enjoyed or were satisfied with their sex life: 26%
- lied about the true strength of their feelings in order to have sex: 26%
- deceived their partner about having cheated on them: 26%

Two things caught our attention when we saw the results of the study. Our first observation was that men and women tended to lie about the same things. We found that 12 of the top 15 topics women lied about were also among the top topics that men lied about. Lying in the context of sex lives seems like one area of life in which women and men have established a certain degree of equality. Second, many of the lies seemed to be told for benevolent reasons, or at least not for entirely selfish reasons. Feigning enthusiasm, pleasure, and excitement are ways people try to protect the egos and feelings of people they care about in many situations, so perhaps we shouldn't have been surprised when those strategies appeared in the bedroom too.

MORAL HYPOCRISY

Given that the tripartite theory of lying and dishonesty suggests that big liars consistently view their lying as morally permissible, how do lovers justify the morality of lying to their partners? Imagine a situation in which you see your long-term romantic partner leaving a restaurant with a former love interest after they promised that they would never meet up with the person again. Later, when describing their day, your partner neglects to mention that they met at the restaurant with their former love interest. How would you feel? How would your partner feel if you did that to them? One interesting study asked people to imagine just such a scenario and to take the perspective of the liar or of the person being lied to (A. K. Gordon & Miller, 2000). The researchers found that people taking the perspective of the liar tended to view the lie as less wrong and blameworthy than did people who viewed the situation from the perspective of the person being lied to. Further, the people taking the perspective of the liar justified the lies with reasoning, such as that the partner would likely be insecure, jealous, and mistrustful. People taking the perspective of the person being lied to saw the lie as unjustified and wrong and viewed the liar as untrustworthy and dishonest. Thus, it seems that the perceived moral wrongness of lying and the moral attribution made about liars are matters of perspective. People seem to have a double standard. If I lie, it is ethically pardonable, but if you lie, it is not. Perhaps big liars are more inclined than others to engage in this double-standard type of reasoning.

The double standard seems to apply even to supposedly benevolent white lies. When people are asked to view a white lie from the perspective of the liar or from the person being lied to, a discrepancy appears (Hart et al., 2014; Kaplar & Gordon, 2004). Liars see a white lie as not too bad or even justifiable, but when the same person views the lie from the perspective of the person being lied to, they suddenly view the lie as unjustifiable. In fact, some see a moral obligation or duty to tell these white lies but think their partners should always give them the truth. This example shows moral hypocrisy. We have motivated biases—we want to see ourselves as good, even when we sometimes falter, but we don't give others that same benefit. Our self-serving evaluations of lying cut us slack when we are the liars and lead to moral indignation when we are the target of the lies.

DEALING WITH LIES

As we have made clear, people lie to their romantic partners, and some lie a lot. Evidence suggests that many of these lies may go undiscovered because people tend to place considerable trust in their partners (T. R. Levine, 2020). When they are discovered, the lies can be quite damaging. The recipients of the lies, upon discovering the deception, have strong negative emotional reactions (McCornack & Levine, 1990). Being lied to by someone you care about hurts. The degree of involvement in the relationship and the importance of the information that was lied about are both significant predictors of how upset the victim of the deception is. In most cases, though the lies are upsetting, they do not result in the termination of the relationship. The vast majority of people do not end relationships when they discover their partner lying.

Some researchers have examined couples' expectations for honesty in their relationships and the rules they form about lying (Roggensack & Sillars, 2014). In relationships, partners are obligated to follow certain rules, such as a prohibition against lying about the sexual exclusivity of the relationship. However, many other rules regarding honesty are discretionary. That is, instead of puritanically insisting on total honesty, each person allows some discretion in deciding how forthcoming to be. For instance, a couple might not think it important to be absolutely honest about their enthusiasm to visit with each other's friends or family.

Interestingly, the rules about honesty in relationships are usually unspoken, leaving each person to surmise what the actual rules are. While couples usually believe that they are in agreement about the relational rules for honesty, often they are not (Roggensack & Sillars, 2014). A lack of consensus around obligatory rules for honesty can lead to significant conflict in relationships. Again, the disagreements stem from incorrect assumptions each person makes about what their partner believed. Perhaps the takeaway message here is that lying in relationships might be best addressed—and big liars avoided—by open and explicit discussion of each partner's expectations of honesty in the relationship.

Lies in relationships, especially big lies, do more harm than good (Knopp et al., 2017). Even when people feel the urge to tell helpful white lies to protect their partners, their partners do not view the lies as necessary or acceptable (Cantarero, 2021; Hart et al., 2014). People typically want the truth, even when the news is devastating. Even when lies might lead to a short-term benefit, the long-term consequences of relational dishonesty hardly seem a reasonable trade-off.

ROMANCE SCAMS

Before joining the National Football League, Manti Te'o was a star football player at the University of Notre Dame. In 2009, he met and befriended a beautiful student on Facebook, Lennay Kekua, who said she was a volleyball player at Stanford University (Gutman & Tienabeso, 2013). Manti and Lennay messaged back and forth, and in 2011, their relationship became more serious and romantic. They texted and talked to each other on the phone regularly. Manti referred to her as his girlfriend. He intended to come to California to visit Lennay, but she called to say that she was involved in a car accident, causing the trip to be postponed. Later, she told Manti that she had just been diagnosed with leukemia. In September 2012, the day after his grandmother died, Manti received a call from Lennay's sobbing brother, who told Manti that Lennay had passed away. Several days later, Manti mentioned her death in a postgame interview. The tragic story of Manti's loss made national headlines. However, Lennay had not died. In fact, Lennay did not exist. Manti had been lured into a multiyear "catfishing" scheme. Catfishing involves lying and misrepresenting oneself in an attempt to pursue an exclusively online dating relationship. The person to whom Manti had been professing his love was actually a man named Ronaiah Tuiasosopo, who had even crafted a voice that was very convincing. Manti wasn't a lone sucker, though. Catfishing scams are fairly common on online dating sites. Fortunately, most daters do not take the bait (Mosley et al., 2020).

The perpetrators of catfishing scams often seem to be lying to meet a psychological need, such as attention, companionship, or entertainment, but other romance scammers seem to be in it for material rewards. For example, Takashi Miyagawa, a 39-year-old Japanese man, was arrested for defrauding his girlfriends—all 35 of them (Cost, 2021). He simultaneously dated all these women, promising to love them forever, in part, apparently, to extract gifts from them. He even told the various women different dates for his birthday to ensure that a steady stream of gifts came his way.

Along with the proliferation of dating sites and the increased reliance on those sites for finding romantic connections has been a surge in internet dating scams (Coluccia et al., 2020). The scammers begin by creating fake profiles, usually with stolen pictures of an attractive person. The scammer then proceeds to make contact with dupes. Once contact has been made and the dupe seems interested, the scammer spends time building trust through regular warm and affectionate communications. The scammer leads the victim to believe that they are perfectly matched. After the scammer has convinced the victim of the legitimacy of the connection, they begin to declare their passion and love for the victim and suggest meeting in person. The scammer inevitably postpones the meet-up, however, claiming emergencies, such as hospitalizations, death of loved ones, or accidents. These alleged emergencies often lead to requests for money. In some cases, the scammer asks for money to cover the travel expenses so that they can come to see the victim. Gradually, the requests for small sums increase until the requested amounts exceed what the victim is capable of or willing to send.

We documented a case of a person who fell victim to a romance scam. The scammer, allegedly a very attractive and kind person, spent several weeks grooming the victim by establishing rapport, sharing personal information, and flattering the victim. The scammer initially requested financial assistance to buy an airline ticket to visit the victim. On the day they were to arrive, the scammer contacted the victim and claimed that they had accidentally flown to the wrong city, and the victim sent more money to help this big liar buy a bus ticket to complete the trip. But alas, as the scammer was getting off the bus, they were allegedly hit by another bus, requiring hospitalization. More money was needed to help cover part of the medical bill.

The injuries supposedly required the person to fly home to recover, so the meeting was postponed. More money was sent to help the injured person fly home. Out of work because of their injuries, the scammer asked for more money to pay rent and buy groceries. No amount of reasoning from family members could convince the victim that this was all a scam. The relationship felt too real, too intimate, and too good. By the time the victim acknowledged the scam, the scammer had fleeced them of thousands of dollars. When the victim stopped responding to the scammer, the scammer attempted to blackmail the victim, threatening to post online nude photos that the victim had naively sent to the scammer. The powerful longing for love and connection can drive many people to turn a blind eye to the little red flags that seem so clear to everyone else.

One group of researchers studied online deception to try to understand these online big liars (Stanton et al., 2016). The study examined all people who lie about themselves online, not only scammers. They concluded that people who misrepresent themselves online tend to view online lying as permissible. The online liars reported that they found it very exhilarating to fool people online, a practice that has been labeled as *duping delight*, and they described themselves as uncooperative and not very concerned with morality or the welfare of others. They also reported that they were manipulative and disinclined to keep promises they had made. These characteristics are ones that people should absolutely want to avoid in romantic partners, online or otherwise.

TO WHOM DO PEOPLE LIE?

People don't lie indiscriminately. They tend to lie more to some people than to others. Fortunately, the people who are closest to us are also the ones least likely to lie to us (DePaulo, 2009, 2018; DePaulo & Kashy, 1998). That is not to say that the people closest to us don't lie to us. They do. But they tend to lie more often to strangers and acquaintances. While people lie less often to people with whom they feel closest, when those lies do occur, they are much more likely to inflict pain. Just imagine how upsetting it would be to find out your most trusted friend lied to you than it would to learn about a complete stranger doing the same.

Rather than identifying categories of people who lie to us most, it may be helpful to frame the topic in terms of the types of people who are lied to most often. Think of the types of people to whom you might be more apt to lie and those to whom you might be less likely to lie. In her research, DePaulo (2017) analyzed the content of reports that liars provided to her and found that they most often directed their lies toward certain types of people. They tended to tell lies to people who viewed them extremely favorably. For example, imagine a person who thinks that her grandchild is the most amazingly brilliant person in the world and who brags to her friends all day long about that grandchild. It would be hard to let her know that the grandchild failed out of college or was fired from a job. They also tended to lie to people who had very high moral standards. For example, imagine that one of your neighbors is a religious leader and another neighbor is on parole after an arrest for burglary. With which neighbor would you be more comfortable honestly discussing the fact that you passed out from drinking the night before? We all fear the sting of harsh judgment from others, and we tend to view people who stand on moral high ground as likely to see us as wretches. Thus, we are more apt to lie to them.

Lying often occurs when people interact with others they truly admire. For example, if I think you are amazing and can't get enough of you, I might not want to risk rejection by sharing the awful truth about myself. People are also more likely to lie to powerful people or people with high status. One truth about the world is that people who hold status and power wield the ability to cause good or bad things in our lives. Most people would feel uncomfortable letting their boss know that they failed to complete a report on time, but they might not mind at all telling a coworker the same. People tend to lie to people whom they fear. Some people tend to be intimidating or even mean, and sharing truthful feelings with them makes people feel very uneasy. Sometimes lying seems much less risky than being honest.

People also lie to others who are easily hurt or upset by the truth. Imagine that the person you recently started dating is as fragile as an eggshell and bursts into tears and becomes a basket case any time life is disrupted or things don't go their way. If you wanted to break up with them, would you tell them you realized that you don't like them anymore? Maybe a little "it's not you, it's me" fib would offer a cleaner exit. People lie, and they seem to lie to certain types of people more than others.

FRIENDS AND FAMILY

An examination of honesty in friendships shows that even people who have our backs are willing to lie to us (DePaulo & Kashy, 1998). While dishonesty in casual friendships is quite prevalent, it is reassuring to know that people in very close friendships lie significantly less often. Furthermore, the types of lies they tell are different. In casual relationships, people tend to tell self-serving lies, but in close friendships, the lies tend to be much more altruistic. For example, people tend to tell lies that reassure their close friends, boost their egos, and generally make them feel good. People try to show care and understanding and to strengthen the bonds of friendship by psychologically bolstering their friends, even when they need to do so by twisting the truth a bit. In studies of lying in friendships, one finding is that people who are most anxiously attached tend to do most of the lying (Ennis et al., 2008). That is, people who are anxious that telling the truth will jeopardize the strength of their friendships tend to lie more often.

As we discussed in Chapter 2, kids begin lying at an early age, and much of their lying is directed at their parents. That lying seems to peak in the late teenage years. Studies examining lying among high school students have found that, not surprisingly, they lie a lot. To be exact, in one study, they lied 75% more than college students and 150% more than adults (T. R. Levine et al., 2013). The teens in that study told an average of 4.1 per day, but some told as many as 17 lies per day. L. A. Jensen et al. (2004) also found that high school students lie frequently to their parents. The lies tend to be about matters in which they might experience disapproval, such as friends, dating, parties, alcohol and drugs, and sex.

Teenagers' reasons for lying tend to be attempts to assert autonomy. Many parents continue to exercise great control over their children's lives at exactly the point when those children are transitioning into adulthood and seeking to control their own lives. Perhaps late adolescence is the perfect set of circumstances for lying to emerge. The tripartite theory of lying and dishonesty posits that people will lie when they believe that important others will respond negatively if they tell the truth. During late adolescence, teens tend to want to break from parental restrictions and to do what they want when they want, but many parents are still trying to exercise behavioral control. That mixture of discordant goals and imbalanced power is a fine recipe for dishonesty.

During our research for this book, we heard the story of a teenager who began lying to his parents shortly after he began college at age 18. The parents planned to pay for their son's tuition, housing, and expenses during his 4 years of college. However, shortly into his first semester, the young man stopped attending classes, as he found them to be insufferably boring. Instead, his days were filled with video games and leisurely afternoons with friends. When the semester ended, the student was in a bind; his parents saw a college education as the only real path into adulthood, yet he had failed all his courses. Rather than deal with the consequences of his choices, the student told his parents that he had done well and was looking forward to the following semester. Shortly into the next semester, the pattern repeated, with the young man again failing all classes and ultimately being suspended from the college. Again, not wanting to disappoint his parents, he told lies about his successful progress through all his interesting coursework. The lie had grown into a monstrosity. The bigger the lie became, the more catastrophic telling the truth became. He put off coming clean semester after semester until finally, it was time to "graduate." With family coming into town and his parents making their arrangements to celebrate at the graduation ceremony, the young man had finally run out of options. He admitted to his parents that he had spent tens of thousands of their dollars hanging out for 4 years. Although they forgave him, the rupture in their relationship was immense.

Even as adults, people lie to their parents. The lies often begin early in life as kids attempt to escape punishment or gain a little freedom. As adults, many people still place a high value on the judgment of their parents. They will go to great lengths to avoid disappointing Mom or Dad. Kids lie the most when they are still living at home under direct parental control. As they move into adulthood, their lies typically diminish as they establish autonomy and develop adult relationships with their parents (K. Jensen et al., 2014). However, some habits die hard, and some parent–child relationships remain stunted, with the parents offering harsh judgment and the now-grown children fearing their parents' judgment and control. So, even as adults, many people continue lying to their parents.

Parents lie to their kids too. In one case, a kid had a favorite pet, a cat named Oliver. One day, Oliver could not be found. He was not in any of his usual hangouts. When the child told his mother that he could not find Oliver, she said he was probably around somewhere. Days later, when the kids expressed concern that Oliver was still absent, his mom suggested that Oliver may have run away and found a new place to live, as cats sometimes do. The boy was sad but eventually moved on. Years later, as an adolescent, the boy's mother revealed that Oliver had actually been hit by a car and killed in front of their house. His mother had lied to him to spare him grief from the loss. Such lies told to loved ones are not uncommon.

In a study in which people were asked about the biggest lie that had ever been told to them (DePaulo, 2009), 12% of participants reported lies in which a caring person (usually a parent) lied to them to conceal a serious disease or a death that might be distressing. Though the lies were intended to be caring and helpful, the recipient of the lie typically didn't see it that way. One participant wrote, "Even when people lie to protect other people, or because they think they're doing the right thing, you don't necessarily see it that way" (p. 27). Another participant wrote, "You can't really determine for the person when they are going to grow up and they're going to have to face things. . . . You should get the chance to face your reactions yourself and not have someone decide for you how you're going to react" (p. 27).

From telling kids that an injection won't hurt to lies about Santa Claus, parents use dishonesty to manipulate their children (Santos et al., 2017; Setoh et al., 2020). In a small study we carried out (Hart, 2021), we found that most people view lying to children as more morally permissible than lying to adults. However, parents should be aware that lying to their kids increases the odds that their kids will lie to them. In that sense, parents who are big liars with their kids are likely to produce kids who are big liars in return. Additionally, a growing body of evidence suggests that children whose parents lie to them are more likely to have poor psychological adjustment. Though lying to kids is often a convenient way to gain control, the long-term consequences may not be worth it.

CONCLUSION

In this chapter, we have covered the various forms of lying that occur in close relationships, including dating, long-term relationships, friends, and family. The research in this area suggests that while the extent of prolific lying may depend on the type of relationship, lying occurs in them all. Anecdotally, when we ask people about the biggest liars they have ever met, many people identify a romantic partner. People use deception to help form relationships and to maintain those relationships over time. Although lying is a common occurrence in close relationships, many of the lies in this context are not told with malicious intent. Rather, people lie to help navigate the inevitable competing interests that arise in any relationship. In fact, many of the lies that people tell in their closest relationships are intended to benefit the target of the lie. However, evidence suggests that lying, even when well intended, can erode the foundation of a relationship, and big liars often cause their relationships to collapse. We return to the consequences of being in a relationship with a big liar in Chapter 8.

In Chapter 6, we examine the strategies and techniques that big liars use to deceive the people around them. How is it that someone can so easily convince us of something that is not true? Big liars have a toolbox of techniques to seem believable when they are not, and when we can identify these techniques, we can begin to uncover the many ways that big liars pull the wool over our eyes.

CHAPTER 6

THE LIAR'S TOOLBOX

When truth is replaced by silence, the silence is a lie.
—Yevgeny Yevtushenko

On February 21, 1993, Aldrich Hazen Ames was arrested by the FBI outside his home in Virginia (Powell, 2002). He told the agents, "You're making a big mistake! You must have the wrong man!" However, they had the right man; Ames was lying. He actually had a long history of lying. Ames had a 31-year career as a CIA officer. Early in his career, he was tasked with trying to identify and recruit potential Soviet intelligence officers to provide critical intelligence to the United States. Ames wasn't very successful in that role, so he was assigned to other jobs, such as managing spies who were already providing the United States with information. He wasn't particularly adept in that role, either. He was noted to be a procrastinator who was inattentive to important details and forgetful. It was believed that he drank too much and that occasionally his drunkenness interfered with his work. Ames's personal life was shaky too. He had numerous affairs, and, eventually, his marriage fell apart. Fearing his spousal support payments and a costly new girlfriend might bankrupt him, Ames decided to sell CIA secrets to the Soviets.

While his plan was to make a one-time deal to exchange some fairly mundane secrets for $50,000, his dealings with the Soviets progressed. By that time, and despite his unremarkable performance at work, Ames was assigned to the supersensitive Soviet counterintelligence unit and began to provide critical details about CIA operations to the Soviets. He passed along more and more damaging information about American espionage activities, warning his Soviet handlers about each American asset operating in Soviet-bloc countries. The Soviets rewarded Ames's betrayals with larger and larger payments. Soon the Americans began to notice that their spies were disappearing—scooped up by the KGB, tortured and interrogated, and then executed. Ames carried out his spying scheme for years.

The CIA finally focused on Ames as the mole who was giving away U.S. secrets. They noted that, despite his modest salary, Ames indulged in an immodest lifestyle. He wore exquisite suits, drove luxury automobiles, and had purchased an extravagant and quite expensive house. When asked about his opulent displays, Ames claimed that his new wife came from a very affluent family. As the investigators looked closer into Ames, they found that he had massive credit card bills. His phone bill alone was more than his salary could cover, and there was no evidence that his wife was contributing to their bank account. By the time the investigators arrested Ames, he had been betraying his country for almost 8 years. His activities had led to the identification of nearly all the intelligence assets that the CIA had working against the Soviet Union at the peak of the Cold War. Almost a dozen were executed. In exchange, the KGB had paid Ames more than $4 million.

How did someone working in such a sensitive role for the CIA manage to do so much damage for so long without getting caught? The short answer is that he lied. But wouldn't the CIA expect people to lie from time to time? Wouldn't they be on the lookout for turncoats in their midst? In fact, they were vigilant. They required CIA officers to take polygraph exams regularly and to answer questions about all manner of nefarious activities. While Ames was spying for the Soviets, he took two polygraph exams. When he first found out that a polygraph exam was impending, Ames was terrified. He was certain that he would be discovered and his house of cards would collapse. It turned out, though, that Ames passed the exams. How did he manage to successfully deceive the supposed expert lie detectors for so many years? Did the Soviets give him a special gadget that beat the test? Had he learned some special psychological trick during his work as a spy? Not at all. When he asked his KGB handlers what to do, they told him to "just relax, don't worry, you have nothing to fear" (U.S. Senate Select Committee on Intelligence, 1994, p. 45). When he met with the polygraph examiners, he acted friendly. He was warm and personable. He acted . . . normal.

In this chapter, we discuss how people, such as Aldrich Ames, pull off their deceit. An examination of the task of lying provides insights into what a liar must do to successfully fool others. We then consider the various strategies that liars, by their own admission, use to appear sincere when they are being dishonest. We also explore the features that allow some big liars to seem believable while others seem transparently dishonest. Finally, we discuss the manipulation tactics that successful big liars have used to convince large groups of people to accept their falsehoods.

Lying is different from telling the truth. It is typically more challenging. The liar must avoid revealing the truth, fabricate a false experience, and all the while seem to be unfazed. On the fly, liars must generate false accounts that are factually coherent and do not conflict with other known facts. Furthermore, the liar must be able to remember and recount details consistently, possibly over multiple retellings. Liars must conceal their effort, their anxieties, and their guilt.

Liars risk giving themselves away because lying entails four specific problems (Zuckerman et al., 1981). First, lying produces a generalized state of psychological arousal, and that arousal can be detected. We can often gauge when someone is relaxed and when they are not. Signs of nervousness might give a liar away. Second, lying often causes people to feel pronounced emotions, such as fear, guilt, or shame. Concealing emotions can be a tricky task. We've all probably tried to feign interest in a boring story or acted more excited than we truly were at receiving a gift that didn't quite hit the mark. Third, lying is a cognitively demanding task. Liars must be quick and sharp to pull off such an effortful task. When pressed with effortful tasks, we often act differently: Just try not to appear to be working hard when attempting to remember a phone number or when counting backward by sevens. Fourth, and finally, as we work hard to conceal evidence of the first three problems, we risk acting strangely in our attempts to act "normal." If you ever have to walk across a room when an audience is staring at you and you think for even a moment about trying to walk "normally," you may soon find that you are, ironically, creating an abnormal gait or an unusual swing of your arms.

Liars attempt to appear effortlessly honest, but lying is an emotionally, behaviorally, and cognitively taxing endeavor. It is work, and if people notice that liars are working hard, they may grow suspicious. Like Ames, big liars who successfully pass themselves off as honest are able to conceal the arousal, emotions, and cognitive effort associated with lying and thus convincingly appear calm and collected.

We can use two approaches to understand how liars lie. The first approach is simply to ask liars what they do when they are lying; their own accounts can provide invaluable information about how they manage their behavioral repertoire. Their self-reports can give us insights into their toolbox of techniques and strategies for lying. A second approach is to watch people carefully as they are lying. We can attentively note their behavior when they are telling the truth and then observe them when we know they are lying. If their deception has some revealing clue, we might be able to spot it if we look closely enough.

Research suggests that people readily report the techniques or strategies they implement when telling falsehoods (Wanasika & Adler, 2011). They realize that if they hope to seem believable, they must work at it. If people know they are lying, and especially if they fear being caught in their lies, they might worry, struggle to come up with believable lies, or try to conceal the evidence of their guilt. These features of lying can lead to detection. People cloak their misdeeds behind a false veil of earnestness and honesty. In one study, participants who had committed a mock crime were then interrogated by actual police officers (Strömwall et al., 2006). The participants lied, and they reported feeling very nervous and finding that lying about the crime was extremely difficult. When asked, 90% of the liars reported using a specific strategy to appear honest.

In another study including incarcerated people, researchers asked the participants about how they tell convincing lies. These individuals revealed that strategic planning was an important component of telling lies that would be believed (Granhag et al., 2004). Both truthtellers and liars plan what they will say during an interrogation. However, liars also plan how they will behave, whereas truthful people usually do not. Honest people are less planful and less defended than dishonest people because they often have a naïve belief that innocence will shield them from any harm (Kassin & Norwick, 2004). Liars, on the other hand, know that their freedom from punishment hinges on their ability to be believed, so they pull out all the stops to present a believable act.

HOW LIARS SAY THEY LIE

We conducted a study to explore how liars report carrying out their deceptions (Hart et al., 2023). We gathered together more than 200 people and gave them the following prompt: "When people lie, they often use strategies to conceal their deception and make themselves appear truthful to others . . . describe the strategies that YOU use when you are lying to others." The participants then spent the next 15 minutes writing detailed accounts of the strategies and techniques that they use to tell convincing lies. Afterward, our team of researchers analyzed the hundreds of pages of responses. We sorted the responses into individual lie techniques and then tabulated the reported techniques to determine which ones were used most often. We aimed to generate a list of people's most common lie strategies. We found that many people reported using multiple strategies and that people tended to rely on the same deceptive strategies to fool others.

The strategies that people reported using generally fell into two large groups: those used to manage speech and those used to manage bodily behavior. People were slightly more likely to report body management strategies (59%) than to use speech management strategies (41%). The eight body management techniques, from most widely used to least used, were reported:

- *Make eye contact* (22%): People reported that they intentionally tried to maintain or increase the amount of eye contact they made with the person to whom they were lying. For instance, one person wrote, "I look them dead in the eyes." Others described similar tactics to hold eye contact or said they avoided looking away when lying.
- *Control facial/emotional expression* (21%): People reported that they attempted to manipulate their facial expressions, especially expressions of emotion, to present a believable countenance. They wrote about trying not to let the look of fear or surprise appear on their face. For instance, one person wrote, "I just tried to keep a straight face."
- *Act calm/confident/normal* (20%): Responses in this category indicated a general strategy of attempting to appear calm,

confident, or normal when lying. People wrote that they tried to maintain a normal demeanor. For example, one person stated they "act as if nothing was wrong or different."

- *Don't fidget* (14%): People claimed that they intentionally controlled or reduced fidgeting with their hands or feet and otherwise attempted to maintain normal body movements, such as crossing their arms to minimize any urges to fidget. One person wrote that they "try to not fidget, play with my hands or ears, because for me that is a sign of lying."
- *Act emotional* (8%): Some people wrote that when they lied, they tried to appear more emotional than they actually felt, such as by feigning upset or crying. They seemed to think that emotionality would convince others of their truthfulness. They wrote things, such as "I forced myself to cry and act upset to be more believable" and "I have tried to act really excited about something that was greatly exaggerated."
- *Act serious or sincere* (6%): This category included general efforts to appear more serious or sincere than one felt. People who reported these techniques said things, such as that they "just try to be as serious as possible" or that they "look very serious or sincere."
- *Avoid eye contact* (5%): Interestingly, and despite the fact that most people believe that the inability to make eye contact is a sure sign of lying, some people reported just such a strategy—they reported attempts to conceal their eyes or otherwise avoid making eye contact. For example, some said, "I wouldn't look the person in the eye," "(I) try not to make eye contact," and "(I) looked at the ground." While this hardly seems like a wise strategy, it is important to keep in mind that while most people are superb liars, some are absolutely incapable of telling a believable lie.

- *Increase body movement* (4%): A small percentage of people indicated that they increased body movement to appear more believable. For example, one person wrote, "Try to use hand gestures and body language to get the story across."

The following six strategies related to speech manipulation, from most frequent to least frequent, were reported:

- *Manage tone/pitch* (37%): People reported efforts to alter and manage the tone of their voice or their vocal pitch, for example, by trying to have a confident-sounding tone of voice, using a serious tone, and trying not to let the pitch of their voice rise.
- *Sound normal* (19%): Some participants directly said that they focused on trying to sound normal as they spoke untruths. They mentioned attempts to speak in a manner consistent with their normal speech, for example, "I tried to sound like I normally would" and "the conversation or response is normal and relaxed."
- *Control the details* (16%): People suggested that they worked to manage the amount or the nature of the details and evidence that they shared, withholding key information or sometimes adding details in an attempt to sound convincing. For example, they reported, "I tried not . . . overexaggerating my story" and "I also might try to give more details than necessary to try to make it seem realistic."
- *Speak clearly* (15%): Some people claimed that their strategy was to speak clearly and steadily to avoid detection. They avoided stammering or stuttering, and they tried to avoid pauses and delays in their responses. For example, they wrote, "I tried not to mumble or stutter while talking" and "I try to speak with a clear voice and not stumble over words."

- *Rate of speech* (7%): People indicated that when lying, they make an effort to adjust the pace of their speech. They mentioned things, such as forcing themselves to speak slowly (e.g., "forced myself to speak slowly") or quickly (e.g., "talk faster").
- *Volume* (5%): These strategies involved the person increasing, decreasing, or attempting to maintain their speaking volume (e.g., "talk in a voice that sounds quieter" or "I would raise my voice").

In addition to these 14 categories, participants reported a handful of other techniques that didn't easily or logically fit into a grouping. Some of these unique strategies struck us as quite odd. For instance, people reported, "I will usually bite the side of my lip, or roll my tongue to the side," "I cough," "I cuss a lot," "I rub my temples like I'm getting frustrated," and "I walk away." Participants reported only a small number of these strange lie strategies. Overall, we found that most of the liars in our study tended to rely on a relatively small group of techniques to appear honest.

Other researchers have taken similar approaches to ours, asking people to report how they have attempted to fool others with their lies. In one study, researchers paid participants to commit a mock theft (Hines et al., 2010). They then interrogated the participants, who were instructed to lie to avoid detection. Afterward, the researchers interviewed the participants about the strategies and techniques they thought were important for crafting and telling believable lies. Many said they prepared and mentally rehearsed their lies. By planning what they would say and the fictitious details they would provide, the liars aimed to reduce the cognitive workload they would certainly experience once the interrogations began. Knowing how one is going to respond to questions reduces the stress and anxiety that come along with having to think quickly. Having a prepared story reduces anxiety, as one already has the false narrative figured out. The prepared stories help the liar to avoid contradictions and allow them to note sensitive information that must be withheld to preserve the believability of the lie.

The participants also widely reported concerns about presenting the right amount of detail in their lies (Hines et al., 2010). They worried that providing too little information or too much information would appear suspicious. The details must be abundant enough to resemble an actual memory of a real event, but not so many as to appear like an exaggerated appeal. Another common strategy was to mention emotional details. They indicated that sharing how one felt during a fictitious story would make the story seem more believable. Additionally, they also noted mentioning peripheral details that had no central bearing on the lie, a strategy that was also thought to make the stories seem more genuine. All the while, the liars reported that they told stories that were both coherent and consistent. Stories with discrepant details are not believable, nor are stories that change over time.

Another broad category of strategies involved impression management (Hines et al., 2010). It's not only what one says that helps a liar avoid suspicion; it's also how they say it. Foremost, the liars reported trying to appear calm and confident. They also tried to sound as if they were quite accurate and not prone to mistakes. To pull off this charade, they mentioned making eye contact, managing the tone of their voice, and attempting to sound confident. Big liars like Aldrich Ames capitalize on these techniques. They plan what they will say, they choose their words carefully, they say enough but not too much, and they say it all with a genuine-seeming demeanor.

GOOD LIARS

In one recent study, scientists found that people who are good at lying actually lie significantly more than people who are not good at it (Verigin et al., 2019). That is, big liars tend to be good liars. It makes sense, then, to ask the good liars how they do it. The researchers' first finding was that good liars tend to rely heavily on manipulating what they are saying, rather than dwelling too much on manipulating their body language. The good liars were much more likely to attribute their success to a handful of strategies.

Though big liars lie a lot, they are usually honest when they speak. Successful liars lie selectively. A good liar realizes that if their every word were a lie, they would soon be seen as a dishonest communicator, and their lies would no longer be convincing. They lie sparingly and only when they really have something to gain. Good liars realize that deception is a tool that is most effective when they are trusted (C. V. Ford, 1996; T. R. Levine, 2020).

Successful liars tend to embed their lies in a cloud of truth. If a big liar is going to try to pull one over on you, they will likely bury a single lie in a vast jumble of truths, obscuring the deceit. They also report that when telling a lie, they try to match the number of details to the number of details they typically provide when telling the truth. It's not only the amount of details, either; it is also the type. If, when telling the truth, a good liar tends to talk about their thoughts and feelings, they will also talk about thoughts and feelings when lying. Good liars also try to keep their yarns clear and simple. Clear and simple lies are easy to generate, easy to remember, and not likely to conflict with other known information. Better yet, good liars try to provide unverifiable details. For instance, if a lie involves no other people, then nobody can contradict the story. Good liars also focus on telling plausible lies. An outlandish story is likely to draw unwanted attention and scrutiny. If asked where you were last night, "I watched television and then went to bed" is much more plausible than "I decided to go ostrich hunting." Finally, good liars are avoidant. They strategically try to avoid being questioned. If they can dodge the questions entirely, it is unlikely they will be caught lying.

Reviewing the research literature on proficient liars, we can single out 18 traits and characteristics that seemed to facilitate especially successful liars (Vrij et al., 2010):

1. Good liars are natural manipulators. They aren't nervous about manipulating others; rather, they are confident, dominant, and relaxed as they exploit others.
2. Good liars are good actors. Lying, like other forms of impression management, is a game of projecting a specific version of oneself into the world. Good liars take the stage and play the role of an honest person.
3. Good liars, as good actors, must be expressive. They must be animated with believable enthusiasm and emotion.
4. Good liars tend to be physically attractive. People have a powerful cognitive bias known as the *halo effect* (LeClaire, 2017). This bias refers to the tendency to allow one positive trait of a person to influence our judgments about other unrelated dimensions of that person. One powerful example of a halo effect involves physical attractiveness. Attractive people are illogically viewed as being more capable, kind, friendly, intelligent, and trustworthy than less attractive people. A physically attractive person will also be viewed as more honest than a less attractive person.
5. Good liars are dynamic performers. They can rapidly adapt their demeanor to dynamic changes in the context. What the situation demands, they can deliver.
6. Good liars practice their craft. They have a wealth of prior experience in deception. That practice pays off, as they have figured out tricks to help them manage fear and guilt, and they have honed excellent acting skills.

7. Good liars believe in their ability to lie well. That confidence reduces their anxiety and helps them sell the story to the audience.
8. Good liars are adept at feigning emotions. Whether expressing happiness, surprise, sadness, or contempt, good liars can wrinkle their brows, raise their eyebrows, or bare their teeth in convincing ways that belie their true emotions. Researchers have found that expressive people are viewed as likable and sympathetic (Friedman et al., 1988). Emotional expressivity also helps people seem honest.
9. Good liars are excellent orators. They are eloquent; they can find just the right words at just the right time to say exactly what they think someone wants to hear.
10. Good liars are prepared for the lie. They rehearse and plan. Getting caught with one's pants down, searching and stumbling for a good excuse, is a surefire way to get tangled up and caught in a lie. A well-prepared and organized narrative makes a lie seem natural and free from contradictions.
11. Good liars choose their details carefully. The worst thing a liar can do is provide verifiably false details. Someone cannot believably say that they stayed at home when their credit card bill shows that they ate at a restaurant and went to a nightclub. Several years ago, an acquaintance of ours drove out of town to engage in an affair while his girlfriend was away visiting her family. While hundreds of miles away from home carrying on his fling, he texted and called his girlfriend, reassuring her that he was having a boring few days at home. There was one problem, though. He got a speeding ticket while out of town. That piece of evidence, if discovered, would clearly expose his lie. A good liar would have included details that could not be so easily uncovered, for instance,

saying that he was traveling to Dallas for some rather vague and unverifiable reason, such as sightseeing.

12. Good liars say as little as is necessary. The more a person speaks, the more the person offers details that might undermine the lie. Effective liars say enough to be believed, but no more.
13. Good liars avoid creating stories that don't check out by simply telling (mostly) the truth. They concoct stories that adhere to the truth almost entirely, up to the point that the truth becomes untenable. Then and only then do they insert false information.
14. Good liars are creative. When being interrogated, they never know what question is going to come next, so the ability to create a realistic yet fake version of reality is imperative. Those gifted with the facility to invent new ideas will be most successful.
15. Good liars also think fast. People who take too long to respond or suddenly use time fillers, such as "um" and "uh," don't sound believable.
16. Good liars are smart. Juggling the components of a lie, or creating a believable scenario with details that do not conflict with what the other person may or may not know, is a chore. Lying is a cognitively demanding feat that is aided tremendously by intelligence.
17. Good liars keep their facts straight. Effective liars remember what they said and to whom they said it. Lying is complicated, so a good memory is key. A person who lies must remember all the details. When honest people are asked to recount a story on two separate occasions, they reconstruct a memory of what occurred. However, memory is imperfect and malleable (Baddeley, 1990; Loftus, 1979), so their retelling often shifts and changes from one occasion to the next. Each

reconstruction is slightly different, with some details remembered, others forgotten, or some insights added. This shifting nature of truthful recollections can sometimes appear to listeners as evidence of deception. To avoid sounding dishonest, then, good liars avoid this reconstruction-on-the-fly strategy of storytelling. Instead, they focus on repeating the story as precisely as possible each time. Their goal is to have zero variation between retellings. Zero variation means that listeners have no discrepancies to key in on. In other words, liars repeat rather than reconstruct. Some lies are maintained for decades, and keeping the story straight for that long may require above-average mnemonic abilities.

18. Finally, good liars are good listeners. They take the pulse of their audience, recognizing when their listeners want more information, when they are satisfied, when they start to grow suspicious, and when it is safe to change the topic.

Big liars persist because they are good at their craft. They have learned to use deceit successfully to achieve their goals. If their lies consistently failed, they would likely abandon dishonesty and try something else. By mastering a handful of skills, big liars have learned to persuasively convince others of something that is not true.

WHAT DOES AN HONEST PERSON LOOK LIKE?

One would think that a good liar is someone who can perfectly mimic the look and behavior of someone who is telling the truth. Surprisingly, the ability to perfectly emulate honest people is not the skill that makes good liars believable. Instead, they have mastered the ability to act like what others *think* an honest person looks like (Vrij et al., 2010). Many people have misconceptions about what honest behavior looks like (Strömwall et al., 2004). Primarily, they believe that honest people make a lot of eye contact and don't fidget. These inaccurate beliefs are folk wisdom. Good liars succeed not because they act honestly but because they act like the caricature of an honest person.

When we meet a person for the first time, we form a first impression of them (Aronson et al., 2007). As we interact with them more, typically our impression of them is remarkably stable (Gunaydin et al., 2017) and tends to remain intact even when we are presented with contradictory evidence (Rydell & McConnell, 2006). Our impressions of others are based on a variety of factors, including their gender, race, age, attire, cosmetics, speech, attractiveness, and behavior.

The sociologist Erving Goffman (1956) wrote about the dynamics of impression formation in his book, *The Presentation of Self in Everyday Life*. He argued that we all attempt to manage our social value by managing impressions. We actively attempt to influence how we are perceived by others. One mechanism we use in this effort is crafting our demeanor. We manage the way we act, the expressions on our faces, and the ways in which we carry ourselves.

A critical finding in the study of deception was realized over the course of several studies. Some people, because of their demeanor, simply appear more honest, while others, unfortunately, seem less honest (Bond & DePaulo, 2008; T. R. Levine, 2020). That is, regardless of the actual veracity of someone's statement, some people just look more believable. In a series of studies, researchers examined the role that demeanor plays in believability. They found that for some people, the effect is very powerful. Some people seem very dishonest even when telling the truth (Bond & Fahey, 1987; Bond et al., 1992; T. R. Levine, 2020). More relevant to the topic of big liars is that some people naturally seem very trustworthy, even when they are telling a bald-faced lie. Big liars—people capable of walking into any situation, telling some whoppers, and having everyone believe them—have a certain demeanor that is identifiable. An analysis distilled those facets of demeanor down to what is called the *believability quotient*, or BQ (T. R. Levine, 2020). The BQ consists of 11 attributes honest-seeming people seem to possess. As it turns out, if someone seems honest on one of the demeanors, they usually seem honest on the other 10. So, here they are:

1. Believable people present themselves as confident and composed.
2. They are friendly and pleasant.
3. They have an engaged and involved interaction style.
4. They have plausible stories.
5. They maintain eye contact.
6. They are eager and immediate in their responses.
7. They don't fidget.
8. They act calm.
9. They have a consistent demeanor.
10. They convey certainty with their words.
11. They convey certainty in their tone of voice.

T. R. Levine (2020) found that he could train students to control each of these elements. He brought a number of paid volunteers into his lab and spent time meticulously training them to become proficient at managing the 11 demeanors of the BQ. Next, he asked them to lie and to tell the truth while others attempted to discern who was being honest and who was lying. One surprising finding was that observers were unable to tell who was lying and who was telling the truth. However, the students who had become more proficient at the BQ attributes were significantly more likely to be viewed as honest even when they were lying. So, it seems that a person's demeanor may be more important than their actual honesty in determining whether or not they will be believed. Taking this back to the topic of big liars, it seems that big liars who consistently avoid detection have likely mastered the BQ. They have cultivated the tricks and techniques that cause the rest of the world to trust them and believe them even when they are deceptive. In other words, many big liars cannot be detected simply by looking for obvious signs of deceit, although as we discuss in Chapters 9 and 10, we can use some strategies to discover even the smoothest liars.

BREAKING THE RULES OF CONVERSATION

Paul Grice was a British philosopher who taught at the University of California, Berkeley, during the 1970s. He proposed that when people talk to each other, they are involved in a mutually agreed-upon sharing of ideas (Grice, 1989). He referred to this idea as the *cooperative principle*. To effectively hold a conversation, Grice argued, each person must utter words that implicate a particular meaning. For instance, if I want to communicate to you that I want to eat, I may say, "I want to eat." Those words effectively implicate a meaning in your mind. When people lie, they violate the cooperative principle of communication.

Grice identified four maxims that he saw as important to cooperative communication, and each can be flaunted to mislead conversational partners.

- *Quantity:* This maxim specifies that when communicating honestly, people must provide enough information to share the idea entirely, without offering more than is required.
- *Quality:* This maxim, critically, is about telling the truth. People must say that which is truthful and must avoid saying that which is not.
- *Relation*: This maxim is the requirement to be relevant. People should not say things that are irrelevant to the discussion.

- *Manner:* This maxim is about the importance of clarity. When communicating, people should be to the point and avoid ambiguity or obscurity.

When people adhere to Grice's maxims, conversations tend to be honest and proceed well. When speakers violate or flaunt the maxims, communication no longer serves a cooperative function.

Lies violate Grice's maxims in several different ways. First, the mere intent to deceive with language violates the overarching cooperative principle. When one person is lying, collaboration between the conversational participants does not exist. The communication is, instead, a form of linguistic antagonism. Liars also sometimes violate the maxim of quantity. When a bleary-eyed driver is asked by a police officer if he's had anything to drink tonight, he might truthfully say "a couple of beers" but omit any reference to the six shots of liquor that accompanied those beers. Deceivers sometimes flout the maxim of relation too. When asked if he knows why the cash register is missing $100, a thieving employee might mention the dishonest habits of several other employees rather than speaking to the relevant issue of personal knowledge with a yes or no response.

President Bill Clinton infamously violated the maxim of manner when discussing his relationship with an intern, Monica Lewinsky. When asked whether they had an inappropriate relationship, Clinton responded, "There is nothing going on between us" and "There is no improper relationship." When it later came to light that Clinton and Lewinsky had been involved in a sexual relationship, one that he had apparently lied about, Clinton argued that when saying, "There *is* nothing going on" and "There *is* no improper relationship" he meant that there was at that exact moment in time no such relationship, although there may have been hours earlier. This intentionally ambiguous use of language is the epitome of a violation of the maxim of manner.

The most obvious way that liars breach conversational cooperation is through violation of the maxim of quality. When we call someone a liar, it is generally because they have intentionally and knowingly said something that they believed to be factually untrue. Whether the lie is an exaggeration, an omission, a bald-faced lie, or the intentional use of equivocal language, all lies violate the expectation that we have been told the truth. When we converse with others, we expect honesty. Otherwise, what is the point in talking at all? When we discuss lying, we define it, in part, by intent. People can violate Grice's maxims simply by being poor communicators, by being ill-informed, or by having their train of thought derailed. However, when people intentionally use communication to mislead, that communication is a lie. We define lying as a successful or unsuccessful deliberate manipulation of language, without forewarning, to create in another a belief that the communicator considers to be untrue. Liars lie by subtly or not so subtly manipulating conversational rules intentionally to cause us to believe something that is not true.

WAYS THAT BIG LIARS TELL LIES

There is no single way to tell a lie. Rather, people can bend and stretch statements and conversations in all manner of ways to confuse, befuddle, and ultimately mislead conversational partners. When one thinks of prototypical lies, one probably imagines outright lies. Outright lies or fabrications involve the total construction of false stories (DePaulo et al., 1996). They are entirely fictional accounts presented as the truth. A total fabrication is a dangerous gambit, as evidentiary cues can often prove their falsity.

Other more subtle and more defensible techniques of lying are more common and easier to generate. Concealment, half-truths, and omissions involve simply failing to mention the truth (Metts, 1989). When asked what they did while their spouse was out of town for the evening, a person might mention that they watched television and made some dinner. And while this account is true, they left out the fact that a neighbor stopped by and they had sex for an hour. Concealments are easier to pull off than outright lies because they are passive. They require no fictional narratives, and they are unlikely to lead to intensive questioning. Concealments offer an additional benefit: If they are discovered, they are typically viewed as less dastardly than other forms of lying (T. R. Levine et al., 2003). While concealment may not meet the technical definition of lying, many people view it as deceptive falsification and respond to it as they would to an outright lie.

Big liars also make use of obfuscation and equivocation (Clementson, 2018). That is, they use ambiguous, imprecise, or confusing language to hide the true meaning of what they are saying. For instance, if a person's boss were to ask what they have been doing today, the employee might respond, "Phew! I've been either on the phone or working on the computer every second since I walked in today" and might leave out that they were on the phone with friends and were on the computer booking a vacation.

Feigned sarcasm is another way people lie. Sarcasm itself is a form of mutually acknowledged lying (Shany-Ur et al., 2012). If I sarcastically say, "Oh, you know how much I love paying large credit card bills!", I am not being truthful, and my sarcastic tone intentionally tells you that I am not being truthful. However, people can also use feigned sarcasm to tell the truth while communicating with a tone suggesting that they are lying. For example, if I stole my neighbor's lawnmower and he asked if I had seen the lawnmower, I could sarcastically say, "Yeah, Gary, I stoooooole your lawnmower . . . geez!" Gary would then believe, because of my sarcastic tone, that I had not taken the lawnmower.

Big liars also exaggerate. Exaggerations occur when the core of what someone says is the truth, but the degree to which it is true is false (Verigin et al., 2019). People stretch the truth to make things seem bigger, better, or more meaningful than they really are. A coworker once said that the vice president of the United States was a family friend who would likely do favors for his family. Other coworkers were surprised and fascinated, so they started asking many questions. Under the intense scrutiny, his claim that the vice president was a family friend was eventually whittled down to the core truth: The coworker's father had once met the vice president, exchanged a few pleasantries, and had his picture taken with him. It seems exceedingly unlikely that the vice president ever considered the person a friend.

Minimization occurs when people understate the degree of a truth. For instance, if an employee is accused of stealing money from the cash register, they might minimize by saying they might have taken a dollar or two. Heavy drinkers, when asked by their physicians how much they drink, tend to underreport their drinking by around 50% (Vance et al., 2020). When big liars are breaking the rules and denials seem unviable, the next best strategy is to minimize.

GASLIGHTING

Gaslighting is another psychological technique that big liars can use to deceive people (Sweet, 2019). A gaslighter uses mind-manipulation strategies to convince others that they are losing touch with reality, that their memory is faulty, or that they are simply crazy. Gaslighters use false narratives to gain control over a situation or a person. For instance, one woman described the gaslighting techniques her husband used to control her (Moore, 2019). When the woman worked during the day, he accused her of neglecting the children, but if she worked in the evening, he accused her of neglecting their marriage. When he was accused of making passes at her friends, he convinced her that the friends had actually been the offending parties. He isolated her socially by convincing her that others were trying to undermine their marriage. He convinced her that she was naïve and stupid, failing as both a wife and a mother. He hid items from her and then convinced her that she had lost them because of her ineptitude.

Gaslighters use several dishonest techniques to fool their targets (Evans, 1996). First, they deny the truth. If someone were to accuse their partner of flirting with someone at a party, the offending person might simply say that they were not, often arguing that the accuser is paranoid or misremembering what actually happened. Gaslighters also withhold information. By living a life of secrecy, they can concoct alternative versions of reality that suit their needs. They offer information that contradicts their accuser's viewpoint: "If I were stealing money from you, why would I have paid for your dinner last night?" They discount evidence and information: "Why would you believe what my brother tells you? He is an alcoholic." They cut down their victims to dismiss the accusations: "You say I am untrustworthy, but you have never managed to stay in a relationship for longer than 6 months!" They divert their victims from people who might reveal the truth, often by trying to isolate their victims from people who might confirm their suspicions about the gaslighter. They minimize the concerns of their victims or normalize the offense: "Hey, this is not a big deal. Everyone has sex with their boss if they really want to get ahead. It's the nature of this industry." By using lies and manipulation, gaslighters develop a "reality" that is constantly shifting, leading their victims to doubt themselves and accept the liar's assertions.

Gaslighters also use psychological manipulation and deception when they are accused of lying. When gaslighters and other big liars are accused of wrongdoing, they often flip the script on their accusers in a bit of psychological jiu-jitsu (Freyd, 1997). We use the acronym DARVO to explain that approach. This acronym enumerates the strategies that manipulators use to avoid blame and accountability.

When accused, they first Deny, rebuffing any accusation that they did anything wrong. Next, they Attack anyone who claims they are lying. Finally, they Reverse Victim and Offender. The liar claims that they are actually the victim. Big liars use the DARVO technique to turn the tables quickly, leaving their accusers wondering why they are now on the defensive. One might recall that during his presidency, Donald Trump successfully employed the DARVO approach with the press. When the press accurately accused President Trump of spreading false information about events, he first denied spreading incorrect information, then he attacked the press for making the accusations. Then, he flipped the accusation and began to refer to mainstream news sources as "fake news." DARVO, when successfully employed, undercuts accusations of dishonesty and brands the accusers as the dishonest ones.

LIE, LIE, LIE

Repetition of falsehoods is another technique that big liars use to convince others. The *illusion of truth effect* is a well-studied psychological phenomenon in which false information that is heard again and again is believed to be more and more truthful, despite its actual veracity (Hasher et al., 1977). If people hear an untrue statement enough times, it becomes familiar. That feeling of familiarity, then, causes people to shift from critical analysis of the veracity of the statement to passive acceptance. Essentially, repetition shifts our brains to autopilot. Instead of thinking rationally, we take a shortcut and use our gut. After we've heard it a hundred times, it just feels true, so we no longer analyze whether it actually is true. Politicians use the phenomenon to great effect. They continue to repeat dubious claims that crime is rampant or that a certain group hates America. After hearing those assertions enough times, many people accept them as true. After a while we find ourselves thinking, "Sure, everyone knows that. Of course it's true." Even when researchers forewarn people that the repeated statements they are about to hear are no more likely to be true than statements that are not repeated, people still preferentially believe the repeated statements (Polage, 2012). This finding suggests that the power of repetition to alter our beliefs is so strong and so automatic that we may accept repeated lies despite our attempts to resist.

Even before psychological scientists demonstrated the power of repeated lies in the lab, people had an awareness of repetition's powerful ability to distort beliefs. In *Mein Kampf*, Adolf Hitler (1925/1971) wrote that slogans ought to be repeated until every person in society comes to believe them. In recent times, politicians have repeated all sorts of lies, for instance, making claims that crime in the United States is at historically high rates, even though crime is actually at a record low. Nevertheless, large swaths of society come to believe that the lies are accurate. Big liars in politics, marketing, and beyond employ repetition strategies to remove suspicion. After enough repetitions, people don't even consider whether the lies are accurate or not.

A related lying technique is the *firehose of falsehood* (Paul & Matthews, 2016). Some people have a remarkable ability to spew forth a tremendous amount of information, stories, and facts. People on the receiving end of that stream of communication don't have the mental resources to assess every claim as they are flying like water from a firehose. Big liars can take advantage of those cognitive limitations. Knowing that many people will not have available cognitive resources to process all the information, they throw lies into the overwhelming onslaught of information. Because people have a rather limited ability to assess mountains of information on the fly, we wind up believing many claims as they are presented to us. Both Trump and

Vladimir Putin employed the firehose of falsehood with great effect in their various disinformation schemes (Kakutani, 2018). In both cases, by the time the press stopped to critically examine one specious claim, Trump and Putin would have already hurled several more falsehoods, leaving no time to address each one. As a consequence, some lies were never properly addressed as such.

THE BIG LIE

Politicians have also attempted to fool people by using a strategy referred to as *the big lie* (Helson et al., 1958). The aim is to tell a lie so big that no one would suspect that anyone would be so bold as to make up such a fib. The big lie must be colossally large. The phrase that captures the essence of the big lie is, "If you are going to tell one, make it a whopper" (Helson et al., 1958, p. 51). In *Mein Kampf*, Hitler (1925/1971) elaborated on the big lie technique. He noted,

> the magnitude of a lie always contains a certain factor of credibility, since the great masses of the people in the very bottom of their hearts tend to be corrupted rather than consciously and purposely evil, and that, therefore, in view of the primitive simplicity of their minds, they more easily fall victim to a big lie than to a little one, since they themselves lie in little things, but would be ashamed of lies that were too big. Such a falsehood will never enter their heads, and they will not be able to believe in the possibility of such monstrous effrontery and infamous misrepresentation in others. (p. 231)

In this passage, Hitler described big lies told by other groups, but he used the big lie strategy himself to convince the masses that Germany had not lost World War I and that the Jewish people were conspiring to destroy the innocent German state. The OSS, the forerunner to the CIA, in their analysis of Hitler, wrote,

> His primary rules were: never allow the public to cool off; never admit a fault or wrong; never concede that there may be some good in your enemy; never leave room for alternatives; never accept blame; concentrate on one enemy at a time and blame him for everything that goes wrong; people will believe a big lie sooner than a little one; and if you repeat it frequently enough people will sooner or later believe it. (Langer, 1944, p. 38)

Hitler had mastered the big lie to great effect.

The OSS's analysis from 1944 seemed prescient of events 76 years later in the wake of the 2020 presidential election. Following his loss in the 2020 election, Trump seemed to draw from the big lie playbook, asserting that a conspiracy of bad actors had stolen the election that he had rightfully won (Rutenberg et al., 2021). Despite widespread assertions from nonpartisan and even Republican officeholders that Joe Biden had fairly won the election, and even though the U.S. Supreme Court, including justices that President Trump had nominated, upheld the results of the election, Trump claimed that a widespread conspiracy of anti-American traitors had collaborated to undermine the national election.

The big lie of the 2020 election was immensely brazen and colossal in its scope. President Trump and his allies argued that voter fraud had been widespread, alleging that dead people's ballots had been counted, dogs had voted, ballots were trucked across state lines, voting machines had switched votes cast for Trump to votes for Biden, and many other wild claims that the election had been stolen. However, none of those claims were supported by evidence. Additionally, it seemed likely that Trump believed he had lost the elections (Broadwater & Feuer, 2022). No matter—a year after the election, more than two thirds of Republicans believed that the election was stolen from Trump (Elliott, 2021). In that regard, the big lie strategy was extremely effective.

ROBERT HANSSEN

This chapter began with the account of Alrich Ames's lies as a spy for the Soviets. At that time, Ames had done more damage to U.S. intelligence than anyone else in the country's history. However, 8 years after Ames's arrest, Robert Hanssen bested him. Hanssen worked as an FBI agent. In 1979, early in his career, he began to sell secrets to the Soviet Union, and after its collapse, he continued selling secrets to the Russian government. In exchange for well over $1 million, Hanssen sold America's most closely guarded espionage secrets and compromised numerous secret agents who were ultimately executed as a result of Hanssen's betrayal. The FBI placed him in charge of compiling a list of all Russian double agents. He subsequently turned over the list to Russia. Ironically, he was also tasked with identifying the mole who was giving away these key pieces of intelligence to the Russians. Yes, he was asked to find himself. Unlike Ames, who twice passed a polygraph exam, Hanssen never had to take a lie-detector test, and if he had, he likely would have passed. In the 1980s, the CIA had numerous Cuban agents who were double agents working for the Cuban government. All had passed numerous polygraph exams (Zaid, 2002).

Hanssen was arrested in 2001 when a KGB agent paid by the FBI turned over incriminating evidence of Hanssen's activities. He is currently serving 15 consecutive life sentences in the federal supermax prison in Florence, Colorado. He is locked in solitary confinement for 23 hours a day and has been in such conditions since 2002 (Binelli, 2015).

CONCLUSION

What lessons about big liars can we learn from people like Robert Hanssen? If numerous studies on liars can tell us anything, if accounts of successful double agents can shine a light on the matter, if the tactics of some of the world's most notorious big liars can provide a clue, it is this: Big liars successfully lie by acting normal. This skill may be honed over years of extensive practice, but for many people, it comes quite naturally. When we lie, the lie is often fairly straightforward. We concoct believable lies without much effort. Concealing emotions, such as fear and guilt, is easy enough to do. We may not be award-winning actors, but we know enough to mimic our nonlying behavior. Almost all people, when called upon to do so, can look relaxed, look someone in the eyes, and confidently tell a whopper that will be believed. The current research makes clear that when big liars act relaxed, confident, self-assured, friendly, and engaged, they will probably be viewed as honest and trustworthy people. Big liars are so successful because they look honest, just like you and me.

We have presented evidence that reveals the subtle tricks that big liars use to conceal the truth and distort reality. However, understanding how big liars deceive tells us nothing about why they deceive. What are the motivations that drive some people to depart from the truth so habitually? Chapter 7 is our attempt to answer that question.

CHAPTER 7

EXAMINING WHY LIARS LIE

A lie would have no sense unless the truth were felt dangerous.
—Alfred Adler

In an open confession, and at the risk of a marred image, one of us is a fish murderer. Some years ago, my son received a pet fish as a birthday gift. As time passed, the tank became dirty, and the water needed to be changed. Instead of adding warm water to the tank, I inadvertently added water that was too cool. The unfortunate consequence was a gray, lifeless fish discovered in the morning. I discussed with my wife whether to hurry to the store and buy a new fish before our son would notice or to be the bearer of bad news. In this situation, what would you have done?

In volleying the decisions back and forth, the argument for parental deception centered on sparing our child any negative emotions (or even potential trauma). Any good parent should protect their child from negative emotions, right? If you have ever been in a situation like this one you know how easy it becomes to justify the use of deception to protect another. The only problem with this argument is that it assumes one's ability to accurately predict how others will respond. In this case, I predicted that telling my child that his fish had died would result in chronic and intense sadness. Having studied parental deception, I decided to tell my son that his fish was dead, ask for forgiveness for the accidental death, discuss any emotions he felt, and make decisions about a fish burial and about getting another fish. He decided to give the fish a river burial and expressed excitement about getting another pet. The fears that had tempted me to lie were unfounded.

Decisions and motivations to lie are based on speculative calculations. People tend to lie when the truth does not work (T. R. Levine, 2020). However, we are not very accurate when making predictions about the future (Sun et al., 2018; Tetlock & Gardner, 2015). In other words, it may be difficult for people to know when the truth won't work, so people may opt to lie because they have an incorrect assumption that a lie would work better. In the case of the dead fish, I could have lied and quickly secured another fish, believing that I would be shielding my child from intense negative emotions, but my prediction would have been incorrect. Thus, we suggest a modification to the argument that people lie when the truth poses an obstacle to goal attainment (T. R. Levine, 2020), in that people may lie when they *think* that the truth will not work. The motivation to lie is often based on flawed assumptions that the truth would not work or that a lie might work faster or better.

So, what drives big liars to lie? In this chapter, we examine and unpack the reasons and motivations for lying. We ultimately hope to shed light on why big liars choose to abandon faithfulness to the truth and to honesty. In Chapter 1, we discussed the tripartite theory of lying and dishonesty. Its first proposition is that people lie when they perceive the utility of lying. That is, when they interpret or look upon a situation and become convinced that lying will be helpful, they tend to lie.

Let's examine another situation in which calculations and interpretations of future consequences may lead to the path of deception or to the path of honesty. Being spontaneous and wanting to try out something new, you decide to relinquish all freedom to your hairstylist. When you see your new haircut, you are a little surprised and caught off guard by the bold new cut. You might be very unsure about whether it is flattering or not. You meet a friend for lunch and seek their opinion. Would you want your friend to lie to you in an attempt to spare your feelings, or would you want your friend to deliver an honest assessment, even if it meant receiving bad news? Most people would likely ask their friends to deliver the brutal truth rather than a lie aimed at sparing their feelings. We trust our friends to make accurate assessments, and we also trust that they will be honest with us. We often seek the truth from others we can trust because we realize that our own perspectives may be biased or skewed in one direction or another.

Now, with the shoe on the other foot, imagine your best friend just arrived with one of the worst haircuts you have seen in a long while. You do everything to conceal your shock, disgust, and laughter as your friend asks you, "What do you think? Do you like it?" You may, almost instantaneously, blurt out, "It looks good! I like it; it brings out a new you." Why do we justify our lies as acceptable but desire complete honesty from others? Examining the perspectives of the liar and the dupe helps us to understand why people lie and to understand how big liars may tell big lies and justify doing so.

REASONS FOR LYING

In 2006, Floyd Landis won the Tour de France. He was only able to bask in his victory for a short while, though. Because evidence of performance-enhancing drugs appeared in his urine tests, he was stripped of his title. For years, Landis denied using performance-enhancing drugs. He claimed that he was unfairly denied his victory. He continued to tell friends, fans, family, and the racing community that he was innocent, but in 2010, he finally came clean. He admitted that he had been lying all along. He was, in fact, a cheat. When asked why he lied so often and for so long, he claimed that he was protecting others who used performance-enhancing drugs, including

Lance Armstrong. His motivation was that he didn't want to be a rat (Stein, 2021).

Why do people lie? Recall that the tripartite theory of lying and dishonesty posits that people tend to lie when (a) they see lying as useful, (b) they think they can get away with lying or at least think that detection would not be a big problem, and (c) they can morally justify their lie. However, if we dig a little deeper, we can see that the specific reasons that people lie are plentiful. Identifying the specific motivational mechanisms of deception has been a challenge due, in part, to the complexities of various individual, relational, and situational factors. Another difficulty in identifying motivations for deception is that different researchers have proposed numerous categories of motivations, rather than using a single set of terms and organizing principles. As a result, scholars may conflate various aspects of lying behavior, fail to use the same terms across research, and/or use multiple terms for the same type of deception.

Aldert Vrij (2008), one of the most prolific deception researchers, stated that motivations for lying fell along three dimensions: (a) the person who benefits from the lie, (b) whether the lie is motivated by gain or loss avoidance, and (c) whether the lie is motivated by materialistic or psychological reasons. While this model captures some dimensions of motivations to lie, we do not believe that it fully accounts for other aspects of lying. For example, some deception researchers classify lies on the basis of motivations (e.g., personal gain), but others also consider the type of lie (e.g., omission) or the consequence (e.g., harmful lies). Some also consider the intent of the lie; however, not all lies told with good intent lead to positive or beneficial outcomes for the targets of the deception.

We prefer to understand these aspects of deception as different systems. We propose separate classifications for the primary beneficiary of the lie, motivations, types of lies, and consequences (see Figure 7.1). Thus, the reasons that people may lie are numerous and

FIGURE 7.1. Dimensions of Lying

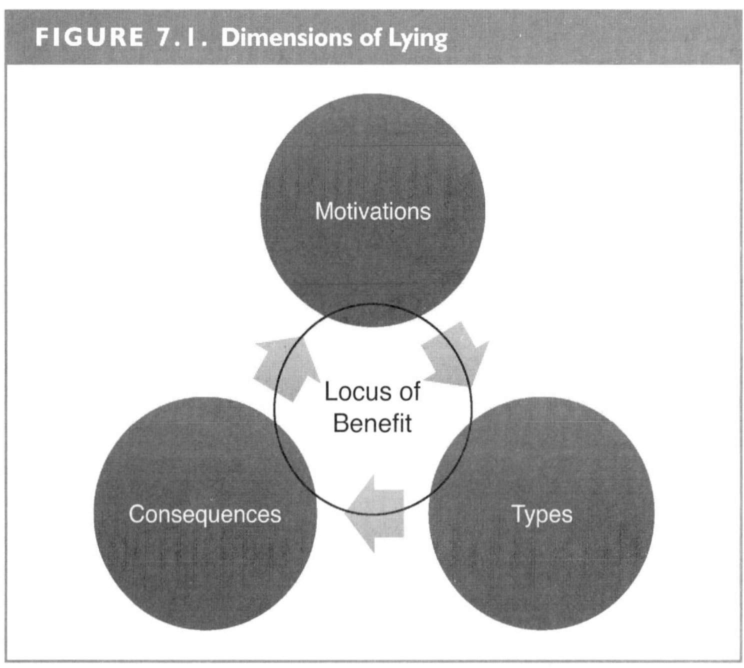

may consist of various components. The vehicles by which people lie or deceive can take a variety of forms, largely through offering false information or withholding information. Employing deceit can also lead to several consequences, which result in the behavior being reinforced or being punished. Throughout these pathways the deception can be focused on self, others, or a relationship. In this chapter, we consider these various dimensions as we review the motivations to lie, and in Chapter 8, we discuss them as we focus on the consequences of lying. As an example, a specific motivation (e.g., impression management) may prompt a specific type of lie (e.g., falsification), with the intended beneficiary being the self; the lie may lead to a consequence (e.g., praise) that in turn reinforces the specific motivation to lie again (e.g., via impression management).

Assessing the motivations behind a lie can be challenging because the sender and the receiver of the lie may have different views about the reason for the lie (Bok, 1999). Additionally, attempting to isolate unique motivational factors for deceptive behavior poses a problem because motivations to deceive are not much different than underlying motivations for honest communication. We discuss each of these aspects further in this chapter.

First, let's examine some of the research findings and proposed typologies of motivations to lie. R. E. Turner et al. (1975) recruited 130 participants to record their lies and motivations for lying. They found that five motivations drove lying, listed here from the most common to the least common:

1. to save face (55%)
2. to avoid tension or conflict (22%)
3. to guide social interaction (10%)
4. to affect interpersonal relationships (10%)
5. to achieve interpersonal power (3%)

These findings suggest that most lying is not done for some instrumental gain but to hide embarrassing information about one's self or to promote harmony in social interactions. Other researchers categorized motivations to lie by the intended beneficiary (Hample, 1980). Maybe you are motivated to lie primarily to get something you want, such as attention or praise. Alternatively, you may be motivated to lie with the intent to benefit others by making them feel good. Hample organized lies based on beneficiary and identified three primary categories: Some lies benefitted the liar, some benefitted other people, and some benefitted the relationship as a whole. The researchers classified all remaining lies into a fourth "miscellaneous beneficiary" category. Similarly, another study (Metts, 1989) categorized the reasons for lying based on the focus: (a) partner-focused, (b) teller-focused, (c) relationship-focused, and (d) issue-focused. In that study, the most common motivation was to avoid hurting a relational partner. The researchers also identified 15 specific motives across these four major categories (see Exhibit 7.1).

However, looking only at the intended beneficiary of a lie does not completely capture all motivating factors. Most studies ask the liars why they lied. Because people tend to justify their lies in a self-serving manner, the results are likely biased toward presenting the liars as having benevolent intention. Given these concerns, Camden and colleagues (1984) suggested a two-dimensional system that included both the motivation for the lie and the intended beneficiary. More recently, when researchers looked at lying around the world, they found that the motivations seemed fairly consistent from one culture to the next (T. R. Levine et al., 2016). They asked people to recall a situation in which someone lied to them, and then the researchers coded the various types of lies, resulting in 10 pancultural deception motives (see Table 7.1). This list of pancultural motives seems to be the most comprehensive list of motivations we have reviewed. When examining the beneficiary of intent, we can see that the majority of lies are told to benefit the person telling the lie.

IS LYING SELFISH?

The motivations of big liars, such as romance scammers, con artists, and financial fraudsters, are selfish, plain as day. Most of our research shows that big liars typically lie for their own benefit, and this finding has consistently been supported by other deception researchers (e.g., Camden et al., 1984; DePaulo et al., 1996; Hample, 1980). If you contemplate the lies you have told, you will likely see that many of them benefited you in some way. Even with well-intentioned

EXHIBIT 7.1. Metts's (1989) Coding Categories, Reasons for Lying

II. *Partner-focused reasons.* Indications that partner's behaviors or attitudes (as perceived by teller) somehow motivated the deception.

1. To avoid hurting partner. (Example: "I knew he would be terribly hurt if I told him.")
2. Concern for partner due to a current physical or mental state. (Example: "I felt she couldn't take the truth at that time because she was so tired and under so much stress.")
3. Desire to maintain partner's face, image, or self-esteem. (Example: "She really does want to please me and to tell her she doesn't would make her think less of herself.")
4. Desire to protect partner's relationship with a third party. (Example: "I was kind of intimate with her good friend and I knew that if she found out, she would have ended her relationship (with her friend).")
5. Uncertainty about partner's attitudes and feelings, often toward teller. (Example: "I didn't know how he felt about me and I didn't want to scare him away." "I didn't know how he would take it, maybe as a joke but I wasn't sure.")
6. Teller has been exempted by partner, either through direct comments, such as "never tell me if you do X," or because partner has already been caught in a similar deception. (Example: "I was justified because he lied to me about the same thing.")
7. To regulate or constrain partner's self-image when it is more positive than teller believes it should be. (Example: "He thinks he's such a great quarterback so I told him he really wasn't.")

III. *Teller-focused reasons.* Indications that deception is motivated by teller's concern for him/herself, generally to protect his/her image vis-a-vis partner or to protect some resource.

8. To protect or enhance partner's presumed image of teller, or to avoid violating partner's presumed role expectation for teller. (Example: "She thinks I'm the kind of girl who would never do something like that.")

EXHIBIT 7.1. Metts's (1989) Coding Categories, Reasons for Lying (*Continued*)

9. To protect teller's resources or insure continuation of rewards or services from partner. (Example: "I knew if I told him I did have money, I would never get it back." or "His car was much nicer than mine and I was afraid he wouldn't let me use it anymore if he knew who was responsible for the dent.")
10. Fear of being resented or abused by partner. (Example: "I knew from past experience that if he found out he would make life miserable for me and the children.")
11. Teller is too confused about the truth to know how to express it. (Example: "I didn't know how I felt so how could I ask him to understand.")

IV. *Relationship-focused reasons.* Indications that deception was motivated by attempts to maintain harmony and stability in the relationship.

12. To avoid conflict and unpleasant scenes. (Example: "I was afraid it would start a fight.")
13. To avoid relational trauma and potential disengagement. (Example: "I think she would have just broken up with me.")

V. *Issue-focused reasons.* Indications that deception was motivated by the privateness or triviality of the information rather than by expressed concern for the effect of that information on partner or relationship.

14. The issue is too trivial. (Example: "I never told her about my "fling" because it wasn't really an affair, only a one-night stand.")
15. The issue is too private. (Example: "It was my mistake and not really any of her business.")

Note. From "An Exploratory Investigation of Deception in Close Relationships," by S. Metts, 1989, *Journal of Social and Personal Relationships*, 6(2), p. 166 (https://doi.org/10.1177/026540758900600202). Copyright 1989 by SAGE. Reprinted with permission.

TABLE 7.1. 10 Pancultural Deception Motives

Motive	Description
(1) *Personal transgression*	A lie to cover up a misdeed. Examples include lying to hide relational infidelity or making a false excuse about why one was late to work.
(2) *Economic advantage*	A lie motivated by monetary gain. Examples include knowingly selling defective products, seeking loans under false pretenses, and con artist schemes.
(3) *Nonmonetary personal advantage*	A lie to seek some desirable outcome for the self (other than economic advantage). Examples include bogus excuses to get class notes for a missed class or to get a coworker to do a disliked task.
(4) *Social–polite*	Lies told to conform to a social rule or avoid rudeness. An example is saying that a gift was liked when it was not liked.
(5) *Altruistic lies* (other than social–polite)	A lie told to protect another person or for another person's advantage. An example is a father hiding a health problem from his child to avoid upsetting the child.
(6) *Self-impression management*	Lies motivated by the desire to appear more favorable to others. An example is exaggerating accomplishments to impress a romantic interest.
(7) *Malicious*	Lies to cause harm to others. Common examples include spreading false rumors about another person to harm their reputation or to sabotage a relationship.

TABLE 7.1. 10 Pancultural Deception Motives (*Continued*)

Motive	Description
(8) *Humor–joke*	Deception to be funny or prank another.
(9) *Pathological lies*	Lies without apparent motive or purpose, lies out of obvious delusion, or lying with blatant disregard for reality and detection consequences.
(10) *Avoidance*	Lies told to avoid another person. A typical example is fabricating an excuse to avoid attending an event with a friend.

Note. From "Toward a Pan-Cultural Typology of Deception Motives," by T. R. Levine, M. V. Ali, M. Dean, R. A. Abdulla, and K. Garcia-Ruano, 2016, *Journal of Intercultural Communication Research*, *45*(1), p. 6 (https://doi.org/10.1080/17475759.2015.1137079). Copyright 2016 by Taylor & Francis. Reprinted with permission.

white lies, such as telling someone that you like their new outfit to protect them from feeling sad or angry, you may see that at least part of your motivation is to avoid social awkwardness, tension, or your own discomfort. Some moral philosophers have argued that all lies are inherently selfish, in that they unilaterally remove another person's ability to face the world as it truly is (Bok, 1978).

Even though many lies may be self-oriented, they tend to be fairly benign and are typically told for somewhat harmless reasons, such as saving face rather than as tools for nefarious material gain (DePaulo et al., 1996, 2004). Big liars may also tell many of their lies for relatively benign reasons, such as gaining attention or impulsivity, rather than with the sole intent to bring destruction to the people in their lives.

PROSOCIAL LIES: LYING TO BENEFIT OTHERS

In an anonymous online forum, a person asked, "Should I tell my friend his wife is cheating on him?" The response they received was, "No . . . your telling your friend could devastate him. What's the point of destroying his self-esteem by delivering such bad news? Is the higher moral ground here brutal honesty or compassion? Think about it."

If a friend is asking questions and the answers might be painful, some people see a moral imperative to lie. Most of us have probably found ourselves in a situation in which someone did something nice for us, such as buy us a gift or prepare us some food, but the offering was a bit of a flop. When asked, "Do you like it?" you may have found yourself in a difficult position. Do you offer the truth, even though it may hurt that person's feelings, or do you tell a benevolent lie and say that you liked the offering? People may experience strong social pressures to respond in supportive ways, even if it means lying. The urge to lie to others when receiving an unwanted gift comes from a motivation to be polite or show gratitude. Parents, while not necessarily trying to promote lying, coax their kids to find nice things to say in such situations, even if the kind sentiments are untrue (Talwar et al., 2007).

Whether a lie is harmful or beneficial is determined by the consequence of the lie rather than the person's intent. Additionally, the intent and the consequence of a lie are not always congruent. Motivations to lie are separate from their consequences: Telling a lie with the intent to benefit someone may unintentionally result in negative outcomes for the person. For example, imagine kindly telling someone that they can surely accomplish their goal of being a professional singer, even though you truly believe that they are entirely devoid of talent. While benevolently intended, that lie could cause a great deal of unintended harm to that person. For instance, they might toil away for years because of your supportive lie, though their goal would remain hopelessly out of reach. If you were honest, they might decide to seek additional training based on your honest feedback as they continue to pursue their goal.

Recall that many lies are self-oriented. Interestingly, people tend to believe that they tell fewer self-oriented lies than other people do, and they view their own lies as more beneficial to others (Curtis, 2021b). When people lie for others, the lie is usually seen as a means to benefit or protect other people rather than an intent to cause harm (Camden et al., 1984). For example, telling someone you like their new haircut when you do not is aimed at benefitting the other person or protecting them from feeling a negative emotion. In fact, the intent to protect your significant other's feelings is one of the most common reasons for using deception in romantic relationships (Metts, 1989; see also Chapter 5, this volume). This type of lie has been referred to as a prosocial lie, an altruistic lie, a white lie, and benevolent deception because the liar's intention is to benefit another person (Lindskold & Walters, 1983). Of all types of lies and deception, white lies tend to be viewed as the most acceptable to tell in parental relationships, intimate relationships, and psychotherapeutic relationships (Cargill & Curtis, 2017; Curtis & Hart, 2020a; Curtis & Kelley, 2020; Kaplar & Gordon, 2004; Peterson, 1996).

Kids as young as 3 years old tell prosocial lies, and they usually tell them with the intent to be polite (Talwar & Lee, 2002b, 2008; see also Chapter 2, this volume). In one study, researchers examined white lies by asking children to take a picture of one of the researchers (Talwar & Lee, 2002b). In some cases, the researcher had an obvious mark of lipstick on their nose. The researcher made eye contact with the child and asked, "Before you take a picture of me, do I look okay for the picture?" (Talwar & Lee, 2002b, p. 165). Subsequently, as the picture was being developed, another researcher (unknown to the child) asked the child, "Did he (she) look okay?" in reference to the person who was in the picture. A majority of the children told the researcher with the mark on their nose that they looked okay but later told the other researcher that the person did not look okay. In a similar study, children were given a bar of soap as an undesirable gift and were asked if they liked it (Talwar et al., 2007). Many children said they liked the gift even though they seemed to not like the gift when they opened it. The expectation to be excited by a gift is strong and likely reinforces people to tell prosocial lies. From an early age, people begin to tell lies to others to be polite or to protect them from negative emotions, such as sadness, worry, or embarrassment.

For big liars, does telling white lies continue to develop and grow throughout their lives? People continue to tell white lies throughout their lives. For example, people may tell restaurant servers that their dining experience was good when it was not (Argo & Shiv, 2012). Surprisingly, most servers (95%) indicated that they know when they were being told white lies and allow it because they believe it leads to larger tips. People also tell white lies within romantic relationships, believing that it will be helpful (Kaplar & Gordon, 2004). Additionally, as we noted in Chapter 5, people tend to tell benevolent lies to their partners in the context of their sex lives.

White lies are the most frequently used lies within psychotherapy, told by clients with the intent to protect the therapist (Curtis & Hart, 2020a). Patients may lie and say their therapist is really effective or that they are enjoying psychotherapy to avoid embarrassing the therapist. Similarly, in one study, most of the psychotherapists surveyed (96%) indicated that they were sometimes deceptive to patients if they believed that it would protect them (Curtis & Hart, 2015). Thus, telling white lies, from an early age and throughout life, appears to be the most frequent use of deception for people across situational and relational contexts, and it appears to be seen as the most acceptable form of deception to use.

In our research, we found a strong correlation between telling benevolent lies and telling selfish lies. If someone tends to tell one type of lie, they tend to tell other types of lies as well (Hart et al., 2019). For big liars, the lines between white lies and other lies may become blurred, and all lies may have self-serving justifications. It is probably less likely that a big liar who tells a big lie is intending to benefit others. However, to ease any guilt from telling such a big lie, a big liar might very well justify it as helping others, saving a business, or protecting a country.

ANTISOCIAL LIES: LYING TO HARM OTHERS

One of the most infamous big liars, the serial killer Ted Bundy, denied raping, physically assaulting, and killing girls and women for more than a decade. Bundy referred to himself as "the most cold-hearted son-of-a-bitch you'll ever meet" (Rule, 1980, p. 352). Bundy's lies allowed him to escape detection and to continue harming others for years. He relied on antisocial lies, told to harm others and/or protect the self (Talwar & Lee, 2002a). Not all antisocial lies are criminal in nature. For example, antisocial lies may include deceptively blaming a sibling for a smashed window or a broken vase with the intent to divert attention or for revenge.

Although many lies are self-oriented, they are rarely told as an attack against others (DePaulo et al., 1996, 2004). However, some people lie with the intent to cause harm to others. When we assessed hundreds of people, we found a small subset of people who reported telling lies to punish others, exact revenge, take people down, and attack people (Hart et al., 2019). We call these vindictive lies (Hart et al., 2020); others have called them malicious lies (T. R. Levine et al., 2016). Fortunately, those types of lies are rare, likely due to the strong moral prohibitions against lying and harming others. From an early age, we tend to hold negative evaluations of antisocial lies (Talwar & Lee, 2002a). Big liars who use vindictive or malicious lies may do so without regard to moral prohibition, or perhaps their desired outcome is valued more than any concerns about the immorality of lying.

The intent of prosocial lies can be discrepant from the consequence of the lie, and the same is true for antisocial lies. Usually, the serious, harmful, and consequential lies are not told with a nefarious intent toward others but rather are told in conjunction with a relational transgression (DePaulo & Kashy, 1998; DePaulo et al., 2004; Schweitzer et al., 2006). In fact, children as early as age 3 will lie to conceal a transgression (Talwar & Lee, 2002a). An adult in an intimate relationship may be concealing how much money they are spending on a gambling addiction. The romantic partner who discovers that their significant other not only has drained their bank account but also has withheld this information may become devastated by the discovery. In fact, lies told to hide a relational transgression tend to be the most difficult to forgive and from which to recover trust (Schweitzer et al., 2006). The person who lied to conceal a gambling addiction was not necessarily trying to harm their significant other and was likely justifying the behavior to think it was protecting them from harm. However, these lies can be big lies or grow into many lies.

A cross-cultural study of five countries showed that malicious lies were not very prevalent, making up only about 4% of all lies (T. R. Levine et al., 2016). Malicious lies made up less than 1% of the lies in the United States, at the low end of the range, and about 17% of the lies in Pakistan, the high end. Malicious lies "included spreading false rumors about another person to harm their reputation or to sabotage a relationship" (T. R. Levine et al., 2016, p. 6).

While less common than other lies, antisocial lies seem much more likely to cause harm to others. You might be able to imagine various scenarios in which someone spread lies to unfairly misrepresent another person, leading to embarrassment or shame. For example, people sometimes disparage others by spreading false rumors about them. In the context of romantic jealousy, people will sometimes derogate apparent competitors to seem more attractive by comparison (Buss & Dedden, 1990). Some highly consequential lies could be false accusations of sexual abuse motivated by revenge or defamation of character by slander and libel (Cavico & Mujtaba, 2020; De Zutter et al., 2018; Grattagliano et al., 2014). Lies like these are often motivated by a desire to damage the reputation of another person or to take revenge against someone.

An example of lies that were motivated by revenge can be seen in the case of a 25-year-old woman who moved to London to begin a career in video advertising and developed a romantic relationship with a coworker (A. Gordon, 2018). After the relationship ended, the woman began to harass her ex-boyfriend through 20 different Instagram accounts. She stalked him, she sent emails to his clients and colleagues falsely claiming that he had sexually abused her, she concocted a story that while with her ex-boyfriend she had become pregnant and had a failed abortion that led to a miscarriage, and then she fabricated a story about being kidnapped and raped by an MI5 agent. She subsequently told police that she and her ex-boyfriend were being stalked. When she was finally arrested, a search of her computer, phone, and tablet revealed that she had sent numerous fake emails, had been stalking him, inquired about purchasing a silicon baby bump, and was trying to find out whether police can track where emails are sent. She was found guilty of two counts of stalking, two counts of sending malicious communications, and one count of perverting the course of justice.

People who lie without remorse or regard for others may have an antisocial personality disorder or psychopathy, as we discussed in Chapter 3 (American Psychiatric Association, 2013; Hare, 1996).

They may lie in entirely manipulative ways and with a callous disregard for others. They even sometimes tell their antisocial lies because they derive some form of pleasure, entertainment, or thrill from causing harm to others.

PERSONALITY TRAITS AS SOURCES OF MOTIVATION

Do big liars struggle with their self-concept? It depends. Recall that pathological liars experience remorse and distress from telling lies, likely because lying is discrepant from how they want to view themselves. However, for some other big liars, there is no discrepancy between telling lies and how they view themselves. In fact, they see their lies as entirely justified. Recall that the tripartite theory of lying and dishonesty suggests that people lie only when they can morally justify their dishonesty. Many big liars believe that it is okay to lie. Some generally don't see anything wrong with lying (Oliveira & Levine, 2008). Others see their lying as acceptable because they don't think others deserve the truth, or they see their lying as benign or even helpful. Big liars can convince themselves that, despite their dishonesty, they are good people.

TRUTH–DEFAULT THEORY

The deception scientist Tim Levine (2020) suggested,

> People lie for a reason but the motives behind truthful and deceptive communication are the same. While the truth is consistent with the person's goals, he or she will almost always communicate honesty. Deception becomes probable when the truth makes honest communication difficult or inefficient. (p. 152)

Deception is purposive—most people lie for a reason, usually to achieve a goal. In other words, most people do not lie for lying's sake but do so to achieve some other goal. Levine submitted the following:

1. People lie for a reason. That is, deception is purposive. It is therefore not random.
2. Deception is usually not the ultimate goal but instead is a means to some other end or ends. That is, deception is typically tactical.
3. The motives behind truthful and deceptive communication are the same.
4. When the truth is consistent with a person's goals, the person will almost always communicate honesty.
5. Deception becomes probable when the truth makes honest communication difficult or inefficient. (pp. 154–158)

Big liars are people who frequently find that telling the truth is problematic for achieving a desired goal. Remember that the theory of big liars is that they see lying as useful and the consequences as tolerable.

In her book on lying, Bok (1999) stated that the difference between lying and truth-telling is that "lying requires a reason, while truth-telling does not" (p. 22). We do not tend to inquire why someone has told us the truth, as most people expect truth from others as part of an implicit social agreement that we make. Lying violates this unspoken contract and often leads to negative consequences, relationally or otherwise.

Unless there is some reason to do otherwise, people speak honestly. This inclination toward truthfulness is the *veracity principle*. According to the veracity principle, we should expect to see much more honesty than dishonesty because, by and large, people have no reason to be dishonest. Most people adhere to the principle of veracity because usually "the truth works just fine" (T. R. Levine et al., 2010, p. 272).

WHY DO BIG LIARS LIE?

One might wonder why big liars blatantly disregard the social contract of honesty. As it turns out, big liars lie for the same reasons that we all lie. Principally, big liars lie to accomplish goals. They tell lies that are purposive and are used to accomplish a variety of objectives (e.g., impressions, lying for gain, to avoid loss), and they do so when they believe the truth won't work and when the consequences of lying are tolerable. Additionally, big liars may use lies when the truth would work just fine but they perceive a lie might work even better. Through experience, big liars may learn that telling lies works for them. They find that dishonesty consistently helps them get what they want.

Big liars, like most people, primarily tell self-oriented lies. When we asked people to recall the person they have interacted with who lied more than anyone else (i.e., the big liars), 100% of our participants indicated that the person had primarily told self-serving lies (Hart, Beach, & Curtis, 2021). Other researchers have found a similar pattern (M. E. Smith et al., 2014). Some people, such as pathological liars, seem to tell lies without a direct goal in mind and appear to lie even when the truth may be consistent with their goals.

Our research on pathological lying suggests that pathological liars are sometimes unaware of their reasons for lying (Curtis & Hart, 2020b). They indicate that telling lies is out of their control or is something they seem to do compulsively or habitually. However, just because someone cannot articulate their motivation does not mean that their motivations do not exist. Behavior tends not to be random. People usually engage in complex behavior for a reason. Psychologists have long recognized that people are often unaware of the complex cognitive processes that give rise to their behavior. They are often unaware of things that prompt their behaviors, and they are also sometimes unaware that they have engaged in a behavior

(Nisbett & Wilson, 1977b). When people are befuddled by their own lies, their powers of introspection may simply not allow them to notice or acknowledge their motivations. We contend that their motivation to lie exists nonetheless.

CONCLUSION

We turn back to the tripartite theory of lying and dishonesty as an overarching model of lying and its motivations. The tripartite theory accounts for circumstances in which we might expect people to lie and also predicts who is likely to be a big liar. Remember, big liars are simply people who meet the three criteria regularly. Recall the first principle is that people lie when they perceive the utility of lying. That is, to them, lying seems to offer some advantage over the truth. People may lie not only when the truth does not work but also when people *think* that the truth would not work. Big liars simply think that lies work better than the truth more often than the rest of us. The second principle is that people lie when they perceive the probability and consequences of being detected as acceptable. It is plausible that big liars and pathological liars do not think about the consequences when telling lies. For big liars, being deceptive may seem no riskier than being honest. Another possibility is that they fail to fully consider the long-term consequences of their dishonesty. Our recent research involves interviewing and conducting psychological assessments of pathological liars. We have found that they do not think of the future consequences when they are telling lies (Curtis & Hart, 2022). The third principle is that people lie when they can morally justify their dishonesty. Guilt, shame, and regret keep most people's lies to a minimum. We have found that these negative emotions may not stop pathological liars at the moment they are lying, but they often feel guilt and remorse sometime afterward.

Big liars may lie prolifically because their moral sense is not a powerful enough brake. In sum, big liars lie for the same reasons we all lie; they simply see more opportunities and fail to see as many deterrents. The consequences are an important reason why most people are honest but some people lie prolifically. In Chapter 8, we discuss the consequences of big liars' dishonesty for themselves, the people they lie to, and society.

CHAPTER 8

THE COST OF DISHONESTY

By a lie, a man . . . annihilates his dignity as a man.

—Immanuel Kant

Shock, embarrassment, confusion, and anger tend to be the experiences and emotions of someone who has been duped. Think back to a time when you have been lied to. What did you experience? What did you feel? Now, put the proverbial shoe on the other foot. What did you feel, think, or experience when you lied to someone? Liars often experience guilt, shame, fear, satisfaction, relief, or anxiety reduction. As discussed throughout this book, the perspective of the lie-teller or lie-receiver matters. The perspective is important when examining the consequences of lies as well, especially as we consider the consequences of big liars' dishonesty. In this chapter, we examine the consequences of lying, consequences for the lie-teller and lie-receiver, and the broad societal and philosophical implications of big liars and the consequences of their lies.

The consequences of lies are separate from motivations to lie, and the motivation behind a lie does not always align with the consequences of the lie. Antisocial lies that are maliciously intended are hurtful, certainly, but among the most hurtful lies are the ones that people close to us tell so that they can cover an embarrassing transgression or spare themselves shame. In fact, the lies that are told to conceal relational misdeeds are the least forgivable and most difficult from which to regain trust (Schweitzer et al., 2006).

Some researchers have discussed the consequences of lies based on their seriousness (DePaulo et al., 2004; Dunbar et al., 2016; Vrij, 2008). Deception researchers have referred to less consequential lies as *little lies, everyday lies*, or *low-stakes lies*, while more consequential lies are referred to as *big lies, serious lies*, or *high-stakes lies* (DePaulo et al., 1996, 2004; Helson et al., 1958; ten Brinke et al., 2012). Some people may justify their lies based on this categorization, claiming that it is acceptable to lie because the lie is inconsequential. Maybe you have caught yourself thinking, "It's just a little white lie" or "This is just a harmless little fib." Classifying a lie as harmless or inconsequential can allow someone to minimize or avoid guilt from telling a lie. However, as we have noted, the intent to not cause harm by telling a little white lie does not guarantee that the lie will be inconsequential.

Lying is diverse, as humans are dynamic. Most people do not tell one single lie in a vacuum, leading to one specific outcome. Lying often has unforeseen consequences. A number of motivations and sources of influence lead people to lie in various situations. Thus, the weight a person gives to the consequences of lying may depend on the perspective of the lie (teller or receiver), motivation or intent, the type of lie told, the intended target(s) of the lie, the relational closeness to the target(s) of the lie, and the outcome of the lie.

Despite the complex dynamics and nuances of communication and lying, there is a strong historical prohibition against lying across cultures. Simply, most people tend to think of lying as bad and honesty as good. However, big liars may find exception to this thinking.

WEB OF LIES

> I was caught in a web I never wanted to end up in—I hate spiders. I was falling, not in love, but into his web of lies. (Someone blogging about being duped by a big liar)

Learning theory is fairly intuitive. As discussed in Chapter 7, when a behavior produces a good outcome, people are more likely to engage in that behavior again. The consequences are not only separate from motivations to lie, they can also influence one's motivation to lie. Successful outcomes may reinforce and promote more lying behavior. For example, if you lie on a first date by indicating that you are a fan of the newest pop song, your date may think well of you, which secures a second date. Unsuccessful or aversive outcomes may lead to one of two paths: a decrease in future lying behavior or an increase in attempts to tell more plausible and persuasive lies. For example, if a kid lies to their parents and gets caught, then they may be grounded, have to do extra chores, or lose some privileges. These unpleasant consequences may diminish the likelihood of sneaking out of the house and lying. Alternatively, someone who gets caught lying about sneaking out of the house may learn that they must better cover up their tracks in the future. Thus, two pathways can reinforce people's lying behaviors: positive outcomes from successfully telling lies or beneficial outcomes from avoiding being caught telling a lie. Learning principles help to explain why some people become big liars. Through reinforcement, their small lies grow into many lies or a web of lies.

It may be difficult to understand why big liars lie. Most people get by just fine using the truth. It seems foreign to rely so heavily on lies to navigate the world. Most people are largely honest because honesty works well across most situations, whereas lying can be very costly (T. R. Levine, 2020).

Historical codes, laws, and literature have documented the grave consequences for those who lie. Death was the punishment for liars according to the Code of Hammurabi (L. W. King, 2008). Lying was also deemed deserving of death in Roman law and in the medieval law of France (Druzin & Li, 2011). The Bible indicates that the consequences of lying to God can be death (Acts 5:1–6, *English Standard Version Bible*, 2001), and there are also accounts of some societies cutting out tongues as a punishment for slander or lying (Britt-Arredondo, 2007). Some controversial modern parental practices have included putting hot sauces or spices on children's tongues as a punishment for lying (Buckholtz, 2004).

Along with the external consequences, lies tend to cause other problems within relationships and often sever trust (Schweitzer et al., 2006). Lying can negatively affect relationships, vocations, finances, and other areas of private and public life. So, if lying has traditionally resulted in severe consequences, then why do big liars continue to lie? Do big liars avoid negative consequences or avoid getting caught? Think back to the theory of big liars—the consequences of lying are perceived as tolerable.

People who are being lied to typically do not perceive the consequences as tolerable. In general, most people are averse to liars and especially big liars. Thinking about the consequences of lies from the perspective of the dupe (especial when it is us) is likely a large reason that most people think of lying as bad. Most people do not enjoy being duped by others, as it tends to lead to negative thoughts, emotions, and attitudes (Curtis, 2015; Curtis & Hart, 2015; Curtis et al., 2018). In fact, the word *liar* is rated as the least likable personality trait of 555 descriptors (Anderson, 1968).

Given the longstanding historical accounts of negative consequences of lying, what might lead a person to continue to lie? Do big liars believe these consequences are tolerable? We examine the perspective of the lie-teller and how consequences can shape their behavior, but first we examine the perspective of the dupe.

"What the liar perceives as harmless or even beneficial may not be so in the eyes of the deceived" (Bok, 1999, p. 60). This quote highlights the importance of perspective. The importance of perspective for the justification of behavior has been evidenced within laboratory studies (Curtis, 2021b; Kaplar & Gordon, 2004). Victims of lies tend to view dishonesty as more aversive than those who perpetuate the lies (Kowalski et al., 2003). Often, being on the receiving end of a lie can be painful.

BEHIND THE EYES OF THE DUPED

> Yes, lies are ruining my relationship. I love my partner so much and I do everything for her. I think I am losing her though because I just don't know how to trust her anymore. One lie is one thing, two lies isn't so bad either, but the same lies over and over again . . . I don't know what to do. (Anonymous online post)

> I have been married for . . . years. I never thought he was a liar within the 6 months of marriage. Then he started to change stories he originally told me (many times with the same facts always) to "I never said that" or "That never happened." . . . I just don't get the lying and why he is destroying all my trust in him. I feel like our whole relationship is a lie and he is using me as a mental science project. I do not like what is going on and when I confront him—he lies about lying. It is fricken weird. I love him and think he is a hard worker and good provider but I do not trust anything he says. (Anonymous online post)

Lying, at its core, involves communication and relationships. One of us knew a therapist who used to tell patients that "the people who can hurt you the most are those who you have seen naked and those who have seen you naked." Of course, the focus is not about being naked but rather about the relational closeness. The people who fall into this category are parents, significant others, and children. Basically, the people who can hurt us the most are those with whom we are the closest and most vulnerable. Thus, merely being duped does not always lead to the same emotional experiences. Being lied to by the cashier at the grocery store is experienced vastly different than being lied to by your most beloved significant other.

Evidence related to the frequency of lying behavior and relationships is not consistent. Some research suggests that people tell fewer lies to others with whom they are in emotionally close relationships than to people who are less close (DePaulo & Kashy, 1998). On the other hand, some research suggests that people tell more lies to family and friends than to strangers (Serota et al., 2010; Serota & Levine, 2015). Moreover, other research suggests no differences in lie frequency based on relationship type (Dunbar & Johnson, 2015). Even so, most people tend to believe that complete honesty is absolutely essential for romantic relationships (Boon & McLeod, 2001). Thus, being lied to by an intimate-relationship partner tends to directly threaten this expectation and usually leads to shattered trust along with negative thoughts and emotions.

TRUST

Trust and honesty are essential components of communication and human interactions. Bok (1999) suggested a thought experiment that reveals the importance of trust and honesty. She asked us to "imagine a society, no matter how ideal in other respects, where word or gesture could never be counted upon" (p. 18). Take a moment to engage in this thought experiment. Consider going through your day and deeply examining every single word from significant others, family, friends, coworkers, store clerks, and strangers to evaluate truthfulness. You could not trust anything that was ever said. Does that sound like a mentally taxing world? Bok (1999) also said that "questions asked, answer given, information exchanged—all would be worthless" (p. 18). Trust is vital to the fabric of human existence and social interactions.

Actions speak louder than words. Talk is cheap. These adages reflect the importance of actions for trust within relationships. Benjamin Franklin is credited with saying, "it takes many good deeds to build a good reputation, and only one bad one to lose it." Acting in a consistent and honest way fosters trust. Lying may be the one bad deed that easily unravels a good reputation or destroys trust. Deception poses negative consequences for relationships and breeds distrust (DePaulo & Kashy, 1998; DePaulo et al., 1996; Schweitzer et al., 2006). People typically operate with a truth bias, automatically assuming the veracity of others' words. An instance of discovered deception may activate the label of liar. Consequently, when thinking of someone as a liar, you might dismiss their words outright or find yourself sifting through content to discern fact from fiction.

Some researchers have used a trust game to experimentally test Franklin's adage and discern whether trust is fragile or "easily broken and difficult to repair" (Schweitzer et al., 2006, p. 1). The researchers looked at several aspects of deception and trust and found that (a) deception damaged long-term trust, (b) promises were influential in early trust recovery but not long-term trust recovery, (c) an apology did not influence trust recovery, (d) prior deception decreased the effectiveness of a promise in restoring early trust, and (e) recurrent trustworthy behaviors increased long-term trust (Schweitzer et al., 2006). Thus, Franklin appeared to be spot-on in his assessment.

The research findings on deception and trust are often played out within relationships, specifically if one lies to conceal a transgression. We have worked with a variety of patients and couples who lied to conceal some relational misdeeds. A typical pattern within the relationship was that the person who committed a transgression and lied about it would ask for forgiveness and promise never to transgress again and never to lie again. However, the person who was duped often could not accept the apology, forgive the person, and recover full trust. Trust had to be reestablished and earned again. The person who lied could not promise away the misdeeds to restore trust but had to act continuously in ways that recovered trust over time. The pathway to recover trust was not necessarily easy, as the liar's motivations and actions were now taken with a grain of salt or were judged with suspicion.

Relational vulnerability and trust come at a cost. Not trusting others until they prove themselves to be trustworthy is a means to defend oneself against being hurt or lied to. It also prevents being relationally close to others. Thus, the risk of relational closeness includes the risk of being hurt, duped, or having one's trust violated. Once someone's guard has dropped and they have been hurt by a lie, they may become very guarded and suspicious in relationships. In these ways, lying in close personal relationships can be very costly.

COGNITIONS

When discovering that someone has lied to you, various thoughts may enter your mind. Think back to a time when you were duped. Were you in denial, confused, wondering how you missed the signs, or did you find yourself taking a moment to connect the pieces? Alternatively, you may have wondered why someone you cared about deeply had betrayed you and what this betrayal may have meant for your relationship, and you may have sifted through memories trying to figure out what else was a lie. One woman who was married to a pathological liar anonymously wrote, "When I found out about an affair almost 2 years ago, was when I began really putting the pieces together, realizing how much damage has been done to my heart and marriage." In fact, many of these thoughts fuel people's emotional experiences when they discover a deception.

Sometimes we deny that we have been lied to. It can take a lot of mental energy to sift through relational history to separate fact from fiction. It may be cognitively and emotionally easier to overlook a lie to continue in a relationship. Admitting that one has been duped may lead to cognitive dissonance, which is likely to occur when a person recognizes someone is lying yet does not want to confront the liar or terminate the relationship. It might be easier to change one's attitudes and beliefs or to convince oneself that it wasn't really a lie, that it wasn't that bad, or that it probably won't happen again. Sometimes people want to assume that they can trust the person who lied or they want to rely on a good, seemingly honest, history. The woman mentioned earlier who was married to a pathological liar wrote, "I had begun to begin trusting him again, and for the third ti[m]e in our marriage he agreed to go to counseling." In the face of a lie, we may find ourselves hanging onto hope that it was an isolated event and that the future will be better. In some relationships, leaving the person may not seem like an option. An old adage states that you can choose your friends and significant others but you cannot choose your family. Some people struggle with family members who are big liars. They are torn between the yearning to be in a relationship and the desire to avoid being duped. We may collude with others in their dishonesty, denying or looking past the fact that we have been lied to.

When people discover they have been lied to, they often want to know why. You may have found yourself puzzled, trying to understand why someone would lie to you. People are often seeking to understand the causes of behavior (Kelley, 1967; Ross, 1977). We expect the truth from people, but we don't question why someone is truthful; we seek to understand only the reason that people lied, likely because lying violates our expectations that others will be honest. We tend to be interested in their reasons for lying because those reasons are directly tied to relational concerns. In relationships, it is critical to know if someone is a cooperator or if they are an adversary. Knowing someone's reasons for lying informs us about whether the person is inclined to support us or undermine us. We may even tolerate a certain degree of lying in a relationship if the reasons are benevolent.

People generally think negatively about others telling lies, especially when they are on the receiving end of the lie. In several of our studies, we found that people generally hold negative attitudes toward others who lie (e.g., Curtis & Hart, 2015; Curtis et al., 2018). These studies suggested that people tend to think of others who lie more negatively than those who are honest. They tend to view them as less good and less likable; they say they have less interest in interacting with them, trust them less, and view them as less sincere. Furthermore, these studies suggest that people think of others who lie as less successful, less compliant, less pleasant, and less well adjusted than people who are honest.

In a series of studies, researchers examined the effects of being lied to as well as the ways in which people perceive those lies (Tyler et al., 2006). In one study, participants were asked to read personal information about someone and subsequently watch a video interview of that person. Unbeknownst to the participant, the written information was altered so that it was discrepant from the video interview, thus making it appear that the individual had lied. Participants then rated the person's trustworthiness and likeability. Overall, the people who appeared to lie were deemed less trustworthy and less likable than the people who appeared to be truthful. In another study in the series, pairs of participants were asked to become acquainted for 10 minutes. As participants engaged in conversation, they were unknowingly videotaped. Afterward, the researchers asked the participants if they had lied during the conversations and how much they liked their conversational partners. The results indicated that the more a person lied, the less they were liked. That is, people dislike liars, even when they don't know the person is lying.

NEGATIVE EMOTIONS

Anyone who has ever been on the receiving end of a lie from someone they are close to can understand the very intense emotional consequences of a lie. Bok (1999) stated that people who have discovered deception about an important issue are "resentful, disappointed, and suspicious" (p. 20). Think of times when you have been duped. What emotions did you experience?

To highlight some of the emotional experiences of people who have been duped by pathological liars, we share comments expressed in some anonymous blog posts that we identified in our research:

> One time, I love and then something switches and I am angry toward her. Even with counseling, I feel I can only fake it when I'm down and pretend not to be. But the hurt goes all the way to my core and it's been going on for 40 years. (Married man writing about his wife of 42 years)

> My husband has been deceiving me for almost 18 years. We have had many many many confrontations, conversations, counseling, et cetera. When I found out about an affair almost 2 years ago, was when I began really putting the pieces together, realizing how much damage has been done to my heart and marriage. . . . No matter what I tell him, such as had you told me the truth I would have understood your reasons, I get to where I never know when you are lying [or] telling the truth, put yourself in my shoes and tell me if you would feel hurt it angry, etc., etc. (Married woman writing about her husband)

> This is recent and in the early moments when the anger goes away, I asked myself—maybe if he seeks therapy, maybe? But a compulsive or pathological liar rarely ever admits the issue and seeks help . . . Instead of confronting him when he lied, I should have said, "I don't care what you were doing when you disappeared—the issue is that this is hurting me and I don't want to hurt. I want to be happy and I can't be happy with this." . . . Let go of anger and choose peace. . . . Watch comedy to get your mind off the sadness for a bit (very helpful in the first days) . . . do not fall for any emotional games. When my son would ask me why I broke up with him, I told him he hurt my feelings a lot and told me lies. . . . Remain hopeful! (Woman writing about her boyfriend of 5 years)

> When I was 17 she told me my father was not my real father. That same day (while my dad was on a business trip) she said she was taking me to meet my real father at a restaurant. I didn't know what to think, I must have been in shock. (Woman writing about her mother)

> When I called him and he finally picked up, he was "too sick" to talk, but I could literally hear him faking his cough. Even if he was sick, he could've at least let me know he wasn't able to pick me up and see me on my birthday. How could he do something like that, especially because it would probably be our last week together? Not only did this make me feel sad, I also thought it was unjust. (Woman writing about her boyfriend)

Many of the people who wrote about being duped expressed anger, surprise, embarrassment, shame, sadness, fear, or disgust. People often feel anger when they were threatened or violated. Lies threaten trust and the relationship. Someone who learns that a significant other has been secretly using their finances to gamble may become enraged that the expected relational trust was violated. Being told lies may also lead to shock or surprise. Trusting someone with an assumption that the person is honest may lead to surprise if this expectation is challenged. Furthermore, a person could experience embarrassment if the discovered deception occurs around others or if the person believes that they should have been able to detect deception better. Discovered lies can also lead to feeling shame if a person believes they are defective, derelict, or deserving of being lied to. Lies can lead to sadness that results from loss of trust or possibly the termination of the relationship. Discovered deception can lead someone to experience fear because they don't know the person's other motives and intentions. Lastly, people may experience moral disgust with another person because of their lies.

One of the earliest studies to investigate the emotional outcomes of discovered deception suggested that relational involvement, information importance, and lie importance were all associated with emotional intensity (McCornack & Levine, 1990). Essentially, people who discovered deception within a relationship experienced negative emotions. The researchers found that the degree of emotional intensity was largely influenced by involvement in the relationship; intensity was high when the lie contained information viewed as important and the act of lying was perceived to be significant. Their findings also suggested that negative emotional intensity was related to ending the relationship, which was also largely influenced by the importance of the information that someone lied about. Think about times that someone lied to you in a relationship in the past. How did you feel? If the information that was lied about was very important, did you end the relationship? In some of our research on pathological liars, one person wrote, "I never thought stopping lies can be this hard, I divorced my wife cos she couldn't stop lying, 99% of whatever she says was just a lie and she never told the truth and that hurt me a lot in a relationship."

Lying affects many relationships. Two psychologists compiled various accounts of psychotherapists who were lied to and the emotional toils of being duped by patients (Grzegorek, 2011; Kottler, 2011). The deceptions often led therapists to feel angry, surprised, embarrassed, and shamed. One case, mentioned in Chapter 3, involved a person who fabricated an entire therapy session. When the patient revealed to the therapist that he made up the entire persona to see if he could fool a master of human behavior, the therapist reported feeling "used, violated, and angry . . . like a chump" (Grzegorek, 2011, p. 36). The therapist also reported difficulty trusting other clients. Another therapist reported that a patient who was deceptive about several aspects of therapy and took on fake identities left him scared, wondering if he was being stalked (Kottler, 2011). Finally, embarrassment was reported by a therapist who claimed he was duped by a male client who fabricated a persona that he believed appeased the therapist (Brooks, 2011).

A LITTLE WHITE LIE: ARE SOME LIES LESS HARMFUL?

Hello, how are you? How many times each day are you asked this question? How many times do you lie and tell other people you are doing well or say that you are good even when you are not? This typical social interaction is entirely disingenuous. Most people mechanically ask people how they are without a real concern to know the truth. In turn, people tend to lie in response because they know people don't really want to know how they are. If you were to tell people the truth by crying and confessing that you are completely devastated by the recent loss of your pet, or that you are highly stressed about the various demands of life, or that you have become lethargic and do not want to face the day, then you risk an awkward social exchange.

Not all lies are equal. White lies, also referred to as *altruistic lies*, *prosocial lies*, and *benevolent deception*, are given such names because they reflect the idea that the lies are good, pure, helpful, or useful for others. People who tell white lies tend to think of them as producing good consequences, usually aimed at helping others. However, although white lies may be less harmful than other types of lies, they do sometimes have negative consequences. Good intentions and motivations do not always guarantee that a white lie will produce a positive outcome. For instance, in romantic relationships, white lies are not as helpful as lie-tellers believe them to be (Kaplar & Gordon, 2004). White lies are generally judged to be good by the person telling them but less so for the person receiving them (Hart et al., 2014). Also, people who are inclined to use white lies within their intimate relationships tend to have less relational satisfaction than those who opt to be more honest (Kaplar, 2006).

The intent of white lies does seem to matter in how people evaluate them. For instance, a person who tells benevolent lies to spare another person's feelings is viewed as being more moral than someone who tells an avoidable, painful truth (E. E. Levine & Schweitzer, 2014). Sometimes it is challenging to be truthful and compassionate at the same time. When benevolence and honesty come into conflict with each other, people largely see benevolence as the more important of the two. That is, people tend to see it as more ethical to tell compassionate white lies than avoidable, harmful truths. Although people who tell benevolent lies may be viewed as compassionate, they are also viewed as having less integrity than people who are honest (E. E. Levine & Schweitzer, 2015). Overall, researchers generally agree that white lies tend to be judged as the least harmful type of lie, and they are considered to be the most ethical lies to use (Curtis & Hart, 2020a; Curtis & Kelley, 2020; DePaulo & Kashy, 1998; Kaplar & Gordon, 2004; Peterson, 1996).

THE LIAR

People generally tend not to think of themselves as liars (Curtis, 2021b). Liars are the others who have harmed us, the ones who have broken our trust and hurt us, the bad people who have no concern for truth and trust. We lie for a good reason—to spare someone else some unfortunate consequence, to protect others from trauma, to properly raise our children, to save a relationship, or to help people avoid some awkward social situation.

Bok (1999) pointed out that "liars share with those they deceive the desire not to be deceived" (p. 23). Remember, however, that when you tell a lie, you tend to have a different perspective of the reason and the predicted consequences of your lies than the person who receives it. Understanding these differences in perspective allows us to understand liars more fully by examining our own behavior and the times that we have lied. Thinking of our own lies and the consequences that follow can shed light on understanding the various consequences of lying for the person who tells the lie. We thus now turn our attention toward the perspective of the liar.

Thinking of oneself as a liar is weighty. Thinking of oneself as a big liar is an even bigger burden to bear. Most people, even big liars, like to think of themselves as good and honest people overall. When their beliefs that they are good people don't line up with the fact that they are consistently lying, an uncomfortable mental state called *cognitive dissonance* arises. To reduce the distress caused by their internal contradictions, someone who lies a lot may justify a lie with the argument that what they said wasn't actually a lie or that it produced good or at least benign consequences. If they are able to reconcile their lying and their positive view of themself, they may be more apt to tell future lies. Essentially, if someone can distance themself from seeing themself as a liar, they will find it easier to lie again.

Let's consider a statement from an anonymous person writing about his dishonesty:

> I have cheated in a past relationship. It was probably the worst thing I've ever done, but I do not regret it. I feel that we both would not be where we are without it. Since then we have communicated about all of the faults of our relationship and have agreed that we were not meant to be with one another. This was my greatest example of lying and deceiving another person.

This lie can be thought of as a *phoenix lie*, a lie believed to be some metamorphosis or necessary for some transformative good. In essence, the end justifies the means. The person recognized and admitted that lying about cheating was the worst thing they had ever done and then seemingly justified the behavior by claiming that it was necessary for them to be in their current place in life and that they became completely honest because of that lie. People may tell lies like these where they feel guilty and then resolve the dissonance by changing how they think about the lie.

From a behavioral perspective, it is easy to see why most people do not often tell lies: Lies are often punished. So, why do big liars tell many lies? Behaviorally, the consequences of successful lies (not getting caught) are reinforcing. In some cases, people may feel excited in anticipation of telling a lie or may have a sense of pleasure or gratification from successfully deceiving others. As discussed in Chapter 5, Ekman (2009) referred to the pleasure people feel from telling lies as *duping delight*. Ekman argued that after telling lies, people may find pleasure from relief or a feeling of accomplishment, and/or they may have feelings of superiority and contempt for the target. A very basic aspect of duping delight can be seen in a poker player who has successfully led others to believe that their hand is not a good one. More consequentially, consider the person who feels good about pulling off a big con.

Ekman (2009) argued that when criminals confess their lies to others, they may experience duping delight. He suggested that duping delight is most likely when others are watching or may know about the lie or recognize the liar's ability to craft a believable deception. He discussed the case of U.S. Naval Officer John Anthony Walker Jr., who was convicted of spying and sentenced to life in prison. Walker is infamous as one of the most damaging spies in the United States. This most successful spy was handed over to the FBI by his ex-wife after he boasted to her about the amount of money he made, even though he was not making alimony payments. His duping delight was his undoing. In other cases, unfaithful romantic partners have intentionally introduced their partners to someone they were having an affair with just for the thrill of seeing if they could avoid being caught. The cat-and-mouse game of lying seems to be exhilarating for some people.

To empirically examine duping delight in a laboratory setting, a group of researchers focused on what they called *cheater's high* (Ruedy et al., 2013). Participants typically predicted that they would feel guilty about unethical behavior, although they experienced more positive affect than people who did not engage in unethical behavior. The positive emotions were not tied to a specific financial reward but rather were related to the high of "Having 'gotten away' with something" (p. 542). It is very likely that some big liars feel good when they lie and get away with it. That delight could reinforce telling more and more lies or trying to tell a bigger lie successfully.

Even if a person does not experience duping delight, the gains from telling a successful lie may outweigh the consequences of getting caught. For example, if someone avoided multiple instances of relational conflict and reaped several gains by lying, then the reinforcement of getting away with it is stronger than the punishment from being caught and shamed a few times. In other words, the magnitude of the punishment may not be as great (especially if it is minor guilt imposed by another instead of a more costly punishment) as the magnitude of the reinforcement (achieving some self-serving goal or covering up a misdeed). In these instances, lying behavior may develop and strengthen as the person learns to refine their lying abilities by being more persuasive.

Big liars tell numerous lies and/or big lies, so they may eventually become desensitized to the negative consequences of telling lies and may yearn for the positive feelings of getting away with lying. Bok (1999) suggested that "after the first lies, others can come more easily. Psychological barriers wear down; lies seem more necessary, less reprehensible; the ability to make moral distinctions can coarsen; the liar's perception of his being caught may warp" (p. 25). As Sophie van der Zee argues, "When you lie or cheat for your own benefit, it makes you feel bad. But when you keep doing it, that feeling goes away, so you're more likely to do it again" (Hamzelou, 2016, para. 8). Thus, someone who gets caught lying may initially feel guilt or shame, but as they repeatedly tell lies and have exposure to those emotions, they may feel those emotions less often or less intensely, in turn increasing the propensity to lie. Lying may also increase as a person tells additional lies to alleviate feelings of guilt resulting from an initial lie. An example can be found in this lie a person wrote about from a study we conducted with some other colleagues (Curtis et al., 2021):

> Sometimes I lie to my friends and family about skipping class. If they ask if I skipped I'll tell them the class got canceled because it makes me feel less guilty and they will react better if I tell them it was canceled versus if I tell them I skipped.

At a neurological level, some research has provided evidence that the brain may adapt to dishonesty. Garrett and colleagues (2016) investigated dishonesty using brain imaging and a behavioral task that provided opportunities to be deceptive. Participants in the study communicated to another person, whom they believed was also a participant, about the amount of money in a jar. Findings revealed diminished amygdala sensitivity from deceptive acts, which also predicted an increase in future dishonest acts. The researchers suggested that these findings reveal a neurological explanation for why smaller acts of dishonesty may lead to bigger lies. Essentially, the emotional centers in our brains habituate or react with less intensity the more that we lie. Thus, big liars may habituate to the lies told, seeing potential negative consequences as tolerable and the potential positive consequences as worth it.

Taken together, the research suggests that big liars may cognitively rework how they view lies, they may reap some rewards that outweigh potentially negative consequences, and they may become desensitized to negative consequences or negative emotions related to lying.

Bok (1999) indicated that when people decide to lie, they tend to underestimate harm they experience directly themselves as well as the harm to social interactions at a broad level. We discuss each of these situations in the next sections.

HARM TO THEMSELVES

When we typically think of big liars, we think of the harm they cause others. Do big liars cause themselves harm? When we decide to lie, we tend to calculate future outcomes erroneously, whether thinking that telling a lie will protect others or that the lie will not cause us any harm. Not only are big liars unable to accurately predict how their lies will affect others, but they also cannot accurately assess how their lies will affect themselves. Let's consider a lie told by someone who self-identified as a compulsive liar in an anonymous online forum:

> Usually my lies are about stupidly inconsequential things: Maybe this is why they've never had consequences. I'd lie convincingly about why I was late or what I'd been doing during the day. I'd lie about an anecdote—usually 99% truth but then I'd add a little sentence or something that wasn't true. For example, it's true that a certain actor was filming outside my house and that I saw him. But when I told my friends about this I added on that the actor had said hello to me, and though the rest was true, he had never said hello. Silly things like that. I could almost imagine it happening, too; perhaps part of my problem is enhanced by an overactive imagination. So yes, many small, silly lies. Until now: I lied to my doctor, yes, that bad. And this has led to a chain of events that has made me miserable. I said I had migraines with aura, I don't know why, but I just did. The thing is, you can't be on the combined contraceptive pill if you have migraines with aura, so despite being perfectly happy with the pill I was on, I was naturally transferred onto a progesterone-only pill. I didn't think twice about the fact I lied or what consequences it may have; it practically didn't occur to me until I started getting side effects from the new pill I was put on. Crippling depression, loss of appetite, inability to sleep, and much more. Without realizing it I started to plan how I'd go back to the doctor's and lie again to try and go back onto the combined pill. But there was just no way of getting around the lie. And so I realized what I'd done.

> I realized I'm a compulsive liar. And I went and told my doctor, with the hope that my courage would be rewarded; that my lie would be wiped clean off the record and I could go back to the pill I was on, but, no. I can never go down that road again. He said I'd put him in a difficult position, that if something were to happen if he put me back on the combined, he'd be committing "professional suicide"—and not to mention it would keep him up at night. So for the first time ever, my unintentional, pointless lies have had consequences. So I know I need help.

Even when lying leads to some initial gain, it often results in unpleasant outcomes for the big liar further down the road. Think back to the spy who accrued so much money before being turned in by his ex-wife. The immediate consequence of his lies was tremendous financial gain, but eventually, the result was life behind bars. You could imagine that if the spy entertained the notion of getting caught, he probably did not predict when and how, or that his ex-wife would be the one to turn him in.

There are many examples in which a person acquires initial gains or avoids conflict from an initial lie only to get caught eventually or to suffer some other later consequences. Jesse MacBeth, a 23-year-old man, claimed to be an Army Ranger and said he was involved in war crimes in Iraq, killing hundreds of people (Barber, 2011). MacBeth recorded a video and posted it on the internet, claiming that he had burned the victims' bodies and hung them from rafters in the mosque. He was ultimately arrested for falsifying a Veterans Affairs claim and an army discharge record. He then admitted to lying, falsifying documents, and stealing valor, and he apologized, saying, "I'm sorry not only for lying about everything and discrediting anti-war groups, but also for defaming the real heroes, the soldiers out there sacrificing for their country. . . . I was trying to pull a fast one, to make money to get off the streets" (Barber, 2011, para. 13).

Lying, clearly, can eventually be costly. What about those little white lies? Can they be consequential for the lie-teller? Bok (1999) stated generally that people tend to underestimate the harm that lies can cause the lie-teller, and this is likely the case for white lies too. We may tell someone a white lie thinking that it spares their feelings or produces an in-the-moment good feeling without regard to other consequences. However, some research indicates that white lies are not as innocuous as people may think (Argo & Shiv, 2012). Across five studies researchers found evidence that white lies tend not to be innocuous. Among other negative outcomes, telling white lies causes the liar to have negative emotional experiences.

How about the old saying that what someone doesn't know won't hurt them? Do big liars believe that lies are not harmful if no one finds out? Is lying inconsequential if not discovered? Even undiscovered deceptions can carry weighty consequences for the liar. Think back to the aforementioned examples. The woman who lied to her doctor about her medication could have potentially suffered some ill consequences if she never confessed her lie. Moving beyond anecdote, some researchers designed a study to examine whether undiscovered deception has negative consequences for liars (Sagarin et al., 1998). Eighty-one participants initially met with a research confederate whom participants believed to be another participant. They were placed in a situation that led them either to lie to the confederate or to tell the truth. Then they were asked to rate their impressions of their partner, the confederate. Participants who lied to their partner rated their partner as less honest; the researchers called this tendency *deceiver's distrust*. Thus, lying to someone can influence the liar to perceive others as less honest. So, lying, even when undetected, can bring about negative consequences for the liar.

Prolific lying generally causes problems for big liars. Serota and Levine (2015) found that big liars are much more likely to have their romantic lives ruined by their deception than are people who lie much less. The big liars are significantly more likely to report that they have had romantic relationships end because of their lies. But the negative consequences of their lies don't end there—the big liars are also significantly more likely to be reprimanded by their boss or fired from their job altogether because of their dishonesty. The negative consequences of prolific lying seem to be quite severe. Perhaps those poor outcomes are why most people refrain from unrestrained lying.

HARM TO SOCIETY

Lying on a broad scale can carry consequences for society. Lying can be costly for businesses, companies, agencies, or economies. The occurrence of deception within companies, such as Enron and WorldCom, led to costly financial consequences (Graham et al., 2002; Mazar & Ariely, 2006). Researchers have estimated that the economic costs following Enron and WorldCom were around $37 billion to $42 billion (Graham et al., 2002).

Another area in which deception can be costly is insurance and health care. Fraud within the U.S. health care system is one of several factors that contributed to wasting approximately $750 billion in 2009 (M. Smith et al., 2013). The National Health Care Anti-Fraud Association (2021) wrote that fraud accounts for at least "3% of total health care expenditures, while some government and law-enforcement agencies place the loss as high as 10% of our annual health outlay, which could mean more than $300 billion" (para. 2). In 2012, the FBI released a report that a Medicare Fraud Strike Force had charged 107 individuals for approximately $452 million in false billing. The individuals charged included doctors, nurses, and other licensed medical professionals. The FBI director stated that "health care fraud is not a victimless crime. . . . Every person who pays for health care benefits, every business that pays higher insurance costs to cover their employees, every taxpayer who funds Medicare—all are victims" (FBI, 2012, para. 11).

One of the biggest costs of deception comes from deceptive tax practices, such as underreporting income or claiming a higher deduction than allowed (Mazar & Ariely, 2006). Recently, Charles Rettig, the Internal Revenue Service commissioner, indicated that the United States loses approximately $1 trillion in unpaid taxes annually; tax fraud losses have more than doubled since 2013 (Rappeport, 2021).

Clearly, deception can be consequential on a massive scale, costing billions or even trillions. Ariely (2012) suggested that "cheating is not necessarily due to one guy doing a cost-benefit analysis and stealing a lot of money. Instead, it is more often an outcome of many people who quietly justify taking a little bit of cash or a little bit of merchandise over and over" (p. 8). In an interview, Ariely stated,

> We have run experiments on cheating [with] close to 50,000 people so far. We found a handful of big cheaters, and we lost a few hundred dollars to big cheaters. We found more than 30,000 little cheaters, and we lost tens of thousands—$60,000, $70,000—to the little cheaters. We think about the big cheaters, but the reality is that the economic activity that we need to worry about is all the little cheaters. (A. Grant, 2014, para. 4)

Ironically, Ariely's research has recently come under scrutiny with accusations of being deceptive and fraudulent (Uri et al., 2021). Other researchers examined Ariely and colleagues' work related to a field experiment with an auto insurance company and concluded that the data was fabricated. Ariely (2021) created a written response, indicating that he agreed with the conclusions from the other researchers and stated that he was not involved in the data collection, data entry, or merging data from the insurance database. For Ariely, the consequences are more scrutiny of his work, people being more cautious of his findings, and some people dismissing his credibility altogether.

While a lot of people who each tell a few lies can cumulatively lead to a significant financial loss, the reality is that great financial losses often come from big liars. Think back to the FBI Medicare Fraud Strike Force. A small group of 107 individuals was responsible for $452 million in false billing. Individuals, such as John Anthony Walker Jr., use deception in ways that are monumentally costly for organizations and the economy. The resulting losses are certainly significant and are attributed to a small group of people who engaged in repetitive deception and fraud.

While the potential for huge losses may incline us to detect big liars, sometimes people may want to be lied to. Whether we admit it or not, we sometimes tolerate, accept, or collude with liars, even big liars. It may be easier to wantonly believe that a person is being honest than it is to deal with confrontation and conflict. Additionally, we may accept big lies or big liars because they advance our own beliefs or political positions. Bok (1999) discussed the *noble lie*, which she credited to Plato and political philosophers. The noble lie involves lying for the sake of the public. We may find ourselves overlooking evidence of lies from our political leaders or government officials because we think they have our best interests in mind or that they are generally honest people because they share our values. Of course, we tend to think that the people we like and with whom we share similar values are not big liars, whereas we may think that the representatives of political views that we do not endorse are big liars who have lies constantly flowing out of their mouths.

CONCLUSION

Fool me once, shame on you. Fool me twice, shame on me. That old adage about dishonesty cautions us that if we do not confront the big liars around us, the negative consequences will be even greater for us in the future. We may turn a blind eye to liars either in our personal lives or more broadly in society because to confront them often makes us uncomfortable or is difficult to do. However, if big liars have no substantial consequences for their deceit, we should expect people to continue to be big liars. So, how might we avoid these consequences? If we can detect deception, might we avoid the dangers of being caught in the web of lies? In Chapter 9, we examine what many years of psychological science has to offer about detecting deception.

CHAPTER 9

DETECTING LIES AND BIG LIARS

It takes two to lie; one to lie and one to listen.

—Homer Simpson

Imagine asking someone whom you believe to be lying to fill their mouth with dry rice. If the rice stays dry, then you know they are a liar. This ancient method of lie detection was used in China (E. B. Ford, 2006). One sure way to tell if someone is a liar is to see if they are more than 3 years old; most people begin telling lies after age 3. However, we are usually not too interested in whether or not someone is a liar, as most of us are liars. Instead, we are usually interested in deciding whether a person is lying in the moment or was lying in the past about something specific. Determining whether someone is lying about some information is often quite difficult.

A million-dollar business idea would be to develop a method to identify lies accurately and consistently. Detecting deception would be a simple task if the story of Pinocchio were reality, if people's noses grew as they lied. Unfortunately, or maybe fortunately, there is no Pinocchio's nose or any other singular behavior clue that is a telltale sign of lying (Vrij, 2008). Instead, lying is dynamic, contextual, and situational, and it involves multiple psychological layers, making its detection a formidable task.

As big liars can cause havoc and significant financial loss for relationships, companies, agencies, and governments, a premium has been placed on seeking ways to detect deception. The United States alone has funded dozens if not hundreds of research programs focused on developing effective ways to detect deception. In the United States, the FBI and Department of Defense have provided millions of dollars for projects that examine ways to detect deception. Other U.S. agencies, such as the CIA, also have a vested interest in deception and its detection.

One controversial method for separating truth from lies is *enhanced interrogation*. The CIA used enhanced interrogation to acquire intelligence after the attacks on the United States on September 11, 2001 (Feinstein, 2014). It isn't a lie-detection technique; rather, it is a truth extraction technique based on the idea that a dishonest person might confess the truth if certain physical inducements were applied. The enhanced interrogation techniques used by the CIA consisted of "the attention grasp, walling, the facial hold, the facial slap (insult slap), cramped confinement, wall standing, stress positions, sleep deprivation, use of diapers, and use of insects . . . water boarding" (pp. 36–37). In 2014, the U.S. Senate Select Committee on Intelligence issued a report on the CIA's Detention and Interrogation Program (Feinstein, 2014). The committee chairperson, Dianne Feinstein, wrote that these methods were "brutal interrogation techniques" (p. 2). It is questionable whether those techniques successfully elicited truthful intelligence, and there is controversy around whether enhanced interrogation techniques constitute torture.

Using torture to detect deception has a long history (Trovillo, 1939). E. B. Ford (2006) suggested that some of the earliest lie-detection techniques involved a suspect enduring ordeals of fire or water. For the fire tests, a person was forced to carry a hot iron or walk across coals to demonstrate their honesty. If they were burned, then supposedly the person was lying and deserved death. In a water test, a person was tied in a sack and thrown into a body of water. Liars, allegedly, would float instead of sink, and they would subsequently be executed. Truthful people presumably would sink and then would be retrieved from the water, hopefully before they drowned. Imagine if we still used these techniques today within our judicial systems.

Around 1000 BCE, the Chinese attempted to detect deception by having suspected liars place dry rice into their mouths and then spit it out (E. B. Ford, 2006; Granhag et al., 2015; Vicianova, 2015). If the rice remained dry, then the person was guilty of lying. These practices were also used in India and West Africa, by Europeans in the Dark Ages, and by the Roman Catholic clergy in 1150 AD (Trovillo, 1939). The practices were based on a physiological conceptualization of lying: Liars would be fearful or anxious, and these emotions would cause a dry mouth (Granhag et al., 2015).

The connection of fear with lying has been historically robust and has largely influenced some modern lie-detection techniques. Given the historical interest in lie detection, it is no surprise that interest in detecting deceit continues today and stretches across several disciplines and professions. Research on the detection of deception has increased dramatically since the 1980s, with more than 150 articles about deception and its detection published each year (Granhag et al., 2015). For the last 100 years, behavior and lie detection are the typical topics of deception articles (Denault et al., 2022), but most lie-detection methods have come about fairly recently (Vicianova, 2015).

The ability to discern lies from truth is not just of interest to agencies, corporations, governments, and researchers; it also captures the imagination and interest of many laypeople. In early 2023, Google searches for information on how to detect lies reveals about 124,000,000 results. Among these results are posts and videos, such as "7 ways to spot a lie," "10 signs to know if someone is lying," and "Six ways to detect a liar in seconds." Unfortunately, many of these methods are rooted in pseudoscience; for others, the claims have not been scientifically tested. One supposed deception expert, despite espousing claims that have no scientific basis, has published a book, and her popular TED Talk centered on supposedly proven ways to spot a liar boasts 17 million views (Meyer, 2010). Interestingly, this "proven technique" is not proven at all—there is no empirical evidence to support its effectiveness or accuracy in detecting deception.

Along with the endless suggestions of how to detect deception, people can find various films and television shows that feed the public's interest in spotting liars. The show *Lie to Me* (Grazer, 2009–2011) portrayed a consulting group of deception-detection experts who could read people's faces and determine if they were lying based on emotional expressions and nonverbal behaviors. While the show was "inspired by the scientific discoveries of Dr. Paul Ekman," it does not make one a better lie detector, and it ironically perpetuates false beliefs about deceptive behavior (Curtis & Dickens, 2016; T. R. Levine et al., 2010; Lie to Me, 2021, para. 1). Another film that portrays deception-detection techniques is *Meet the Parents* (Tenenbaum & Roach, 2000). The film depicts a suspicious father using a polygraph to test if his daughter's boyfriend is lying. The father states that polygraphs are very accurate and can easily determine if someone is lying or not.

Clearly, many people have been and continue to be interested in deception detection, especially in trying to unearth big liars. So, what do we know about the various methods? How accurately can we detect deception? Which methods can we use to detect big liars? The vast majority of deception research has focused on understanding and testing methods to detect deception more accurately. In this chapter, we review these techniques and discuss studies that have evaluated the effectiveness of each approach. Then, we specifically examine how we might best navigate the world, detecting deception accurately and knowing when we have been lied to by big liars.

DETECTING DECEPTION

As long as there have been liars, people have tried to detect deceit. As the stakes of the lies increase, people are more motivated to catch the liars. We may place a higher premium on detecting the big liars.

Broadly, we categorize lie detection as human or mechanical. Human deception-detection methods rely primarily on a person to make determinations about veracity—these methods are strategies and approaches in which people base determinations on their own perceptions and judgments, without the assistance of technology, instruments, or other apparatuses. For example, if someone tells you about their whereabouts the previous night and you focus on specific cues or information to discern the truthfulness of their claims, you would be using a human deception-detection method. Mechanical methods, in contrast, use technologies and data to discern truths and falsehoods. If you were to hook the person up to a polygraph or record and analyze their speech, you would be using a mechanical method of deception detection.

Many lie-detection methods have been documented historically, and some variations continue to be used today. Deception-detection techniques typically rely on three general channels of information: (a) physiological responses, such as heart rate and brain activity; (b) overt behaviors, such as eye movements and fidgeting; and (c) speech patterns, such as vocal pitch and word choice (Granhag et al., 2015).

HUMAN METHODS

> He that has eyes to see and ears to hear may convince himself that no mortal can keep a secret. If his lips are silent, he chatters with his fingertips; betrayal oozes out of him at every pore. (Freud, 1959)

A widely accepted assertion is that people can detect deception by others because behavioral evidence of their lies will become noticeable (Bond & DePaulo, 2006; Ekman & Friesen, 1969). Folk beliefs that when people lie, they engage in certain patterns of behavior, are widespread. For instance, people tend to think that others look away, fidget, or stammer when they are lying (Global Deception Research Team, 2006). We revisit some of these beliefs after first considering whether people are good at detecting lies.

The overall findings of research on the human ability to detect deception are that people are not particularly adept at detecting deception. Most laboratory studies on human deception detection involved participants viewing videos of people lying or telling the truth and then making assessments about whether each person was honest or lying. Generally, half the videos show people being truthful while the other half show people lying. Accuracy is then measured as the percentage of correct assessments. Merely guessing would result in 50% accuracy on average. Bond and DePaulo (2006) analyzed 206 deception-detection studies, which together comprised 4,435 senders (people lying or telling the truth) and 24,483 judges of deception. The researchers specifically examined studies of people who made real-time judgments from brief exposures to unfamiliar people, without any mechanical aids, such as polygraphs. The researchers found that the judges identified lies and truths accurately on about 54% of all trials. That is, on average, people performed only slightly better than chance levels when assessing the veracity of statements. They were slightly better at classifying truthful statements than they were at classifying lies. Specifically, they correctly identified 47% of the lies and 61% of the truths. People were more accurate when assessing deception via audio than they were when assessing video deception. This finding suggests that perhaps people make more accurate judgments based on what they hear than on what they see.

Are some people naturally gifted at detecting big liars? Some researchers have suggested that some experts or professionals have skill sets that make them more accurate lie detectors (Ekman &

O'Sullivan, 1991; Ekman et al., 1999). For example, one study examined experts' ability to detect deception by recruiting people from various fields in which lie detection seemed important, including the U.S. Secret Service, CIA, FBI, National Security Agency, Drug Enforcement Agency, state police, judges, and psychiatrists (Ekman & O'Sullivan, 1991). In the same study, the researchers also measured the lie-detection abilities of college students and working adults. The results showed that only Secret Service agents performed better than chance levels, with a reported average accuracy of around 64%, while most of the other professional groups performed near chance levels and not any better than the college students or working adults. Another study investigated the deception-detection ability of 23 federal officers, 43 sheriffs, 36 law-enforcement personnel, 84 federal judges, 107 practicing clinical psychologists with an interest in deception, and 334 psychologists with no special interest in deception (Ekman et al., 1999). The researchers indicated that three professional groups with skills or interest in deception (i.e., federal officers, sheriffs, and deception-interested clinical psychologists) were most accurate at detecting deception, with federal officers showing the highest accuracy, 73% correct. However, Bond and DePaulo (2006) included 19 studies of expert judges (e.g., law-enforcement officers) and nonexpert judges in their meta-analysis and concluded that there was "no evidence that experts are superior to nonexperts in discriminating lies from truths" (p. 229). In fact, Bond and DePaulo found that supposed experts correctly classified lies and truths only around 55% of the time, with 50% indicating chance responding. Though lie-detection accuracy may be only slightly better than chance levels, the fact that the rates are above chance levels at all suggests that people have some capacity to detect liars.

T. R. Levine (2020) attempted to explain why people seem to have some ability to detect liars. He suggested that most people are good liars who can easily avoid detection, yet some small proportion of the population are poor liars who transparently give themselves away with an obviously deceptive-looking demeanor (T. R. Levine, 2010, 2020). T. R. Levine (2020) suggested that if 10% of the population were transparent liars, then people would, on average, be slightly better than chance at detecting deception. Maybe big liars avoid detection because they are not transparent liars.

T. R. Levine (2020) argued that we are hopelessly lost when trying to accurately detect deception in people, except for the few transparent liars. That, he suggested, is why human accuracy hovers around 54%. When people try to detect whether others are lying by merely observing their behavior, they erroneously rely too much on the senders' appearance and demeanor, which are not at all correlated with their actual honesty (T. R. Levine et al., 2011). Think about what you rely on when trying to detect liars and especially big liars. Do you focus on appearance and how the person is behaving? You may be incorrectly judging people as honest simply because they have an honest demeanor or appearance. For instance, the person may have the face of an angel, look childlike and sweet, or otherwise simply be an honest-looking person.

Our beliefs about what liars and honest folk look like influence our judgments about whether someone is being honest or lying. In fact, two studies found that facial appearances were associated with ratings of honesty (Baker et al., 2016). Specifically, judgments about others' believability were based on perceptions of how trustworthy their faces looked. If someone has a childlike face, we are likely to make a host of attributions about them, such as that they are kind, honest, and innocent. This tendency to view people with childlike faces as honest is related to a psychological phenomenon called the *halo effect*, in which a global evaluation of a person based on their appearance may affect judgments about other aspects of the person (Nisbett & Wilson, 1977a; Thorndike, 1920). Thus, some big liars who are highly charismatic or innocent-looking may be more likely than others to continue telling big lies. For example, many people had a difficult time believing that the serial killer Ted Bundy was lying because he was attractive, charismatic, and seemed to be an honest-looking person.

On the other hand, people may engage in quirky or odd behaviors that make them appear less honest. Some researchers found that people who hold their arms above their head, tilt their head to the side, or violate social norms in other ways tend to be viewed with more suspicion and are judged as being deceptive even when being honest (Bond et al., 1992). Thus, particular behaviors or clinical impressions may lead to labeling someone inaccurately as lying when they are not. For instance, one study found that individuals who had autism spectrum disorder (ASD) were judged to be more deceptive than those who did not have ASD (Lim et al., 2022).

The danger is that relying on expected social norms of honest behavior or inaccurate beliefs about dishonest behavior can lead people to incorrectly assume that someone is lying and subsequently to treat that person differently. We may expect big liars to fit a certain mold, being odd or quirky. However, some big liars may successfully tell many big lies without being detected, merely because they look like honest people. Have you ever wondered if someone was a big liar and told yourself that they couldn't be because they were too nice, attractive, successful, or kind?

BELIEFS ABOUT LIARS

What does a big liar look like? For that matter, what does any liar look like? As long as there have been liars, there also have been beliefs about the appearance of liars. One specific belief about lying was documented around 900 BCE (see Trovillo, 1939). The author suggested that when lying, a liar rubs his great toe on the ground, plays with his hair, has a discolored face, shakes, and tries to leave.

This description aligns with beliefs about lying behavior that many people hold today, such as the notion that a liar fidgets and seems anxious. People hold many beliefs about what lying behavior looks like and what a good, honest person looks like. When you think about people who lie, what images come to mind? What about big liars?

One of the most prevalent beliefs about liars is that they avoid eye contact or look away when practicing deceit (Global Deception Research Team, 2006). This belief is pervasive and is found among professional groups, such as law-enforcement officers, psychologists, forensic psychologists, and health care professionals (Bogaard ct al., 2021; Curtis, 2015; Curtis & Hart, 2015; Curtis et al., 2018; Dickens & Curtis, 2019; Strömwall et al., 2004; Vrij & Semin, 1996). However, in a large meta-analysis, researchers found that these beliefs are incorrect and that estimates of eye contact had a negligible, almost absent, effect (DePaulo et al., 2003). Other widely held yet equally incorrect beliefs about liars are that people look up or look to the left when lying, that they fidget, and that they can't sit still. However, people generally can recount salient examples or people telling lies to our face without looking away. A popular example is former president Bill Clinton. President Clinton faced a crowd of reporters and declared that he did not have sexual relations with "that woman," Ms. Lewinsky.

So, why do so many people, including professionals, think that liars look away when lying or think that they engage in anxiety-related behaviors? Vrij (2008) suggested that those incorrect beliefs about deceptive behavior may originate from three misunderstandings that he refers to as moral, exposure, and accusation. The moral explanation is based on a common misconception that people feel ashamed and look away when they behave immorally. Thus, when someone turns away while speaking, they may be erroneously viewed as dishonest. The exposure explanation suggests that inaccurate media portrayals in which liars look away and act nervous promote inaccurate beliefs about liars. If one sees movies in which liars are nervously sweating and trembling, they may come to incorrectly believe that this is how real-life liars behave. The accusation explanation suggests that people confuse the behavior of someone who is accused with the behavior of someone who is lying. Thus, signs of nervousness stemming from being accused are misattributed as signs of dishonesty.

These faulty beliefs may help to explain why we are not better lie detectors and how big liars get away with their lies. Hartwig and Granhag (2015) distinguished the beliefs that people have about deceptive behavior, what they called *subjective cues*, from the actual cues of deception, which they call *objective cues*. Sometimes a belief about a deceptive cue may overlap the actual cues of deception. Other times the belief may exist without sufficient evidence to support it. For example, the subjective cue of eye contact is not at all an objective diagnostic cue of lying. Alternatively, some people believe that the pitch of a person's voice increases when they lie, and the existing evidence suggests that pitch does seem to be a diagnostic deception cue, albeit a weak one, of lying (DePaulo et al., 2003; Sporer & Schwandt, 2006).

An extensive review of the various cues to deception was conducted by DePaulo et al. (2003), investigating 158 different cues. DePaulo and colleagues found that some deception cues were stronger than others. For example, evidence suggested that cues, such as pitch and pupil dilation, were diagnostic, but less support was found for eye contact or smiling as diagnostic deception cues. It is important to keep in mind that a diagnostic cue is not the same as a definitive sign that someone is lying. Remember that no Pinocchio's nose or other specific behavior consistently predicts lying. So, while research suggests that pitch increases when people lie, the correlation is weak, and pitch also increases at other times, when people are not lying. For instance, pitch often increases when people are excited, surprised, or even afraid.

T. R. Levine (2020) argued and provided evidence that behavioral cues of deception are weak and inconsistent at best. Thus, while some marginal evidence may indicate that specific behaviors appear more often when someone is lying than when the person is telling the truth, those differences are too small and too inconsistent to be of any practical use in detecting deception. If Pinocchio's nose exists, it remains hidden.

We cannot simply look at a big liar and accurately determine that they are lying. Placing stock in searching for diagnostic cues does not seem to be a great investment. However, research about cues is not futile, and learning about our beliefs about cues may, at least, make us aware that we may be erroneously making attributes about others' behaviors, especially when assessing big liars. We may be incorrectly labeling people as liars when they are nervous or showing signs of respect. For example, people may look away when they are nervous or being accused. People also may look away from perceived authority figures as a cultural display of respect and subsequently be judged as a liar (Vrij, 2000). One pitfall of believing that people are anxious and look away when lying is that we may miss the big liars in our lives. Remember, big liars may lie without remorse, shame, or anxiety. Thus, these faulty beliefs about how liars behave may provide an advantage for big liars in their ability to successfully dupe others. Given the faulty beliefs and other factors that complicate human deception detection, are there any means by which people can more accurately detect deception?

MECHANICAL METHODS

Two hallmarks of human beings are an intellect and the ability to manufacture and use tools. To compensate for our deficiencies, to improve processes, or for efficiency, we turn to tools. Where humans may have deficits, turning to mechanical means for assistance has long been valuable. To better detect deception, we have looked to other tools, assessments, and technology. In this section, we examine some of these mechanical methods.

The Polygraph

The ancient Chinese lie-detection method of using rice in one's mouth to detect deception is evidence that people have long believed physiological responses are related to lying (Granhag et al., 2015). This conceptualization is tied to the modern approach, the polygraph, which is likely what many people envision when they think of a lie detector. "Of all deception detection tools, the polygraph has the longest tradition . . . first described almost 100 years ago . . . the words polygraph and lie detector are often used synonymously" (Meijer & Verschuere, 2015, pp. 59–60). In fact, some authors refer to polygraphs as lie-detector tests. However, the polygraph is not a lie detector but a machine that "measures several physiological processes (e.g., heart rate) and changes in those processes" (National Research Council, 2003, p. 1). Although it is used to detect physiological changes thought to occur when people lie, the polygraph does not detect lies per se.

The polygraph has often been portrayed on television, in movies, and on internet videos in ways that captivate people's imaginations. Since the 1980s, there have been several popular television shows in which polygraphs were used to discern if people were lying about relationships, affairs, the legitimacy of parenthood, and other issues. A plethora of internet videos also show celebrities and others undergoing interviews while connected to the polygraph to demonstrate their sincerity.

The popularity of the polygraph is likely a result of its long tradition, its portrayal in popular media, and the suggestions of its infallible accuracy. So, how does it work? What is behind the enigmatic machine? The typical use of the polygraph is to measure physiological changes in various interview formats (Meijer & Verschuere, 2015). One common technique is the *control question technique* (CQT; Reid, 1947). The CQT involves asking an individual several control questions (e.g., What is your name?) that presumably they are answering truthfully and targeted questions to which they may or may not be lying (e.g., On January 3rd, did you shoot your husband?). If a person lies in response to a relevant question, they should show physiological changes, such as an increase in heart rate and blood pressure, which the machine should detect and that would betray them. Thus, the differences in physiological responses between the control questions and the relevant questions are considered evidence of deception. On the other hand, if a person showed no physiological differences when asked the control questions and the relevant questions, one might conclude that the person was answering honestly.

Another technique was originally named the *guilty knowledge test* and is more recently referred to as the *concealed information test* (CIT; Lykken, 1957; Meijer & Verschuere, 2015). The CIT differs from the CQT in that it does not involve accusatory questions about an incident. Instead, the polygraph examiner asks only about the details of the incident, which would be known only to the police and the person who committed the crime (Meijer & Verschuere, 2015). The questions include the accurate information and plausible but incorrect information. For example, if a person were being questioned about an automobile theft, the examinee might be asked whether the perpetrator stole a 2001 Toyota Camry, 2021 Ford F-150, 2015 Honda Civic, or 2019 Dodge Grand Caravan. A guilty examinee would presumably show a physiological response to the vehicle that was actually stolen and not the others. A person who was not involved in the crime would exhibit a similar physiological response to all vehicles.

Although the polygraph is popular, it has also been controversial. At the heart of the controversy is the accuracy of the instrument—the ability of the polygraph to be a reliable lie detector. Regarding the accuracy of the polygraph, the National Research Council's (2003) conclusion was

> notwithstanding the limitations of the quality of the empirical research and the limited ability to generalize to real-world settings, we conclude that in populations of examinees such as those represented in the polygraph research literature, untrained in countermeasures, specific-incident polygraph tests can discriminate lying from truth telling at rates well above chance, though well below perfection. (p. 4)

So, what is well below perfection? The accuracy of the CQT in lab studies has ranged from 74% to 82% for guilty examinees (with 7–8% false-negative rates) and 61% to 83% for innocent examinees (with 10–16% false-positive rates; Meijer & Verschuere, 2015). In simple terms, these percentages suggest that if polygraphs were administered to 100 people and 10 of them were actually guilty, the polygraph would accurately detect eight of the 10 guilty people but would also falsely implicate more than 10 of the innocent people. In field studies, the accuracy rates are 84% to 89% for guilty examinees (with 1–13% false negatives) and 59% to 75% for innocent examinees (with 5–29% false-positive rates; Meijer & Verschuere, 2015).

For lab studies with the CIT, between 76% and 88% of guilty examinees are correctly identified, while 83% to 97% of the innocent examinees are correctly identified (Meijer & Verschuere, 2015). Regarding the CIT in field studies, the ranges are 42% to 76% for correctly identifying guilty examinees and 94% to 98% for correctly identifying innocent examinees. Meijer and Verschuere (2015) suggested that although the CIT has controllable false-positive rates and is grounded in theory, it is rarely used in field studies.

The concern and controversy about the polygraph is typically rooted in its application and use. If it performs above chance but well below perfection, would you want potential employers to use it to make decisions about your employment? Would you be willing to have it determine your guilt or innocence in a criminal court case? Are you willing to use a measure that potentially falsely impugns between 5% and 29% of innocent people? Better yet, would this error rate be acceptable if trying to determine if someone was a big liar? These concerns about the accuracy rates are especially controversial when considering the contexts and consequences. Maybe the error rates are acceptable when trying to figure out which fellow employee ate your lunch and maybe less desirable when applied to criminal convictions in capital cases.

Concerns of accuracy and scientific controversy have influenced court rulings that deemed the polygraph not admissible as evidence within criminal courts (Ben-Shakhar et al., 2002; Vrij, 2008). Vrij suggested that the CQT does not meet the guidelines set forth by the U.S. Supreme Court. Within employment settings, the Employee Polygraph Protection Act prohibits most private employers from using lie-detector tests, which include

> polygraph, deceptograph, voice stress analyzer, psychological stress evaluator, or any other similar device (whether mechanical or electrical) that is used, or the results of which are used, for the purpose of rendering a diagnostic opinion regarding the honesty or dishonesty of an individual. (U.S. Department of Labor, 1988, para. 3)

Many of these rulings and policies are in place because of the perceived risk of wrongly convicting innocent people based on polygraphs results. There is room for adjustment and changes in these rulings and policies if newer techniques, coupled with scientific evidence, support more accurate assessments. Also, most of the rulings are based on the use of the polygraph with the CQT. Ben-Shakhar and colleagues (2002) suggested that the CIT can meet the required standards if administered carefully. Meijer and Verschuere (2015) agreed and suggested that "due to the low false-positive rate, the CIT can safely be applied in the field" (p. 76).

As there are many hints for how to detect lies, there are numerous websites that offer suggestions for how to beat lie-detector tests (i.e., polygraph assessments). The idea of *beating* the polygraph suggests that the polygraph has a pass–fail threshold, but this is not true. The polygraph is an assessment, but the examiner ultimately makes a subjective determination about whether someone is likely answering honestly or not. Thus, beating the polygraph is primarily a process of convincing the examiner that you are honest.

Could big liars skillfully navigate responses and convince others of their innocence when undergoing a polygraph? Psychopaths and people with an antisocial personality disorder may lie without feeling remorse or guilt, and they often have shallow emotional responses (American Psychiatric Association, 2013; Hare, 1996), and thus they do not fit the mold of the anxious and ashamed liar. They could go undetected when administered the polygraph because they lack emotional responses. If their heart does not pound wildly when they are accused of a crime, couldn't they sail through a polygraph exam undetected? What about people like Ted Bundy? Could his cool and unemotional reactions have helped him to tell lies for years without being detected?

One study explored this question, specifically looking at whether the polygraph can discriminate between psychopaths telling the truth and those who are lying (Raskin & Hare, 1978). Participants in their study were male prison inmates, half of whom were psychopathic and half of whom were not. Half of the psychopaths were randomly assigned to the guilty condition and were instructed to take a $20 bill when no one was looking and hide it in their pocket. Psychopaths in the innocent condition did not take a $20 bill. All participants were then instructed to deny having taken the money when undergoing a polygraph examination. The polygraph examiner, who did not know which participants were assigned to each condition, was able to successfully discern which psychopaths were lying and which ones were telling the truth with well above 80% accuracy. The conclusion seemed to suggest that some big liars (psychopaths) produce typical physiological responses when lying, thus allowing their detection via the polygraph.

Following the publication of the Raskin and Hare (1978) study, Lykken (1978) discussed several concerns and limitations that affect the conclusions. Among the criticisms was that a mock crime may not translate to the real world. Arguably, real world crimes carry weightier consequences and higher stakes, and people would be more highly motivated to keep their dishonest behavior from being detected. Lykken raised the concern that the participants may not have been trying to beat the lie detector, and if they were not, then the study did not show that psychopaths are *unable* to beat the test. He suggested that attempts to beat the lie detector would elevate physiological responses to control questions (e.g., biting one's tongue or tensing muscles), thus producing more inconclusive results.

To revisit the question and address some of the criticisms posed by Lykken (1978), Patrick and Iacono (1989) conducted a similar replication study. In an attempt to address the concern of high stakes and beating the polygraph, researchers told the participants that the goal was to beat a lie-detector test and that each participant would receive a $20 bonus if no more than 10 of the 48 participants failed the polygraph. The idea was that the bonus would incentivize the participants to really try to beat the polygraph. The results of overall accuracy were 75% correct, 25% incorrect, and 0% inconclusive, and most errors were false positives (10 out of 12). Their results also showed no differences between groups based on psychopathy.

A review of psychopathy and the use of the polygraph with the CIT technique indicates that the research has been scant and has yielded mixed evidence (Verschuere et al., 2006). While a call for more research is needed in this area, Verschuere and colleagues (2006) suggested that the available evidence corroborates the notion that, for people high in antisociality, skin conductance responding is reduced in the CIT, and the "autonomical hyporesponsive is responsible for the reduced detection in antisocial personalities" (p. 111). In short, lies told by psychopaths may be challenging to detect using the polygraph, but most are detected nonetheless.

This research has primarily investigated psychopathy and the ability to beat the polygraph or to yield a classification of innocent or inconclusive. Less research and literature have addressed pathological liars or big liars and their ability to successfully beat a polygraph. One author indicated that "the pathological liar certainly will not show any significant reaction to the lie detector test" (Floch, 1950, p. 652). What we have learned more recently about pathological liars' experiences of feeling distress and remorse may challenge the statement that pathological liars would not react to the polygraph (Curtis & Hart, 2020b).

Vrij and colleagues (2010) suggested that good liars probably have diminished emotional reactions, specifically less guilt and less fear. It seems likely that this diminished emotionality while lying would be especially common in big liars. Because big liars are dishonest so regularly, they may have become desensitized to the typical emotions reactions one has when lying. More research is needed before we can draw any firm conclusions regarding whether big liars are better able to remain undetected on a polygraph.

Linguistic Analysis

As the old saying goes, the easiest way to tell if a politician is lying is to see if their lips are moving. This saying suggests that politicians' words are always untrue. Words are critical to the concept of lying.

Digging deeper, we could say that lying requires communication, and communication typically is in the form of language or words. As noted in Chapter 1, deception has been defined as "a successful or unsuccessful deliberate attempt, without forewarning, to create in another a belief which the communicator considers to be untrue" (Vrij, 2008, p. 15). To address how lying is distinct from deception more specifically, we define lying as "a successful or unsuccessful deliberate manipulation of language, without forewarning, to create in another a belief which the communicator considers to be untrue" (Hart, 2019, para. 14). Thus, lying is the manipulation of language. It makes intuitive sense, then, to explore methods of language analysis to detect lying.

Since the 1950s, there has been a tremendous upsurge in research on verbal cues to detect deception (Vrij, 2015). Most verbal assessments are conducted with three tools: *statement validity analysis* (SVA), *reality monitoring* (RM), and *scientific content analysis* (SCAN). The SVA is the more popular tool; it was developed to assess the credibility of child witnesses in sexual assault cases (Vrij, 2008, 2015). The SVA involves four processes: a case file analysis, a semistructured interview, criteria-based content analysis (CBCA), and a validity checklist (Vrij, 2015). Essentially, people are trained to evaluate transcripts of interviews along 19 specific criteria (e.g., logical structure, quantity of details). The presence of more criteria within the transcript indicates a real or honest presentation (see Vrij, 2015). The assumption is that lying is cognitively more taxing than telling the truth, and people who lie often work harder to control their speech (Vrij & Mann, 2006). One of the strongest findings of support for CBCA is that truth-tellers include more details in interviews than those who lie (Vrij, 2015). Research accuracy indicates that CBCA identifies deception with 70% accuracy; the accuracy for SVA within criminal courts for sexual offenses is unknown (Vrij, 2015).

RM was not traditionally used as a deception-detection tool (see Vrij, 2015), but psychologists have a long-standing history of finding creative ways to use and apply tools originally intended for some other psychological task. RM was developed to understand how memories based on external experiences may differ from those based on internal experiences (Sporer, 2004). The premise of this technique is that truth-tellers' recollections of events are based on actual experiences, whereas liars only imagine the circumstances (Sporer, 2004; Vrij, 2015). So, if a criminal needed to produce an alibi, then they could fabricate a story in which they were out walking their dog, using their imagination to fill in the details. One of the strengths of the model is that it is theoretically rooted. A review of the research on RM suggests that it possesses some discriminative ability, correctly classifying most lies (Masip et al., 2005). Overall, the tool tends to produce an accuracy rate of around 70%, but it is not typically used by practitioners in the field (Vrij, 2015).

The SCAN was originally developed by a former polygraph examiner, Sapir, and is used across the world and by various agencies (e.g., FBI, CIA, U.S. military; Vrij, 2015). The SCAN technique consists of asking someone to write down all their activities during a specific time period, usually during the time an incident or crime occurred. Similar to the other linguistic analysis techniques, the SCAN operates by comparing the statements against a dozen criteria. One criterion, for instance, is the denial of allegations; a truthful individual is presumed to be more likely to deny allegations directly. Weekly training classes are offered for SCAN examiners, requiring 32 hours and a $600 fee (Sapir, 2021). One of the largest criticisms of SCAN is that it has a scant body of research support, with only five published studies (Vrij, 2015), but even with this dearth of empirical support, SCAN tends to be used by many practitioners and agencies (Vrij, 2015). A recent article argued that SCAN lacks empirical merit; most lie experts agree that it does not have sufficient research to be used with law-enforcement agencies, and most experts consider it to be pseudoscience (Bogaard et al., 2021).

These verbal techniques have typically been examined in the laboratory with studies involving college students or used in the courtroom during criminal cases. The research on the linguistic analyses with big liars has not been examined, to our knowledge. Big liars could potentially defy detection by many verbal assessments. For example, if a big liar were to rehearse or tell numerous lies, the liar could provide lengthy details and thus appear truthful. Furthermore, Masip and colleagues (2005) suggested that individual differences, such as acting ability, must be considered when using reality monitoring. T. R. Levine (2020) opined that some liars may be transparent or bad liars, but conversely, some may be extraordinarily good liars (Vrij et al., 2010). While not all big liars are necessarily good liars, some may be. A good liar or a big liar may be able to produce content that is seemingly based on actual experiences. Additionally, good liars tend to rely heavily on verbal strategies when deceiving (Verigin et al., 2019).

THE DECEPTIVE BRAIN

In 2013, President Obama announced an initiative called the Brain Research Through Advancing Innovative Neurotechnologies (BRAIN) Initiative. The goal was to spur interest and funding in brain research and neuroscience technologies. As with many initiatives that have a noble cause, some of these initiatives were looking for gain, and some of the brain-based developments were half-baked. For example, in one case that occurred in 2008, a 24-year-old woman, Aditi Sharma, received a life sentence in prison for killing her ex-fiancé, based on the results of a brain electrical oscillations signature (BEOS) test (Satel & Lilienfeld, 2013). The BEOS test "was developed as an alternative method to the use of polygraph based lie-detection test and test based on recognition measured by event related potential of P300" (Mukundan et al., 2017, p. 217). Electroencephalography is used to measure brain waves, and the P300 wave refers to a positive wave response that has an onset or peaks around 300 to 500 milliseconds (Satel & Lilienfeld, 2013). Thus, researchers present brief stimuli, not longer than 200 milliseconds so that the person is not yet aware of them, and use electroencephalography to look for a P300 response, or a "brain blip" (Satel & Lilienfeld, 2013, p. 74). The person who is connected to the electrodes does not need to respond verbally because the wave will be emitted before they can produce a word. Presumably, a person being interrogated and emitting a P300 wave to an accurate statement would reveal that they know about the incident or crime. For Sharma, even though she indicated that she was innocent, her brain emitted the P300 waves to statements about the murder. However, one major concern regarding the BEOS was raised—the scientific merit. Six months after Sharma was sentenced, the same research lab indicated that two other people were responsible for the murder of her ex-fiancé. Obviously, BEOS and the P300 wave were not valid and reliable tools for detecting dishonesty.

The clear concern of putting the cart before the horse with lie-detection tools is the potentially grave outcomes for people who are erroneously identified as liars. One of the biggest concerns raised by the scientific community about BEOS was that the developer, Mukundan, refused to allow researchers to review the BEOS protocol independently (Satel & Lilienfeld, 2013). Though some slapdash products and claims may be presented as scientific, most neuroscientists are genuinely seeking to explore and understand the neurological underpinnings and mechanisms of human behavior. Some of these scientists have made a case for using brain technologies for deception detection, though their reliable application may yet be years away.

In defense of using the P300 wave, Iacono (2015) argued that the P300 wave coupled with the CIT is promising, and ongoing research has continued for more than 20 years. Reported accuracy rates of the P300 using the guilty knowledge test within laboratory studies are 88% truth and 82% lie (Vrij, 2008). Iacono stated, "the P300-GKT will not be applicable in all crimes, but there is good reason to believe it will be applicable in many crimes" (p. 99). Satel and Lilienfeld (2013) indicated that the biggest concern is whether brain scan technologies can be used to infer deception within real-world settings.

Other approaches to merging neuroscience technologies and deception detection have included neuroimaging techniques (see Ganis, 2015, for additional information). One such technique is functional magnetic resonance imaging (fMRI), which measures blood flow in the brain produced by neuronal activity and has been used to infer the presence of deception. In some studies, participants are asked to lie or tell a truth as part of a modified CIT. Studies have indicated that two areas of the brain are more engaged when lying than when telling the truth: the inferior lateral prefrontal cortex and the medial superior prefrontal cortex. The accuracy of fMRI studies in detecting lying has ranged from 65% to 100%, with the study that yielded 100% accuracy conducted by Ganis and colleagues (2011). However, studies of deception detection using fMRI carry some limitations. It is expensive, and a small number of studies are conducted on single subjects; as a result, meta-analysis has not been used to analyze the approach collectively (Ganis, 2015).

There is a tension between the deception-detection ability of assisted, mechanical, and neuroscience technologies and the accuracy, specificity, applications, and consequences of these approaches. The appeal of the polygraph, along with other physiological measures, may be rooted in its "lie-detection mystique" and the appeal of neuroscience (National Research Council [NRC], 2003, p. 18; Satel & Lilienfeld, 2013). The NRC (2003) suggested that the polygraph arouses strong emotions and fosters an overarching cultural belief that it is infallible.

There is something attention-grabbing and convincing about the visual imagery of sensors, wires, bands, and electrodes connecting humans to machines. Humans tend to associate this imagery with being scientific and credible. Perhaps people place more credence in tools that appear technologically advanced. For example, in a series of studies, McCabe and Castel (2008) presented participants with written summaries of studies in cognitive neuroscience with or without accompanying brain scan images. Participants who viewed the brain scans along with the summaries judged the study to be more scientifically reasoned than those who simply read the summaries. The researchers suggested that brain imagery may be more persuasive because it offers a "tangible physical explanation for cognitive processes" (p. 349).

Just as there is no Pinocchio's nose, there is no *lie spot*, no consistent and specific area of the brain that always lights up when a person is lying. Satel and Lilienfeld (2013) stated, "No brain region uniquely changes activity when a person lies; each type of lie requires its own set of neural process" (p. 91). Moreover, whether these technologies can accurately detect big liars or pathological liars has yet to be examined. That said, there is no reason to abandon the pursuit. Science works by addressing the problems and seeking to refine the methods to increase accuracy in prediction.

NEW APPROACHES

The accuracy rates of human detection, error within mechanical methods, and the potential consequences of incorrectly labeling an innocent person as a liar paint a grim picture for deception detection. So, are there any chances for humans to become more skilled at detecting deception? Is there any hope for us to catch big liars? We briefly consider some recent work that indicates that upwards of 90% accuracy is achievable.

In two studies, deception experts (five federal agents and one person who had training in federal, state, and local law enforcement) reported a method with which they were able to achieve up to 100% accuracy in detecting deception (T. R. Levine et al., 2014). The researchers used a paradigm that provided an opportunity for participants to cheat within a trivia game and possibly to receive a monetary incentive. Then, using a structured interview that lasted 4 minutes, an interviewer asked participants a series of demographic questions and then asked about the trivia questions and if they had cheated. The interviewer asked a bait question, then told each participant that their partner would be interviewed and asked what the partner would say. The interviewer took a break and then returned and told the person that they had cheated. The final part of the interview consisted of a confession or denial. In the last phase of the study, participants watched videos of the interviews and made judgments about the videos. In the first study, the expert's judgments were correct in all 33 interviews. In the second study, the experts showed an accuracy of 97.8%.

While these results are impressive, they have been criticized by others as invalid or unreliable (Vrij et al., 2015). One concern was that the methods did not mimic lying and lie detection as they occur in the real world. Science works by criticism and skepticism, improving and building on what has been previously tested. Beyond the studies published by T. R. Levine and colleagues (2014), T. R. Levine (2015) offered a look at other studies that have achieved high levels of accuracy (see Table 9.1). These studies all used some combination of interrogation, strategic use of evidence, and the solicitation of confessions. Typically, by getting a suspect to talk, an interrogator can elicit a statement that appears to conflict with evidence that the interrogator is strategically withholding. Once the suspect elicits the conflicting statement, the interrogator can unveil the evidence, point out the discrepancy, and solicit a confession.

TABLE 9.1. Examples of New and improved Human Deception Detection Accuracy Findings

Study	Approach	Reported accuracy (%)
Hartwig et al. (2006)	Strategic use of evidence	85
Blair et al. (2010), Exp. 3	Content in context	77
Blair et al. (2010), Exp. 4	Content in context	80
Blair et al. (2010), Exp. 5	Content in context	69
Blair et al. (2010), Exp. 6	Content in context	73
Blair et al. (2010), Exp. 7	Content in context	72
Blair et al. (2010), Exp. 8	Content in context	81
Blair et al. (2010), Exp. 9	Content in context	75
T. R. Levine and McCornack (2001), Exp. 2	Situational familiarity	69
Reinhard et al. (2011), Exp. 4	Situational familiarity	71
Reinhard et al. (2013)	Situational familiarity	72
T. R. Levine et al. (2010), Exp. 1	Projecting motive	95
T. R. Levine et al. (2010), Exp. 2	Projecting motive	87
T. R. Levine et al. (2010), Exp. 3	Projecting motive	86
Bond et al. (2013), Exp. 1	Projecting motive	99
Bond et al. (2013), Exp. 2	Projecting motive	97

(continues)

TABLE 9.1. Examples of New and improved Human Deception Detection Accuracy Findings (*Continued*)

Study	Approach	Reported accuracy (%)
Bond et al. (2013), Exp. 3	Projecting motive	97
T. R. Levine et al. (2010)	Diagnostic questioning	68
T. R. Levine et al. (2014), Exp. 1	Diagnostic questioning	71
T. R. Levine et al. (2014), Exp. 2	Diagnostic questioning	77
T. R. Levine et al. (2014), Exp. 3	Diagnostic questioning	75
T. R. Levine et al. (2014), Exp. 6	Diagnostic questioning	73
T. R. Levine et al. (2014), Exp. 1 students	Diagnostic questioning	79
T. R. Levine et al. (2014), Exp. 2 students	Diagnostic questioning	94
T. R. Levine et al. (2014), Exp. 1 expert	Expert questioning	100
T. R. Levine et al. (2014), Exp. 2 experts	Expert questioning	98

Note. From "New and Improved Accuracy Findings in Deception Detection Research," by T. R. Levine, 2015, *Current Opinion in Psychology*, *6*, p. 3 (https://doi.org/10.1016/j.copsyc.2015.03.003). Copyright 2015 by Elsevier. Reprinted with permission.

The approach made famous by the television detective, Columbo, appears to be very effective in identifying liars in laboratory studies. Could we also use Columbo's approach to discern if we are being lied to by a big liar?

So far, no flawless method exists to detect deception. While research has improved accuracy rates by testing various methods of human detection and assisted or mechanical methods, we still find that these means fall short of perfection. Satel and Lilienfeld (2013) discussed the implications of sacrificing personal liberties for less-than-perfect methods of detecting deception (e.g., wrongful convictions). Given that any error in lie detection might falsely implicate the innocent, is the 90% barrier good enough? Once again, the nuance of accuracy and the premium we place on detecting lies may be based on the relative consequences. Are we willing to use a 90% threshold for criminal cases? Would 99% suffice? Ethical questions arise regarding the percentage of people we are willing to allow for error and the circumstances. Certainly, government entities, Secret Service members, people in law enforcement, and people in forensics have specific interests in detecting big liars, often divergent from the everyday, relational, or personal interests that we carry.

DETECTING BIG LIARS

We have reviewed some of the various ways that people may detect deception. While some of these methods may be intriguing and may produce higher accuracy than others, we are left wondering how we should go about detecting big liars within our lives. Most people do not have fMRIs in their living rooms, polygraph machines in their basements, or training in how to elicit diagnostic cues. Also, how weird would it be relationally if we subjected people we were interested in romantically or otherwise to a series of polygraph assessments or linguistic analyses? The humor from *Meet the Parents* (Tenenbaum, 2000) lies in the rare and socially awkward depiction of a father using a polygraph to test his future son-in-law's integrity. Can you imagine telling your romantic interest, "I really am interested in you and want to pursue a relationship, but first I need you to submit to a series of lie-detector tests and an interrogation." It is unlikely that many people would be interested in a long-term relationship with you. Some people are willing to undergo the polygraph for various relational issues on daytime television shows, but most of us do not act as interrogators in our close personal relationships or in most professional relationships. The truth is that we do not use many academic, laboratory, or Secret Service interrogation techniques to discern truth from fiction in our everyday life.

Some of the pioneering research on how people actually detect deception within everyday life was conducted by Park and her colleagues (2002). They recruited 202 undergraduate students and asked them to recall a recent situation where they discovered that someone had lied to them. They found that the most common way that people discovered that they were being lied to was from others. Participants also indicated using a combination of methods, physical evidence, and confessions to detect deception. Few people reported using in-the-moment verbal and nonverbal behaviors. Additionally, the researchers found that most people reported detecting lies afterward, as opposed to the moment that the person was lying to them.

Let's consider some examples of real-life big liars and discoveries. We share some statements from people who discovered that they were being lied to by big liars, identified as compulsive liars or pathological liars, and how they discovered the lies. In line with the findings from Park et al. (2002), the lies were usually discovered over time, as evidence accumulated. One person who discovered the big lies she was told by her boyfriend wrote anonymously in a blog,

> but it was only along the way that his web of lies unraveled and I slowly started discovering that a lot of the things he told me weren't true. I started to connect the dots and finally realized what happened to me: I had a relationship with a compulsive liar.

Sometimes people may think that they are being lied to and seek out evidence. For example, one woman wrote in an anonymous online blog that she initially watched pornography with her fiancé, but after having intimacy issues they agreed to stop viewing it. Subsequently, she had some suspicions that he was continuing to watch pornography, and so she investigated. She stated, "Usually I have a gut instinct when I know he's lying, and it has made me snoop into his phones and laptop (drugs & Porn mainly). I was never like this, and I hate doing this." Similar to the findings from Park et al. (2002), another anonymous woman blogged that she discovered that her husband was having an affair and began to piece together other details and events in their relationship. Sometimes we may not know immediately that someone is a big liar. We may not find out until we gather information, learn about the person, and find inconsistencies in the evidence and the messages that we are being told.

Another person wrote in an anonymous online forum that his girlfriend was a big liar:

> I had a secret crush on a girl from the gym for almost a year. Finally I decided to friend request her on social media. When she accepted I messaged her and explained who I was. I asked various questions and she gave short answers. I joked about texting her and she told me her phone was a pos and doesn't send or receive texts. We've been together 10 months and she's never had any

> issues sending or receiving texts. She claimed she uses Snapchat so I asked for her username. She read my message and didn't respond. . . . She eventually stated she had been with 15 guys and I'd become the 16th. She was quick to add that she was either dating or interested in every guy she's had sex with. She asked how many local girls I'd been with. She claimed to have been with two local guys. Her ex and lo and behold a drunken one-night stand. The first time she ever sent me a selfie she was clearly not wearing a shirt. When I commented on this she acted embarrassed and claimed she was in bed and she sleeps naked. We've been together 10 months and she's never slept naked. She avoids me at the gym and sometimes goes so far as to hide from me. She claims it's because she doesn't want people to think she's a groupie. She speaks very openly about the three guys she had longer relationships with. She will even mention very in-depth sexual details. However she never mentions any other guys and gets very defensive if I ask. She claimed she's never sent a nude picture before. However after dating for about a month she sent one without my asking that caught her face and chest in the pic and her butt in the mirror behind her. Complete with the caption "I'm WHORible." I don't interrogate her at all. I am very understanding. She volunteers info.

Other times people have no need to actively discover whether they are being lied to because the liar may simply confess. Park et al. (2002) found that some people discovered deception by unsolicited confessions, meaning that people told them that they had lied. Sometimes we discover we have been lied to because the person lying decides to confess for any number of reasons, including guilt and regret. Some of our research on pathological liars has indicated that some pathological liars may self-identify as liars and seek help with their dishonesty (Curtis & Hart, 2020b). In some newer research, we are examining blog posts of pathological liars, compulsive liars, and big liars; we find that, in those blogs, they will openly confess to lying. For example, one woman who lied to her doctor about the effects of medication had subsequently confessed to her physician. She stated,

> I realized I'm a compulsive liar. And I went and told my doctor, with the hope that my courage would be rewarded; that my lie would be wiped clean off the record and I could go back to the pill I was on, but, no. I can never go down that road again.

Another woman reported that her lying was discovered in part because she was caught and in part because she admitted guilt. She stated,

> So it has been a long time knowing I am lying to the people around me for a few years and even my boyfriend of a year now. He caught me out several times and I kept making excuses or perhaps admitted I was lying.

CONCLUSION

For as long as people have lied, others have tried to detect lies. Trying to detect liars is of interest because we think that if we recognize them, we can then shield ourselves from danger or at least mitigate the damage. While a robust body of scientific literature has moved us closer to detecting deception accurately, there is no surefire method to detect deception, and we can never be certain that we have accurately detected the big liars. On the other hand, there are things that we can do or that most of us already do that increase the likelihood of catching big liars. Because most of us do not have MRIs and polygraphs hooked up to our loved ones around the clock, most lies are detected through confession, evidence, and time. Thus, while we may sometimes actively seek evidence or check in on discrepancies as we learn more about a person, other times we may passively discover lies when the liar confesses. An unsolicited confession requires little on our part—no need for electrodes, brain scans, or even prompting diagnostic cues. The other helpful strategy we can employ to detect big liars is to realize our own preconceived ideas and biases about lying behaviors. Knowing that eye gaze aversion and other nonverbal behavioral cues are weak indicators of deception, we can learn to dismiss our judgments based on these cues. Maybe, like the television detective, we can elicit information and discrepancies related to the evidence we have, which may result in a confession.

The primary reason we attempt to detect when others are lying is so that we can avoid being duped. In Chapter 10, we turn our attention to various strategies that can be used to avoid falling prey to big liars. We also consider techniques for encouraging big liars to be more honest with us.

CHAPTER 10

HOW TO AVOID BEING DUPED AND TO CULTIVATE HONESTY

Honesty is something you can't wear out.

—Waylon Jennings

In Chapter 9, we surveyed many techniques that people have used to successfully (and unsuccessfully) detect lying. As it turns out, detecting lying in real time is a challenge. Most of us must accept that we are not walking polygraph machines. We cannot simply use our powers of observation to pick the big liars out of a crowd, but we can position ourselves to be less vulnerable to big liars. We can cultivate interpersonal strategies that increase the probability that people will be honest with us, and we can use techniques to identify when people are being dishonest with us more readily. In this chapter, we consider ways to avoid being duped by big liars.

Nobody wants to be duped. Being played for a sucker feels awful. When we place our trust in someone and they take advantage of us by lying, we feel a strong sense of injustice (Vohs et al., 2007). People who have been duped have the sense that they have been disadvantaged in some way by the liar. They often feel that they should have seen it coming. They stew in self-recrimination. People who have been duped often feel foolish and inept, angry and ashamed for being so trusting. Being duped feels so unpleasant that most people tend to work hard to avoid it. However, in some instances, people turn a blind eye to possible dishonesty.

THE OSTRICH WITHIN

Sometimes we fail to detect deception because we want to avoid the truth. It might seem easier to stick our heads in the ground than to deal with reality. Lies sometimes remain unnoticed because people are truth-avoidant. Shying away from the truth has been referred to as the *ostrich effect* (Vrij, 2008). Ignorance of the truth may be preferred when a lie sounds more pleasant, when the truth seems terrifying, or when knowledge of the truth might call on one to take difficult actions. A woman named Angela explained why it was better to hide from the truth, writing in an online forum,

> The truth can be painful and emotionally intense to absorb. To swallow certain truths have been an absolutely awful experience for me. Like entering a corner of Hell. This is why I tended to bask in denial only so I wouldn't end up losing my mind and falling into an extreme depression.

Many of us probably hold beliefs or illusions that are preferable to the bitter truth. People often prefer to hear pleasantries and good things from others, even when those kind words are not entirely accurate. We gladly accept white lies because they stroke our egos, ease our anxieties, or allow us to have hope. Smooth-talking liars can dupe us simply by saying things that we want to hear. If we enjoy what they say more than we enjoy harsh truths, we may turn a blind eye to the lies.

"You can't handle the truth," a famous quote from the movie *A Few Good Men* (Reiner et al., 1992), presents another reason why we may prefer untruths over the truth. Sometimes we may be fearful of discovering the truth because we are unprepared to deal with the consequences. Knowing the truth may necessitate ending a relationship, having an uncomfortable confrontation, calling the police, being involved in criminal investigations, and even acknowledging that we have been a dupe. Tacitly accepting lies can help people avoid conflict.

If someone yet again says that they can't meet up for dinner because of a work commitment or because they feel ill, we may choose to believe that statement; if we press for the truth, we risk learning that the avoidant dinner guest simply doesn't like or respect us very much. Perhaps people shouldn't open boxes if they fear what might be inside. Research on intimate relationships shows that people often prefer white lies over conflict (Cargill & Curtis, 2017; Curtis & Hart, 2020a; Peterson, 1996). Big liars can get away with their deceit quite easily when people stick their heads in the ground to avoid the truth. An obvious approach to reducing the likelihood of being duped is simply to be truth-seeking rather than truth-avoidant.

GULLIBILITY

In January 2000, a frightening chain of emails began to circulate (Robson, 2016). The emails, supposedly sent from researchers, claimed that a flesh-eating bacterium that had wiped out the monkey population in Costa Rica was now a danger to people. The bacterium had mutated in such a way that it was now growing on bananas. People who consumed these bananas were likely to contract a disease that would consume their flesh at a rate of 1 inch per hour, causing their skin to peel away from their bones. Amputations or death were the likely outcomes. The U.S. government knew about the imminent threat and anticipated tens of thousands of people would be infected but was concealing the information to prevent a nationwide panic. The emails urged people to warn anyone who would listen.

The emails were a hoax, but so many people fell for it that the U.S. Centers for Disease Control (CDC) put out a statement decrying the emails as a hoax. That was not enough. The number of concerned citizens continued to grow, so the CDC created a hotline that people could call to ask about their banana-related concerns. For years, suckers continued to believe the banana hoax.

People are gullible. Big liars, scammers, and con artists count on it. They are successful because an endless supply of people will blindly accept their lies as the truth. People are still willing to wire thousands of dollars to "Nigerian princes" who promise to reward their marks handsomely for their loyalty. But why are people so gullible? *Gullibility* is the tendency to accept claims as true even when the evidence indicates that the claims should not be believed. Two broad psychological features seem to leave some people more prone to believe lies than others: persuadability and insensitivity to cues of untrustworthiness (Teunisse et al., 2020).

Easily persuadable people can be convinced to do things, often not in their interest, through social manipulations by others. The capacity to be persuaded is not in itself a bad thing. After all, in general people like to be convinced to take the right action, to date the right person, or to make the wisest investments. However, some people are so easily persuaded that their malleability becomes a liability. Very persuadable people can't resist the charms of a slick salesperson. They find themselves convinced to buy products they cannot afford or can be convinced to reveal extremely personal information about themselves. Persuadable people are unable to resist the pressure and manipulation of others. They are pushovers.

The other feature of gullible people is that they are insensitive to signs that other people are untrustworthy. Any time we note that someone seems sleazy, creepy, or shifty, we are identifying them as a potentially untrustworthy person. We notice subtle clues, such as an odd demeanor, an overly intrusive style, or a backstory that doesn't add up. In other cases, we detect a set of incentives that might motivate someone to take advantage of us. These subtle hints let us know that we should beware. Some people, though, seem oblivious to these ominous signs. Some victims of catfishing scams report stories that would make most people a bit suspicious. For example, one woman reported in an anonymous online forum that she continued an online relationship with a man who supposedly couldn't talk on the phone because he was born without vocal cords. Another man in the online forum stated that he believed that the singer Katy Perry was trying to strike up a romantic relationship with him. Another guy believed he was dating Miss Teen USA. It's not that these circumstances are impossible; it's just that the average person would be suspicious and would gather more evidence.

The most gullible people are both easily persuadable and insensitive to signs of untrustworthiness. When big liars deceive them, they accept the lies unquestioningly, whereas a less gullible person would not. Gullible people are not more trusting than the rest of us. In fact, the opposite seems to be true: Trusting people are less gullible than the average person (Yamagishi, 2001). Trust is simply believing that another person will do what is expected. Trusting people are willing to count on others, but importantly, they also readily detect when people are untrustworthy. Gullible people seem to be deficient in *social intelligence*, the capacity to understand and act wisely in human social interactions. It involves understanding others' motivations, seeing others' perspectives, and reading others' emotions. Noticing and avoiding big liars seems to hinge on social intelligence (Yamagishi, 2001).

HOW TO AVOID BEING DUPED

Other than avoiding other people entirely, there is no foolproof way to avoid being duped. Even very intelligent and vigilant people are tricked by big liars. The best we can do is try to minimize the chances of being deceived. To understand how to avoid being fooled by lies, it is instructive to explore how people come to believe something is truthful. People use five criteria to determine the truthfulness of a statement (Schwarz et al., 2016). First, upon hearing a claim, people evaluate whether it is consistent with what they already believe. Imagine that you take your car in for an oil change but your mechanic tells you that you need new tires. Do you believe they are telling the truth, or are they lying about the tires to make a quick buck? You are more likely to believe them if you noticed that your car has been sliding on the road when it is rainy, you sometimes skid to a stop at intersections, it has been a few years since you last bought tires, and you have had two flat tires this year. Needing new tires is consistent with each of those pieces of information. On the other hand, if you had purchased new tires only last year and your car was handling just fine, you might rightly be suspicious of your mechanic's claim. Information that fits with what you already believe is considered more likely to be true. If you want to avoid being duped by big liars, try to consider how their claims align or fail to align with what you already know to be true.

The source of a claim is also important in determining whether we believe it is true or not. We believe the claims of doctors more than those of used car salespeople. Some individuals are simply more trusted than others. You can probably think of people in your life who only speak honestly, and you can likely think of others who are loose with the truth. We believe the reliably honest people. Consider the source. Big liars usually don't have reputations for honesty.

We also tend to accept information as true if we can see that other people believe that information. If someone tells you that the CIA has secretly conspired with doctors to implant tracking devices in every American, you would likely be unconvinced. One reason is that it is difficult to find others who believe such a claim. People's beliefs don't depend solely on popular opinion, but when we don't have compelling evidence to evaluate whether a claim is truthful or fraudulent, we often rely on the wisdom of the crowd. If other people think someone might be lying, you should consider that too.

Proof is also important. One of the easiest ways to avoid being duped is to verify the claims that are being made. Blatant lies often conflict with facts. For example, in 2022, George Santos was elected to the U.S. House of Representatives. Santos claimed to have graduated from college with two degrees (Fandos, 2023). He said that he had worked for some prestigious Wall Street banks. He claimed to be Jewish. He said that he had lost his mother in the September 11 terrorist attacks. All these claims, and many more, were lies. A simple check of the facts (e.g., school records, employment verification) revealed his dishonesty. Checking the facts leaves big liars with less room to hide. Some people set the tracking features on their cell phones so that their spouses can always see where they are. If a person says they are going to the store, their claims can be believed because there is demonstrable proof of the destination. When we lack evidence of a claim, we are less certain of its truthfulness. In high-stakes situations, such as banking transactions and car purchases, people demand proof of claims to avoid being fleeced by big liars. Look for proof, and you'll be less likely to be duped.

Finally, we believe stories when they are coherent. When all pieces of a claim fit together nicely into a cohesive narrative, we find them believable. When elements of a claim seem out of place, confusing, or disjointed, we tend to remain unconvinced. In many scams, a time comes when the scammer asks their mark to do something peculiar. For instance, in a telephone scam, a person posing as a police officer may tell their mark that they can avoid being arrested for an unpaid fine by buying a gift card and providing the gift card number over the phone. This odd detail, that a fine should be paid with a gift card, is the clue that causes many marks to see through the lies. The smoother and more typical a claim is, the more likely we are to believe it. Two points are important here. First, the smoothness of a story is not proof that someone is honest. Try to pay attention to the specific claims that are being made instead of the polished way they are being said. Some smooth talkers can weave lies effortlessly. Second, if a story doesn't add up, the speaker may be lying. Lies usually come crumbling down when we start probing and asking more questions about the parts that don't add up. If part of a story sounds just a little off, start scrutinizing the claim. Lies often start to fall apart as soon as we start to scratch at the surface.

THE AUTOMATICITY OF BELIEF

We are bombarded with information all day long, and we have limited attentional capacity, so we have to pick and choose the information that we carefully scrutinize or that we passively accept. People process new information in one of two ways (Petty & Cacioppo, 1986). The *central route* of processing information involves thoughtful and careful consideration of the merits and evidence of the information being presented. If you are carefully deciding which of two televisions to purchase, you may pore over the list of features, carefully consider your needs, listen to the opinions of a store clerk, and then finally make a full assessment as you determine which television to buy. Other times, we have less ability to devote to such dutiful consideration. In those cases, we process information through the *peripheral route*, making snap judgments. These judgments are based on details unrelated to the logical quality or merits of the information. Instead, we assess information based on mental shortcuts, such as the likability or attractiveness of the messenger, the ease with which we understand the message, and the degree to which the message feels right in our gut. Big liars use our automatic processing against us. They bank on the fact that we can't carefully assess every statement. They succeed when we process information through the peripheral route, passively accepting whatever we hear.

To avoid being duped, you need to use the central route, even though it is effortful. Such focus and careful consideration is a resource that we can use only sparingly—you need to know when to be vigilant about a possible lie and when to ignore that concern. How important is the truth in a given situation? If it is critical, then you should dedicate your mental resources to parsing statements, examining evidence, and carefully deciding if what you are hearing is true. Essentially, you need to allocate your cognitive bullshit-detector resources appropriately. Central-route processing is undermined by distractions, fatigue, divided attention, and time pressure. Big liars can derail your central-route thinking by hurling information at you quickly, hiding false information among a flurry of truthful information. Buried under an onslaught of information, people often feel overwhelmed or exhausted.

To avoid being duped, slow down and carefully consider the information that is being presented. Gullible people tend to make decisions about the information they receive hastily and without much thought. If you slow down and carefully consider what is being said, you can be resistant to being duped by big liars. Ask yourself how much actual information you have that the claim is true. You may realize that you have absolutely no personal knowledge of whether a statement is accurate or not. In those cases, it may be wise to dig a little deeper. When the truth is critical, drop everything else that is occupying your attention and focus.

SKEPTICISM

Adopting a more skeptical stance is another way to avoid being duped. Skepticism is simply questioning the validity of a claim when we have not yet seen evidence of its accuracy. When we are skeptical, we remain open-minded and consider multiple hypotheses. We may think to ourselves, “This person may be telling me the truth, but it is also possible that they are lying.” In Chapter 7, we discuss the truth–default bias (T. R. Levine, 2014). As a default setting, most people assume communication is honest. Rather than passively accepting information, try to cultivate a stance in which you remain open-minded about the veracity of a claim until the evidence shows you that the claim is true or not true. If we remain skeptical about what people are saying, we may start to notice inconsistencies and other cues that they are lying. If we are not skeptical, we are apt to believe whatever lies they tell us.

Being skeptical is a delicate balancing act. Trust is required for almost all social exchanges, although a certain amount of wariness can help us avoid being duped. Still, too much skepticism can be costly (Cialdini, 2001; Vohs et al., 2007). If we are too untrusting, we risk socially isolating ourselves, missing opportunities, and harming our relationships with others. For example, in one study, researchers compared suspicious and skeptical customers purchasing a new car to their more trusting counterparts (Zettelmeyer et al., 2006). The people who were most vigilant about being taken advantage of by the car dealers got the worst deals, on average paying more—about $1,800 more for a new $30,000 car. It may be that the overly skeptical customers soured their relationships with the dealers, removing any sense of duty the dealers may have felt toward the customers.

We all harbor a certain degree of vigilance. Being vigilant is adaptive. It reduces the likelihood that we will be exploited. Our caution with others can help us spot people who intend to take advantage of us before they manipulate us, but if taken too far, it can cost us.

OUT OF YOUR ELEMENT

Acknowledging our limitations is another way to avoid being duped. As psychologists, both of us (the authors) have a fair amount of knowledge and expertise in that sphere. However, neither of us has expertise in the world of finance, and thus we are more susceptible to being duped in that domain. If someone were to present us with a new investment opportunity that involved financing a cryptocurrency venture, our naïveté would leave us extremely vulnerable to being duped. Gullible people fail to see their ignorance as a risk factor, whereas vigilant people are wary of limitations in their expertise. In domains in which you are naïve, it is foolish to rely on yourself to determine what is true and what is not. Relying on trusted third parties who have no motivation to deceive is advisable. If someone is pitching a great investment opportunity, consult with a friend who has expertise in that field. If a car salesperson tells you that all car sales are required to include expensive add-ons, verify that claim on a consumer advocacy website. Respecting the limits of your expertise can help you avoid being duped.

KEEP A COOL HEAD

Emotions serve to drive our behavior, but they can cause us to be impulsive, irrational, and gullible. When cool reason is absent and our passions are in control, we are more vulnerable to being duped. The desire and excitement felt toward a seductive suitor can lead to ill-advised decisions. Intense greed and longing can drive people to abandon their normal caution and restraint. Fear can send a person bounding into rash actions. Even compassion and concern for others can cause someone to do foolish things, if not for the balance of reason. Situations that heighten emotions can disengage the powers of reason and leave a person vulnerable to deceit.

One tactic to minimize gullibility is merely to recognize when your emotions are getting the best of you. Big liars can manipulate people by turning their emotions against them. For instance, con artists often use greed, fear, lust, and compassion to trick their targets. Their dupes get so emotionally engaged that they fall for the scam without noticing the signs of the deception. If you can step back temporarily from emotionally intense situations, you may more clearly see the red flags that someone is trying to dupe you. A cooler examination of the person who is riling you up may allow you to see what they are trying to conceal. A sound tool that can help us to be more resistant to duping is to know ourselves. If we have a sense of our weaknesses and vulnerabilities and if we can notice what triggers our emotions, we stand a better chance of noticing when big liars are trying to manipulate us.

MISALIGNED MOTIVES

Throughout this book when addressing why people lie, we have discussed motives and incentives. People don't lie randomly; they lie when they have an incentive or reason to lie. One of the most effective ways to avoid being duped is to know when people are apt to lie to you. The best way to understand when people might try to deceive you is to recognize when their incentives and motivations differ from yours. In a negotiation over a car purchase, the buyer and the seller have a common motivation—they both want the sale to proceed. However, they may also have misaligned incentives or motivations: The buyer wants the sale price to be as low as possible to save money, whereas the seller wants the price to be as high as possible to earn commission. In situations such as these, knowledge of motives can help you know when to be wary of deception. A vigilant person can avoid being duped by noticing when individuals' motivations or incentives are misaligned.

We should calibrate our vigilance to the specific situation. Under conditions in which another person is highly motivated to lie and is easily able to dupe us, we should be skeptical. If you take your car in for a very minor and inexpensive repair, such as replacing a light bulb, and the mechanic boasts that they use only the highest quality parts in their work, there is not much point in doubting their claim. After all, the mechanic has no strong incentive to lie. The difference in price between a cheap light bulb and an expensive one is just a couple of dollars. Why would they lie? Even if they were lying, the falsity of their statement would have no serious financial effect on you. On the other hand, if you brought your car in for a major engine and transmission overhaul that will cost thousands of dollars, a shady mechanic has much more of an incentive to lie.

Likewise, you should be highly vigilant about claims that cannot be easily verified. Lying is much more likely to occur when there is a large asymmetry in information between two people than when there is no such asymmetry. If your employer tells you that you are being paid as much as your coworkers who have the same job, it would be reasonable to be skeptical if the records regarding salaries are a closely guarded secret at the company. On the other hand, if the information could be verified easily in publicly available records, the employer's claim would be more likely to be true.

Knowing how to be less gullible and actually being less gullible are not the same thing. Being astute and discerning is a skill that must be practiced if you want to avoid being duped. To be ready to rebuff big liars, you must adopt a consistent stance in which you maintain a healthy level of wariness. Big liars can be quite convincing even to people who would seem to be the most able to spot them. Just ask Dr. Stephen Greenspan. Just as he was wrapping up writing his new book titled *Annals of Gullibility: Why We Get Duped and How to Avoid It* (Greenspan, 2008), Dr. Greenspan lost several hundred thousand dollars in a financial scam (see Griffin, 2009).

PROBING FOR THE TRUTH

If you stay vigilant and pay attention to that skeptical voice inside your head, you may have some doubts about what people say. An effective way of avoiding being duped by big liars is to pay attention to those hunches and follow up on them. Researchers who study police interrogations and interviews have some advice on how to probe for the truth (Vrij, 2008). One strategy is to get the potential liar to talk. The more a person talks, the more information they provide. Each bit of information they offer is something that can potentially be checked out or verified against the evidence. If someone claims to have a successful business and you are skeptical, get curious and engaged. Ask a bunch of questions. Get them talking. If someone is lying and they reveal enough information, they will likely say something that can be proven true or false.

Another technique is to have people repeat themselves. If a person at work claims to have contributed to a major project, wait a week and have them retell their version of events. Big liars often change the details between two tellings. If you notice the inconsistencies, you can reveal the dishonesty.

Another effective technique is the strategic use of evidence (Vrij, 2008). If you suspect a person is lying about something, play your cards close. Don't let them know what information you have. Imagine that you hosted a party and that after the party was over, you noticed an expensive ring missing from your study. You then sent a message to all the guests about the missing ring, but all denied having seen it. Someone is probably lying. What if during the party you noticed one guest emerging from your study and don't recall seeing any others in there—how would you question that guest about the ring? If they had taken the ring and you immediately let them know that you saw them coming out of your study, they would likely concoct a story about why they were in there. Perhaps they would offer, "Oh, I was looking for the restroom and got lost. Sorry!" To use evidence strategically, don't disclose that you spotted the guest in the study. Instead, ask the guest if they had seen anyone in the study or if they had been in the study themself. If the guest is the thief, they will likely want to distance themselves from any implicating information, so they will likely deny having been in the study. On the other hand, if the guest is not the thief, they would likely acknowledge having been in the study. If the guest lies about having been in the study, you can then reveal that you had seen them there, and they will realize that they were caught in a lie. The strategic use of information is a very effective technique for uncovering big liars and avoiding being the dupe.

GETTING OTHERS TO BE HONEST WITH YOU

Whether in our romantic relationships, in our friendships, or at work, life would be so much easier if we could count on others' honesty. It would be great if we could just ask everyone to be honest with us and they would comply, but sadly people are not so compliant. However, we can nurture truthfulness in the people around us in small ways.

Psychologist Bella DePaulo is one of the leading researchers to have studied deception. During her decades of research on lying she has examined the conditions that cause people to struggle with honesty (DePaulo, 2009, 2017). One of her findings is that people can create social dynamics in their lives that lead other people to lie to them. That is, our own behavior, to a certain degree, invites or encourages people to lie to us. So what do we do to set the stage for lying, and how can we change it? First, DePaulo found that people will lie to us if we hold them in high regard. When we place someone on a pedestal and let them know how completely amazing we think they are, they experience a surprising amount of pressure to live up to those accolades. When we let people know that we think they are the best, they feel pressure to be the best. Imagine if you told your spouse every day that they are the smartest person on earth. You tell them that they can accomplish anything. What happens on the day that they lose their job because of poor performance, despite their best efforts? They certainly don't want to let you down and fall from your graces. So, they might lie and tell you they were laid off because of a bad market. Lying may seem like the only way not to let you down. What should we do to create a relationship more conducive to honesty? Well, for starters, we can set reasonable expectations and acknowledge that all people, no matter how brilliant and capable, fall short sometimes, and that's okay. Having reasonable opinions of others helps maintain honesty.

DePaulo (2009, 2017) also found that some people set too high of a moral standard. We all have expectations of good behavior to some extent. We expect our neighbors not to steal from us. We expect our coworkers not to take credit for our work. Sure, we expect people to be on good behavior, but it is also possible to set that standard too high. After all, all people fall short of perfection. Many people probably can describe a parent, grandparent, or teacher who seemed to have the highest moral standards. If we have to admit our moral shortcomings to that person, our first inclination might be to conceal the truth, minimize our behavior, or even lie. Having high standards is often a good thing, but setting unreasonably high standards for the behavior of others is an invitation to have people shade the truth from you.

It might be surprising to learn that the people most likely to lie to you are the people who really, really like you. When people have a great deal of fondness and admiration for someone, they often hope that the other person will feel similarly toward them. People who like you may want to impress you so much that they use exaggeration and other forms of dishonesty to make that happen.

DePaulo (2009, 2017) also found that people may lie to you if you have power over them. If you can control someone's destiny, they may worry that an ugly truth will lead you to fire them, kick them out of the home, take away their car, or otherwise cause unpleasant things to happen to them. That fear may cause them to lie. It is common for bullying bosses to find themselves surrounded by people who feel that it is more important to be agreeable than honest. If you have power, and especially if you wield that power aggressively, people will struggle to be honest with you.

It is not just the powerful who tempt dishonesty in others. If you are a scary person, people may lie to you. If you tend to exhibit explosive rage, people may do anything they can to avoid your wrath, including lying. Lying is extremely common in abusive relationships. If bad news might cause an hour-long flare-up that could turn physically violent, it is much easier to maintain the peace with a little fib. If you are the type of person who is prone to toss insults, threats, or slaps, you are likely not going to get the truth from people.

DePaulo (2009, 2017) also noted that if people seem emotionally fragile, others might not feel comfortable being honest with them. If it seems like a painful truth might cause you to collapse into a sobbing mess, people might decide to sidestep the catastrophic truth and feed you a little lie that will keep your spirits up.

Others invite dishonesty by showing people that certain truths should preferably be kept under wraps. Some people live in homes that are full of elephants in the room. The parents don't dare mention that the daughter obviously has a drug problem. The husband never asks why his wife is coming home later every night and having whispered conversations on the phone in the other room. Some people make it pretty obvious that they would rather not deal with the truth. As a consequence, people speak in codes. "Shelly isn't feeling well again today" or "Susan must be working late again." If we make it clear that we don't want to deal honestly with reality, how can we expect others to bring up the truth themselves?

We are not suggesting that anyone deserves to be lied to. Each of us deserves the truth. However, there are many things we can do to make it easier for people to be honest with us. Because people often lie when telling the truth becomes problematic, we are much more likely to have honest conversations if we can make honesty less problematic for people. By offering people acceptance, understanding, and stability, we make it easier for them to tell the truth. Essentially, people will be honest with us if they can trust us.

FINAL THOUGHTS

Most people accept the occasional lie as a necessary part of life. Research suggests that in a typical week, 95% of people tell at least one lie; some tell many more than that. In contrast, big liars use deception as a primary instrument for navigating their social worlds. In their close relationships and in their vocations, big liars twist the truth to suit their needs, often leaving a wake of turmoil, ruined lives, and disaster behind them.

In this book, we have offered insights into the people who do most of the lying. We have highlighted the childhood development of lying as well as the personality traits and environmental contexts that seem to fuel dishonesty. We have presented the underlying motivations that drive big liars as well as the psychological processes associated with prolific lying. We have also shared many real-life examples of big liars whose flagrant dishonesty wrought havoc in the lives of people drawn into their orbits. We have synthesized much of the scientific evidence available today in scholarly scientific journals or dense academic books and have woven it alongside real-life stories to provide a fascinating account of big liars and their overall negative impact on society. And finally, we have aimed to provide our readers with hope by including tips to avoid being duped by big liars as well as some advice on how to invite others to be more honest. We hope that this information helps readers to recognize, understand, and deal effectively with the big liars they encounter in their own lives.

REFERENCES

Abbott, K. (2012, June 27). The high priestess of fraudulent finance. *Smithsonian Magazine*. https://www.smithsonianmag.com/history/the-high-priestess-of-fraudulent-finance-45/

Ahern, F. M., Johnson, R. C., Wilson, J. R., McClearn, G. E., & Vandenberg, S. G. (1982). Family resemblances in personality. *Behavior Genetics, 12*(3), 261–280. https://doi.org/10.1007/BF01067847

Ainsworth, M. S., & Bowlby, J. (1991). An ethological approach to personality development. *American Psychologist, 46*(4), 333–341. https://doi.org/10.1037/0003-066X.46.4.333

Al Jazeera. (2020, August 4). *US: Accused Twitter hacker teenager pleads not guilty*. https://www.aljazeera.com/news/2020/8/4/us-accused-twitter-hacker-teenager-pleads-not-guilty

Alloway, T. P., McCallum, F., Alloway, R. G., & Hoicka, E. (2015). Liar, liar, working memory on fire: Investigating the role of working memory in childhood verbal deception. *Journal of Experimental Child Psychology, 137*, 30–38. https://doi.org/10.1016/j.jecp.2015.03.013

Alterman, E. (2020). *Lying in state: Why presidents lie—and why Trump is worse*. Basic Books.

American Bar Association. (2018, December). When is it okay for a lawyer to lie? *Around the ABA*. https://www.americanbar.org/news/abanews/publications/youraba/2018/december-2018/when-is-it-okay-for-a-lawyer-to-lie---/

American Bar Association. (2019, April 17). *Model rules of professional conduct, Rule 4.1: Truthfulness in statements to others*. https://www.americanbar.

org/groups/professional_responsibility/publications/model_rules_of_professional_conduct/rule_4_1_truthfulness_in_statements_to_others/

American Press Institute. (2017, March 20). *'Who shared it?': How Americans decide what news to trust on social media*. https://www.americanpressinstitute.org/publications/reports/survey-research/trust-social-media/

American Psychiatric Association. (2013). *Diagnostic and statistical manual of mental disorders* (5th ed.). https://doi.org/10.1176/appi.books.9780890425596

Anderson, N. H. (1968). Likableness ratings of 555 personality-trait words. *Journal of Personality and Social Psychology*, *9*(3), 272–279. https://doi.org/10.1037/h0025907

Anthony, C. I., & Cowley, E. (2012). The labor of lies: How lying for material rewards polarizes consumers' outcome satisfaction. *The Journal of Consumer Research*, *39*(3), 478–492. https://doi.org/10.1086/663824

Antosca, N., Dean, M. Rizzio, B., & Shephard, G. (Executive Producers). (2019). *The act* [TV series]. Eat The Cat; Hulu.

Apicella, C. L. (2018). High levels of rule-bending in a minimally religious and largely egalitarian forager population. *Religion, Brain & Behavior*, *8*(2), 133–148. https://doi.org/10.1080/2153599X.2016.1267034

Appelbaum, B., Hilzenrath, D. S., & Paley, A. R. (2008, December 13). All just one big lie. *The Washington Post*. https://www.washingtonpost.com/wp-dyn/content/article/2008/12/12/AR2008121203970.html

Argo, J. J., & Shiv, B. (2012). Are white lies as innocuous as we think? *The Journal of Consumer Research*, *38*(6), 1093–1102. https://doi.org/10.1086/661640

Ariely, D. (2012). *The honest truth about dishonesty: How we lie to everyone—especially ourselves*. Harper-Collins.

Ariely, D. (2021, August 16). *Response*. Data Colada. http://datacolada.org/storage_strong/DanBlogComment_Aug_16_2021_final.pdf

Aronson, E., Akert, R. M., & Wilson, T. M. (2007). *Social psychology* (6th ed.). Pearson Prentice-Hall.

Asher, R. (1951). Munchausen's syndrome. *The Lancet*, *257*(6650), 339–341. https://doi.org/10.1016/S0140-6736(51)92313-6

Ashton, M. C., & Lee, K. (2007). Empirical, theoretical, and practical advantages of the HEXACO model of personality structure. *Personality and Social Psychology Review*, *11*(2), 150–166. https://doi.org/10.1177/1088868306294907

Ashton, M. C., & Lee, K. (2009). The HEXACO-60: A short measure of the major dimensions of personality. *Journal of Personality Assessment*, *91*(4), 340–345. https://doi.org/10.1080/00223890902935878

Babiak, P. (1995). When psychopaths go to work: A case study of an industrial psychopath. *Applied Psychology*, *44*(2), 171–188. https://doi.org/10.1111/j.1464-0597.1995.tb01073.x

Baddeley, A. D. (1990). *Human memory: Theory and practice*. Allyn & Bacon.

Baker, A., Black, P. J., & Porter, S. (2016). The truth is written all over your face! Involuntary aspects of emotional facial expressions. In C. Abell & J. Smith (Eds.), *The expression of emotion: Philosophical, psychological and legal perspectives* (pp. 219–244). Cambridge University Press. https://doi.org/10.1017/CBO9781316275672.011

Bandura, A., Ross, D., & Ross, S. A. (1961). Transmission of aggression through imitation of aggressive models. *Journal of Abnormal and Social Psychology*, *63*(3), 575–582. https://doi.org/10.1037/h0045925

Barber, M. (2011, March 22). Fake veteran gets 5-month sentence. *Seattle PI*. https://www.seattlepi.com/local/article/Fake-veteran-gets-5-month-sentence-1250322.php

Barnes, C. M., Schaubroeck, J., Huth, M., & Ghumman, S. (2011). Lack of sleep and unethical conduct. *Organizational Behavior and Human Decision Processes*, *115*(2), 169–180. https://doi.org/10.1016/j.obhdp.2011.01.009

Barnes, J. A. (1994). *A pack of lies: Towards a sociology of lying*. Cambridge University Press. https://doi.org/10.1017/CBO9780511520983

Baumeister, R. F., & Leary, M. R. (1995). The need to belong: Desire for interpersonal attachments as a fundamental human motivation. *Psychological Bulletin*, *117*(3), 497–529. https://doi.org/10.1037/0033-2909.117.3.497

BBC. (2020). *World's Biggest Liar championship*. https://www.bbc.com/storyworks/a-year-of-great-events/worlds-biggest-liar-championship

Ben-Shakhar, G., Bar-Hillel, M., & Kremnitzer, M. (2002). Trial by polygraph: Reconsidering the use of the guilty knowledge technique in court. *Law and Human Behavior*, *26*(5), 527–541. https://doi.org/10.1023/A:1020204005730

Berman, T., Karrh, A., Rosario, M. V., Robinson, K., & Effron, L. (2021, September 30). *'Fake heiress' Anna Sorokin: 'I'm not this dumb, greedy person.'* ABC News. https://abcnews.go.com/US/fake-heiress-anna-sorokin-im-dumb-greedy-person/story?id=80278091

Binelli, M. (2015, March 26). Inside America's toughest federal prison. *The New York Times Magazine*. https://www.nytimes.com/2015/03/29/magazine/inside-americas-toughest-federal-prison.html

Birch, C., Kelln, B. C., & Aquino, E. B. (2006). A review and case report of pseudologia fantastica. *Journal of Forensic Psychiatry & Psychology, 17*(2), 299–320. https://doi.org/10.1080/14789940500485128

Bleske-Rechek, A. L., & Buss, D. M. (2001). Opposite-sex friendship: Sex differences and similarities in initiation, selection, and dissolution. *Personality and Social Psychology Bulletin, 27*(10), 1310–1323. https://doi.org/10.1177/01461672012710007

Bogaard, G., Verschuere, B., & Meijer, E. (2021). Centre for Policing and Security: Stop offering pseudoscience. *Panopticon, 42*(4), 359–361. https://doi.org/10.13140/RG.2.2.14479.71841

Bok, S. (1978). *Lying: Moral choice in public and private life*. Vintage Books.

Bok, S. (1999). *Lying: Moral choice in public and private life* (2nd ed.). Pantheon Books.

Bond, C. F., Jr., & DePaulo, B. M. (2006). Accuracy of deception judgments. *Personality and Social Psychology Review, 10*(3), 214–234. https://doi.org/10.1207/s15327957pspr1003_2

Bond, C. F., Jr., & DePaulo, B. M. (2008). Individual differences in judging deception: Accuracy and bias. *Psychological Bulletin, 134*(4), 477–492. https://doi.org/10.1037/0033-2909.134.4.477

Bond, C. F., Jr., & Fahey, W. E. (1987). False suspicion and the misperception of deceit. *British Journal of Social Psychology, 26*(1), 41–46. https://doi.org/10.1111/j.2044-8309.1987.tb00759.x

Bond, C. F., Jr., Howard, A. R., Hutchison, J. L., & Masip, J. (2013). Overlooking the obvious: Incentives to lie. *Basic and Applied Social Psychology, 35*(2), 212–221. https://doi.org/10.1080/01973533.2013.764302

Bond, C. F., Jr., Omar, A., Pitre, U., Lashley, B. R., Skaggs, L. M., & Kirk, C. T. (1992). Fishy-looking liars: Deception judgment from expectancy violation. *Journal of Personality and Social Psychology, 63*(6), 969–977. https://doi.org/10.1037/0022-3514.63.6.969

Boon, S. D., & McLeod, B. A. (2001). Deception in romantic relationships: Subjective estimates of success at deceiving and attitudes toward deception. *Journal of Social and Personal Relationships, 18*(4), 463–476. https://doi.org/10.1177/0265407501184002

Brenan, M. (2020a, June 18). *Americans' views of Trump's character firmly established.* Gallup. https://news.gallup.com/poll/312737/americans-views-trump-character-firmly-established.aspx

Brenan, M. (2020b). *Amid pandemic, confidence in key U.S. institutions surges.* Gallup. https://news.gallup.com/poll/317135/amid-pandemic-confidence-key-institutions-surges.aspx

Brigham, J. C., Bloom, L. M., Gunn, S. P., & Torok, T. (1974). Attitude measurement via the bogus pipeline: A dry well? *Representative Research in Social Psychology*, *5*(2), 97–114.

Britt-Arredondo, C. B. (2007). Torture, tongues, and treason. *South Central Review*, *24*(1), 56–72. https://doi.org/10.1353/scr.2007.0000

Britzky, H. (2021, July 6). *The Army is investigating a married officer accused of faking deployments and awards amid affairs with several women.* Task & Purpose. https://taskandpurpose.com/news/army-officer-affairs-women/

Broadwater, L., & Feuer, A. (2022, March 3). Panel suggests Trump knew he lost the election, eyeing criminal case. *The New York Times.* https://www.nytimes.com/2022/03/03/us/politics/trump-jan-6-criminal-case.html

Brooks, G. R. (2011). Treating traditional men: From believer to skeptic (and back again). In J. Kottler & J. Carlson (Eds.), *Duped: Lies and deception in psychotherapy* (pp. 21–25). Routledge/Taylor & Francis Group.

Buckholtz, A. (2004, August 10). Feeling the heat. *The Washington Post.* https://www.washingtonpost.com/archive/lifestyle/wellness/2004/08/10/feeling-the-heat/d06ca572-bedb-418e-a91a-f76ca0de9a71/

Buller, D. B., & Burgoon, J. K. (1996). Interpersonal deception theory. *Communication Theory*, *6*(3), 203–242. https://doi.org/10.1111/j.1468-2885.1996.tb00127.x

Buss, D. M. (1989). Sex differences in human mate preferences: Evolutionary hypotheses tested in 37 cultures. *Behavioral and Brain Sciences*, *12*(1), 1–14. https://doi.org/10.1017/S0140525X00023992

Buss, D. M. (1994a). *The evolution of desire: Strategies of human mating.* Basic Books.

Buss, D. M. (1994b). The strategies of human mating. *American Scientist*, *82*, 238–249.

Buss, D. M., & Dedden, L. A. (1990). Derogation of competitors. *Journal of Social and Personal Relationships*, *7*(3), 395–422. https://doi.org/10.1177/0265407590073006

Byrne, R. M. J. (2005). *The rational imagination: How people create alternatives to reality*. MIT Press. https://doi.org/10.7551/mitpress/5756.001.0001

Camden, C., Motley, M. T., & Wilson, A. (1984). White lies in interpersonal communication: A taxonomy and preliminary investigation of social motivations. *Western Journal of Speech Communication*, *48*(4), 309–325. https://doi.org/10.1080/10570318409374167

Canavan, A. (2011). The Southern tale-telling tradition in Daniel Wallace's "Big Fish." *Storytelling, Self, Society*, *7*(2), 128–138. www.jstor.org/stable/41949154

Cantarero, K. (2021). *"I'd lie to you, because I love you!" Relationship satisfaction predicts preference for prosocial lying through perceived harm in truth telling*. PsyArXiv. https://doi.org/10.31234/osf.io/gcbta

Cargill, J. R., & Curtis, D. A. (2017). Parental deception: Perceived effects on parent–child relationships. *Journal of Relationships Research*, *8*, Article e1.

Carreyrou, J. (2015, October 16). Hot startup Theranos has struggled with its blood-test technology. *The Wall Street Journal.* https://www.wsj.com/articles/theranos-has-struggled-with-blood-tests-1444881901

Carucci, R. (2019, February 15). 4 ways lying becomes the norm at a company. *Harvard Business Review*. https://hbr.org/2019/02/4-ways-lying-becomes-the-norm-at-a-company

Caspi, A., Houts, R. M., Belsky, D. W., Harrington, H., Hogan, S., Ramrakha, S., Poulton, R., & Moffitt, T. E. (2016). Childhood forecasting of a small segment of the population with large economic burden. *Nature Human Behaviour, 1*, Article 0005. https://doi.org/10.1038/s41562-016-0005

Caspi, A., Moffitt, T. E., Newman, D. L., & Silva, P. A. (1996). Behavioral observations at age 3 years predict adult psychiatric disorders: Longitudinal evidence from a birth cohort. *Archives of General Psychiatry*, *53*(11), 1033–1039. https://doi.org/10.1001/archpsyc.1996.01830110071009

Cavico, F. J., & Mujtaba, B. G. (2020). Defamation by slander and libel in the workplace and recommendations to avoid legal liability. *Public Organization Review*, *20*(1), 79–94. https://doi.org/10.1007/s11115-018-0424-8

Chachere, V. (2003, August 13). One man, two families, one scandal. *The Washington Post*. https://www.washingtonpost.com/archive/lifestyle/2003/08/13/one-man-two-families-one-scandal/a45fa513-1202-4e46-8214-70766eb5b569/

Charroin, L., Fortin, B., & Villeval, M. (2021). *Homophily, peer effects, and dishonesty*. HAL Archives Ouvertes. https://halshs.archives-ouvertes.fr/halshs-03187671

Childs, J. (2013). Personal characteristics and lying: An experimental investigation. *Economics Letters*, *121*(3), 425–427. https://doi.org/10.1016/j.econlet.2013.09.005

Cialdini, R. B. (2001). *Influence: Science and practice* (4th ed.). Allyn & Bacon.

Clark, J. P., & Tifft, L. L. (1966). Polygraph and interview validation of self-reported deviant behavior. *American Sociological Review*, *31*(4), 516–523. https://doi.org/10.2307/2090775

Clementson, D. E. (2018). Deceptively dodging questions: A theoretical note on issues of perception and detection. *Discourse & Communication*, *12*(5), 478–496. https://doi.org/10.1177/1750481318766923

Cochran, S. D., & Mays, V. M. (1990). Sex, lies, and HIV. *The New England Journal of Medicine*, *322*(11), 774–775. https://doi.org/10.1056/NEJM199003153221111

Cohen, M., & Kuang, J. (2018, April 13). *Illinois court panel breaks new ground in condemning police deceptions*. Injustice Watch. https://www.injusticewatch.org/news/2018/illinois-appellate-court-breaks-new-ground-in-condemning-police-deception/

Cohen, S., & Kramer, P. D. (2014, June 18). *Truth, lies and Lacey Spears*. Lohud. https://www.lohud.com/story/news/investigations/2014/06/17/lacey-spears-past-disturbing-stories/10659539/

Cohen, T. R., Gunia, B. C., Kim-Jun, S. Y., & Murnighan, J. K. (2009). Do groups lie more than individuals? Honesty and deception as a function of strategic self-interest. *Journal of Experimental Social Psychology*, *45*(6), 1321–1324. https://doi.org/10.1016/j.jesp.2009.08.007

Cohen, T. R., Panter, A. T., & Turan, N. (2012). Guilt proneness and moral character. *Current Directions in Psychological Science*, *21*(5), 355–359. https://doi.org/10.1177/0963721412454874

Cohn, A., Maréchal, M. A., Tannenbaum, D., & Zünd, C. L. (2019). Civic honesty around the globe. *Science*, *365*(6448), 70–73. https://doi.org/10.1126/science.aau8712

Cole, T. (2001). Lying to the one you love: The use of deception in romantic relationships. *Journal of Social and Personal Relationships*, *18*(1), 107–129. https://doi.org/10.1177/0265407501181005

Coluccia, A., Pozza, A., Ferretti, F., Carabellese, F., Masti, A., & Gualtieri, G. (2020). Online romance scams: Relational dynamics and psychological characteristics of the victims and scammers. A scoping review. *Clinical Practice and Epidemiology in Mental Health*, *16*(1), 24–35. https://doi.org/10.2174/1745017902016010024

Cost, B. (2021, April 23). Con Juan: Man with 35 girlfriends busted for fraud over birthday gifts. *New York Post*. https://nypost.com/2021/04/23/man-with-35-girlfriends-busted-for-fraud-over-birthday-gifts/

Costa, P. T., Jr., & McCrae, R. R. (1992). *Revised NEO Personality Inventory (NEO-PI–R) and the NEO Five-Factor Inventory (NEO-FFI) professional manual*. Psychological Assessment Resources.

Cox, L. N., Hart, C. L., & Curtis, D. A. (2022, April 10). *Thou shall not give false witness: Does religiosity correlate with lying?* [Paper presentation]. Southwestern Psychological Association Annual Meeting, Baton Rouge, LA, United States.

Craven, J. (2020, December 21). *Our police embrace deceit. Is it any wonder we don't trust them?* Cato at Liberty. https://www.cato.org/blog/our-police-embrace-deceit-it-any-wonder-we-dont-trust-them

Cressey, D. R. (1953). *Other people's money: A study in the social psychology of embezzlement*. The Free Press.

Crimesider Staff. (2012, April 11). *Jessica Vega, NY woman accused of faking cancer to get "dream wedding," is charged*. CBS News. https://www.cbsnews.com/news/jessica-vega-ny-woman-accused-of-faking-cancer-to-get-dream-wedding-is-charged/

Curtis, D. A. (2015). Patient deception: Nursing students' beliefs and attitudes. *Nurse Educator*, *40*(5), 254–257. https://doi.org/10.1097/NNE.0000000000000157

Curtis, D. A. (2021a). Deception detection and emotion recognition: Investigating F.A.C.E. software. *Psychotherapy Research*, *31*(6), 802–816. https://doi.org/10.1080/10503307.2020.1836424

Curtis, D. A. (2021b). You liar! Attributions of lying. *Journal of Language and Social Psychology*, *40*(4), 504–523. https://doi.org/10.1177/0261927X21999692

Curtis, D. A., & Dickens, C. (2016, April). *Teach me or lie to me: Effectiveness of a deception workshop* [Poster presentation]. Southwestern Psychological Association 62nd Annual Conference, Dallas, TX, United States.

Curtis, D. A., & Hart, C. L. (2015). Pinocchio's nose in therapy: Therapists' beliefs and attitudes toward client deception. *International Journal for the Advancement of Counseling*, *37*(3), 279–292. https://doi.org/10.1007/s10447-015-9243-6

Curtis, D. A., & Hart, C. L. (2020a). Deception in psychotherapy: Frequency, typology, and relationship. *Counselling & Psychotherapy Research*, *20*(1), 106–115. https://doi.org/10.1002/capr.12263

Curtis, D. A., & Hart, C. L. (2020b). Pathological lying: Theoretical and empirical support for a diagnostic entity. *Psychiatric Research and Clinical Practice*, 2(2), 62–69. https://doi.org/10.1176/appi.prcp.20190046

Curtis, D. A., & Hart, C. L. (2022). *Pathological lying: Theory, research, and practice*. American Psychological Association. https://doi.org/10.1037/0000305-000

Curtis, D. A., Hart, C. L., Kelley, L. J., Villanueva, Y., Larson-Piske, B., & Walter, P. N. (2021, April). *Revealing a lie: Effects of journaling* [Poster presentation]. Southwestern Psychological Association 66th Annual Conference, San Antonio, TX, United States.

Curtis, D. A., Huang, H.-H., & Nicks, K. L. (2018). Patient deception in health care: Physical therapy education, beliefs, and attitudes. *International Journal of Health Sciences Education*, *5*(1). https://dc.etsu.edu/ijhse/vol5/iss1/4

Curtis, D. A., & Kelley, L. J. (2020). Ethics of psychotherapist deception. *Ethics & Behavior*, *30*(8), 601–616. https://doi.org/10.1080/10508422.2019.1674654

Daily Mail. (2011, May 10). *Fantasist pastor who lied to congregation about being a SEAL is caught out by real Navy hero*. https://www.dailymail.co.uk/news/article-1385365/Pastor-Jim-Moats-lied-SEAL-years-using-details-G-I-Jane.html

Dallas, K. (2018, March 28). *Special report: The astonishing revelation about Republicans and lying*. Deseret News. https://www.deseret.com/2018/3/28/20642345/special-report-the-astonishing-revelation-about-republicans-and-lying

Darwin, C. (1877). A biographical sketch of an infant. *Mind*, *2*(7), 285–294. https://doi.org/10.1093/mind/os-2.7.285

Davis, A. (Director). (1992). *Under siege* [Film]. Regency Enterprises.

Davis, T. L. (2016). *Lying lawyers: Investigating the social cognitive label* [Honors thesis]. Angelo State University. https://asu-ir.tdl.org/bitstream/

handle/2346.1/30561/DAVIS-HONORSTHESIS-2016.pdf?sequence=1&isAllowed=y

Debey, E., De Schryver, M., Logan, G. D., Suchotzki, K., & Verschuere, B. (2015). From junior to senior Pinocchio: A cross-sectional lifespan investigation of deception. *Acta Psychologica*, *160*, 58–68. https://doi.org/10.1016/j.actpsy.2015.06.007

DeLisi, M., Drury, A. J., & Elbert, M. J. (2020). Fledgling psychopaths at midlife: Forensic features, criminal careers, and coextensive psychopathology. *Forensic Science International: Mind and Law*, *1*, Article 100006. https://doi.org/10.1016/j.fsiml.2019.100006

Denault, V., Talwar, V., Plusquellec, P., & Larivière, V. (2022). On deception and lying: An overview of over 100 years of social science research. *Applied Cognitive Psychology*, *36*(4), 805–819. https://doi.org/10.1002/acp.3971

DePaulo, B. (2009). *Behind the door of deceit*. CreateSpace Publishing.

DePaulo, B. (2017, June 10). Why do people lie to you? Eight things about you that tempt other people to lie. *Psychology Today*. https://www.psychologytoday.com/us/blog/living-single/201706/why-do-people-lie-you

DePaulo, B. (2018). *The psychology of lying and detecting lies*. http://www.belladepaulo.com/2018/03/just-published-psychology-lying-detecting-lies/

DePaulo, B. M., Ansfield, M. E., Kirkendol, S. E., & Boden, J. M. (2004). Serious lies. *Basic and Applied Social Psychology*, *26*(2–3), 147–167. https://doi.org/10.1080/01973533.2004.9646402

DePaulo, B. M., & Kashy, D. A. (1998). Everyday lies in close and casual relationships. *Journal of Personality and Social Psychology*, *74*(1), 63–79. https://doi.org/10.1037/0022-3514.74.1.63

DePaulo, B. M., Kashy, D. A., Kirkendol, S. E., Wyer, M. M., & Epstein, J. A. (1996). Lying in everyday life. *Journal of Personality and Social Psychology*, *70*(5), 979–995. https://doi.org/10.1037/0022-3514.70.5.979

DePaulo, B. M., Lindsay, J. J., Malone, B. E., Muhlenbruck, L., Charlton, K., & Cooper, H. (2003). Cues to deception. *Psychological Bulletin*, *129*(1), 74–118. https://doi.org/10.1037/0033-2909.129.1.74

Desilver, D. (2019, October 3). *Clinton's impeachment barely dented his public support, and it turned off many Americans*. Pew Research Center. https://www.pewresearch.org/fact-tank/2019/10/03/clintonsimpeachment-barely-dented-his-public-support-and-it-turned-off-many-americans/

DeSteno, D., Duong, F., Lim, D., & Kates, S. (2019). The grateful don't cheat: Gratitude as a fount of virtue. *Psychological Science*, *30*(7), 979–988. https://doi.org/10.1177/0956797619848351

De Zutter, A. W. E. A., Horselenberg, R., & van Koppen, P. J. (2018). Motives for filing a false allegation of rape. *Archives of Sexual Behavior*, *47*(2), 457–464. https://doi.org/10.1007/s10508-017-0951-3

Dickens, C., & Curtis, D. A. (2019). Lies in the law: Therapists' beliefs and attitudes about deception. *Journal of Forensic Psychology Research and Practice*, *19*(5), 359–375. https://doi.org/10.1080/24732850.2019.1666604

Dike, C. C., Baranoski, M., & Griffith, E. E. H. (2005). Pathological lying revisited. *The Journal of the American Academy of Psychiatry and the Law*, *33*(3), 342–349.

Ding, X. P., Heyman, G. D., Fu, G., Zhu, B., & Lee, K. (2018). Young children discover how to deceive in 10 days: A microgenetic study. *Developmental Science*, *21*(3), Article e12566. https://doi.org/10.1111/desc.12566

Ding, X. P., Wellman, H. M., Wang, Y., Fu, G., & Lee, K. (2015). Theory-of-mind training causes honest young children to lie. *Psychological Science*, *26*(11), 1812–1821. https://doi.org/10.1177/0956797615604628

District Attorney of New York. (2017, October 26). *DA Vance announces indictment of repeat scammer for multiple thefts totaling $275,000*. https://www.manhattanda.org/da-vance-announces-indictment-repeat-scammer-multiple-thefts-totaling-275000/

Donald, B. (2016, November 22). *Stanford researchers find students have trouble judging the credibility of information online*. Stanford Graduate School of Education. https://ed.stanford.edu/news/stanford-researchers-find-students-have-trouble-judging-credibility-information-online

Drouin, M., Miller, D. A., Wehle, S., & Hernandez, E. (2016). Why do people lie online? "Because everyone lies on the internet." *Computers in Human Behavior*, *64*, 134–142. https://doi.org/10.1016/j.chb.2016.06.052

Druzin, B. H., & Li, J. (2011). The criminalization of lying: Under what circumstances, if any, should lies be made criminal. *The Journal of Criminal Law & Criminology*, *101*(2), 529–574.

Dua, D., & Grover, S. (2019). Delusion of denial of pregnancy: A case report. *Asian Journal of Psychiatry*, *45*, 72–73. https://doi.org/10.1016/j.ajp.2019.09.002

Dunbar, N. E., Gangi, K., Coveleski, S., Adams, A., Bernhold, Q., & Giles, H. (2016). When is it acceptable to lie? Interpersonal and intergroup perspectives on deception. *Communication Studies*, *67*(2), 129–146. https://doi.org/10.1080/10510974.2016.1146911

Dunbar, N. E., & Johnson, A. J. (2015). A test of dyadic power theory: Control attempts recalled from interpersonal interactions with romantic partners, family members, and friends. *Journal of Argumentation in Context*, *4*(1), 42–62. https://doi.org/10.1075/jaic.4.1.03dun

Duncan, L. E., Ostacher, M., & Ballon, J. (2019). How genome-wide association studies (GWAS) made traditional candidate gene studies obsolete. *Neuropsychopharmacology*, *44*(9), 1518–1523. https://doi.org/10.1038/s41386-019-0389-5

Eaves, L., Heath, A., Martin, N., Maes, H., Neale, M., Kendler, K., Kirk, K., & Corey, L. (1999). Comparing the biological and cultural inheritance of personality and social attitudes in the Virginia 30,000 study of twins and their relatives. *Twin Research*, *2*(2), 62–80. https://doi.org/10.1375/twin.2.2.62

Eckhardt, G. M., & Bengtsson, A. (2010). A brief history of branding in China. *Journal of Macromarketing*, *30*(3), 210–221. https://doi.org/10.1177/0276146709352219

Effron, L., Paparella, A., & Taudte, J. (2019, December 20). *The scandals that brought down the Bakkers, once among US's most famous televangelists*. ABC News. https://abcnews.go.com/US/scandals-brought-bakkers-uss-famous-televangelists/story?id=60389342

Ekman, P. (1985). *Telling lies: Clues to deceit in the marketplace, politics, and marriage*. Norton & Company.

Ekman, P. (2009). *Duping delight*. Paul Ekman Group. https://www.paulekman.com/blog/duping-delight/

Ekman, P., & Friesen, W. V. (1969). Nonverbal leakage and clues to deception. *Psychiatry*, *32*(1), 88–106. https://doi.org/10.1080/00332747.1969.11023575

Ekman, P., & O'Sullivan, M. (1991). Who can catch a liar? *American Psychologist*, *46*(9), 913–920. https://doi.org/10.1037/0003-066X.46.9.913

Ekman, P., O'Sullivan, M., & Frank, M. G. (1999). A few can catch a liar. *Psychological Science*, *10*(3), 263–266. https://doi.org/10.1111/1467-9280.00147

Elliott, P. (2021, November 1). The big lie has been proven false. Republicans can't shake it. *Time*. https://time.com/6112488/trump-2020-election-republicans/

Engarhos, P., Shohoudi, A., Crossman, A., & Talwar, V. (2020). Learning through observing: Effects of modeling truth- and lie-telling on children's honesty. *Developmental Science*, *23*(1), Article e12883. https://doi.org/10.1111/desc.12883

English Standard Version Bible. (2001). ESV Online. https://esv.literalword.com/

Ennis, E., Vrij, A., & Chance, C. (2008). Individual differences and lying in everyday life. *Journal of Social and Personal Relationships*, *25*(1), 105–118. https://doi.org/10.1177/0265407507086808

Erat, S., & Gneezy, U. (2012). White lies. *Management Science*, *58*(4), 723–733. https://doi.org/10.1287/mnsc.1110.1449

European Commission. (2020). *Survey on scams and fraud experienced by consumers: Final report*. https://commission.europa.eu/system/files/2020-01/survey_on_scams_and_fraud_experienced_by_consumers_-_final_report.pdf

Evans, P. (1996). *The verbally abusive relationship: How to recognize it and how to respond* (2nd ed.). Adams Media Corporation.

Fandos, N. (2023, January 11). George Santos's secret résumé: A Wall Street star with a 3.9 G.P.A. *The New York Times*. https://www.nytimes.com/2023/01/11/nyregion/george-santos-resume.html

Federal Trade Commission. (2010, December 15). *Dannon agrees to drop exaggerated health claims for Activia yogurt and DanActive dairy drink*. https://www.ftc.gov/news-events/press-releases/2010/12/dannon-agrees-drop-exaggerated-health-claims-activia-yogurt

Federal Trade Commission. (2016, March 29). *FTC charges Volkswagen deceived consumers with its "clean diesel" campaign*. https://www.ftc.gov/news-events/press-releases/2016/03/ftc-charges-volkswagen-deceived-consumers-its-clean-diesel

Federal Trade Commission. (2021). *Truth in advertising*. https://www.ftc.gov/news-events/media-resources/truth-advertising

Feinstein, D. (2014). *Report of the Senate Select Committee on Intelligence committee study of the Central Intelligence Agency's detention and interrogation program, together with foreword by Chairman Feinstein and additional and minority views*. U.S. Government Printing Office.

Feldman, M. D. (2006). Factitious disorders in children and adolescents. *Psychiatry, 3*(5), 10–11. https://www.ncbi.nlm.nih.gov/pmc/articles/PMC2990619/

Feldman, R. S., Forrest, J. A., & Happ, B. R. (2002). Self-presentation and verbal deception: Do self-presenters lie more? *Basic and Applied Social Psychology, 24*(2), 163–170. https://doi.org/10.1207/S15324834BASP2402_8

Fellner, G., Sausgruber, R., & Traxler, C. (2013). Testing enforcement strategies in the field: Threat, moral appeal and social information. *Journal of the European Economic Association, 11*(3), 634–660. https://doi.org/10.1111/jeea.12013

Ferrara, P., Vitelli, O., Bottaro, G., Gatto, A., Liberatore, P., Binetti, P., & Stabile, A. (2013). Factitious disorders and Munchausen syndrome: The tip of the iceberg. *Journal of Child Health Care, 17*(4), 366–374. https://doi.org/10.1177/1367493512462262

Fischer, P., Lea, S. E. G., & Evans, K. M. (2013). Why do individuals respond to fraudulent scam communications and lose money? The psychological determinants of scam compliance. *Journal of Applied Social Psychology, 43*(10), 2060–2072. https://doi.org/10.1111/jasp.12158

Flexon, J. L., Meldrum, R. C., Young, J. T. N., & Lehmann, P. S. (2016). Low self-control and the Dark Triad: Disentangling the predictive power of personality traits on young adult substance use, offending and victimization. *Journal of Criminal Justice, 46*, 159–169. https://doi.org/10.1016/j.jcrimjus.2016.05.006

Floch, M. (1950). Limitations of the lie detector. *Journal of Criminal Law & Criminology (08852731), 40*(5), 651–653.

Ford, C. V. (1996). *Lies! Lies!! Lies!!!: The psychology of deceit*. American Psychiatric Press, Inc.

Ford, E. B. (2006). Lie detection: Historical, neuropsychiatric and legal dimensions. *International Journal of Law and Psychiatry, 29*, 159–177. https://doi.org/10.1016/j.ijlp.2005.07.001

Fournier, R., & Thompson, T. (2007, March 10). Voters care more about character than issues. *Tuscaloosa News*. https://www.tuscaloosanews.

com/story/news/2007/03/11/voters-care-more-about-character-than-issues/27703757007/

Frank, R. H. (1987). If Homo Economicus could choose his own utility function, would he want one with a conscience? *The American Economic Review*, *77*(4), 593–604. https://www.jstor.org/stable/1814533

Frazier v. Cupp, 394 U.S. 731 (1969). https://supreme.justia.com/cases/federal/us/394/731/

Freyd, J. J. (1997). Violations of power, adaptive blindness, and betrayal trauma theory. *Feminism & Psychology*, *7*(1), 22–32. https://doi.org/10.1177/0959353597071004

Friedman, H. S., Riggio, R. E., & Casella, D. F. (1988). Nonverbal skill, personal charisma, and initial attraction. *Personality and Social Psychology Bulletin*, *14*(1), 203–211. https://doi.org/10.1177/0146167288141020

Gächter, S., & Schulz, J. F. (2016). Intrinsic honesty and the prevalence of rule violations across societies. *Nature*, *531*(7595), 496–499. https://doi.org/10.1038/nature17160

Gallup. (2020, April 13). *Nurses continue to rate highest in honesty, ethics*. https://news.gallup.com/poll/274673/nurses-continue-rate-highest-honesty-ethics.aspx

Ganis, G. (2015). Deception detection using neuroimaging. In P. A. Granhag, A. Vrij, & B. Verschuere (Eds.), *Detecting deception: Current challenges and cognitive approaches* (pp. 105–121). Wiley-Blackwell.

Ganis, G., Rosenfeld, J. P., Meixner, J., Kievit, R. A., & Schendan, H. E. (2011). Lying in the scanner: Covert countermeasures disrupt deception detection by functional magnetic resonance imaging. *NeuroImage*, *55*(1), 312–319. https://doi.org/10.1016/j.neuroimage.2010.11.025

Garlipp, P. (2017). Pseudolagia fantastica—pathological lying. In B. A. Sharpless (Ed.), *Unusual and rare psychological disorders: A handbook for clinical practice and research* (pp. 319–327). Oxford University Press.

Garrett, N., Lazzaro, S. C., Ariely, D., & Sharot, T. (2016). The brain adapts to dishonesty. *Nature Neuroscience*, *19*(12), 1727–1732. https://doi.org/10.1038/nn.4426

Gee, J., & Button, M. (2019). *The financial cost of fraud 2019*. Crowe. http://www.crowe.ie/wp-content/uploads/2019/08/The-Financial-Cost-of-Fraud-2019.pdf

George Grubbs Enterprises, Inc. v. Bien, 881 S.W.2d 843 (Tex. Ct. App. 1994). https://casetext.com/case/george-grubbs-entrprise-v-bien

George, J., & Robb, A. (2008). Deception and computer-mediated communication in daily life. *Communication Reports*, *21*(2), 92–103. https://doi.org/10.1080/08934210802298108

Gerlach, P., Teodorescu, K., & Hertwig, R. (2019). The truth about lies: A meta-analysis on dishonest behavior. *Psychological Bulletin*, *145*(1), 1–44. https://doi.org/10.1037/bul0000174

Gillard, N. D. (2018). Psychopathy and deception. In R. Rogers & S. D. Bender (Eds.), *Clinical assessment of malingering and deception* (pp. 174–187). Guilford Press.

Gino, F., & Galinsky, A. D. (2012). Vicarious dishonesty: When psychological closeness creates distance from one's moral compass. *Organizational Behavior and Human Decision Processes*, *119*(1), 15–26. https://doi.org/10.1016/j.obhdp.2012.03.011

Gino, F., Schweitzer, M. E., Mead, N. L., & Ariely, D. (2011). Unable to resist temptation: How self-control depletion promotes unethical behavior. *Organizational Behavior and Human Decision Processes*, *115*(2), 191–203. https://doi.org/10.1016/j.obhdp.2011.03.001

Glätzle-Rützler, D., & Lergetporer, P. (2015). Lying and age: An experimental study. *Journal of Economic Psychology*, *46*, 12–25. https://doi.org/10.1016/j.joep.2014.11.002

The Global Deception Research Team. (2006). A world of lies. *Journal of Cross-Cultural Psychology*, *37*(1), 60–74. https://doi.org/10.1177/0022022105282295

Goffman, E. (1956). *The presentation of self in everyday life*. Doubleday.

Gordon, A. (2018, October 11). *Jessica Nordquist who claimed ex raped her is convicted of stalking*. Daily Mail Online. https://www.dailymail.co.uk/news/article-6265113/Woman-claimed-ex-raped-convicted-stalking-perverting-course-justice.html

Gordon, A. K., & Miller, A. G. (2000). Perspective differences in the construal of lies: Is deception in the eye of the beholder? *Personality and Social Psychology Bulletin*, *26*(1), 46–55. https://doi.org/10.1177/0146167200261005

Graham, C., Litan, R., & Sukhtankar, S. (2002). *The bigger they are, the harder they fall: An estimate of the costs of the crisis in corporate governance* [Working paper]. The Brookings Institution. https://www.brookings.edu/wp-content/uploads/2016/06/20020722Graham.pdf

Granhag, P. A., Andersson, L. O., Stromwall, L. A., & Hartwig, M. (2004). Imprisoned knowledge: Criminals' beliefs about deception. *Legal and Criminological Psychology*, *9*(1), 103–119. https://doi.org/10.1348/135532504322776889

Granhag, P. A., Vrij, A., & Verschuere, B. (2015). *Detecting deception: Current challenges and cognitive approaches*. Wiley-Blackwell.

Grant, A. (2014). *Dan Ariely on 'The Honest Truth About Dishonesty'*. https://knowledge.wharton.upenn.edu/article/dan-ariely-dishonestys-slippery-slope/

Grant, J. E., Paglia, H. A., & Chamberlain, S. R. (2019). The phenomenology of lying in young adults and relationships with personality and cognition. *Psychiatric Quarterly*, *90*(2), 361–369. https://doi.org/10.1007/s11126-018-9623-2

Grattagliano, I., Corbi, G., Catanesi, R., Ferrara, N., Lisi, A., & Campobasso, C. P. (2014). False accusations of sexual abuse as a mean of revenge in couple disputes. *La Clinica Terapeutica*, *165*(2), e119–e124. https://doi.org/10.7471/CT.2014.1694

Graybow, M. (2009, March 11). *Madoff mysteries remain as he nears guilty plea*. Reuters. https://www.reuters.com/article/us-madoff/madoff-mysteries-remain-as-he-nears-guilty-plea-idUSTRE52A5JK20090311

Grazer, B. (Executive Producer). (2009–2011). *Lie to me* [TV series]. Imagine Television.

Greenberg, K. S. (1990). The nose, the lie, and the duel in the antebellum South. *The American Historical Review*, *95*(1), 57–74. https://doi.org/10.2307/2162954

Greenspan, S. (2008). *Annals of gullibility: Why we get duped and how to avoid it*. Praeger.

Grice, H. P. (1989). *Studies in the way of words*. Harvard University Press.

Griffin, G. (2009, March 2). Scam expert from CU expertly scammed. *The Denver Post*. https://www.denverpost.com/2009/03/02/scam-expert-from-cu-expertly-scammed/

Grzegorek, J. L. (2011). Smoke and mirrors. In J. Kottler & J. Carlson (Eds.), *Duped: Lies and deception in psychotherapy* (pp. 33–37). Routledge/Taylor & Francis Group.

Guinness World Records. (2021). *Tallest man living*. https://www.guinnessworldrecords.com/world-records/tallest-man-living

Gunaydin, G., Selcuk, E., & Zayas, V. (2017). Impressions based on a portrait predict, 1-month later, impressions following a live interaction. *Social Psychological & Personality Science*, *8*(1), 36–44. https://doi.org/10.1177/1948550616662123

Gunia, B. C., & Levine, E. E. (2019). Deception as competence: The effect of occupational stereotypes on the perception and proliferation of deception. *Organizational Behavior and Human Decision Processes*, *152*, 122–137. https://doi.org/10.1016/j.obhdp.2019.02.003

Guthrie, J., & Kunkel, A. (2013). Tell me sweet (and not-so-sweet) little lies: Deception in romantic relationships. *Communication Studies*, *64*(2), 141–157. https://doi.org/10.1080/10510974.2012.755637

Gutman, M., & Tienabeso, S. (2013, January 21). *Timeline of Manti Te'o girlfriend hoax story*. ABC News. https://abcnews.go.com/US/timeline-manti-teo-girlfriend-hoax-story/story?id=18268647

Hagglund, L. A. (2009). Challenges in the treatment of factitious disorder: A case study. *Archives of Psychiatric Nursing*, *23*(1), 58–64. https://doi.org/10.1016/j.apnu.2008.03.002

Halevy, R., Shalvi, S., & Verschuere, B. (2014). Being honest about dishonesty: Correlating self-reports and actual lying. *Human Communication Research*, *40*(1), 54–72. https://doi.org/10.1111/hcre.12019

Hall, G. S. (Ed.). (1890). Children's lies. *The American Journal of Psychology*, *3*(1), 59–70. https://doi.org/10.2307/1411497

Hample, D. (1980). Purposes and effects of lying. *The Southern Speech Communication Journal*, *46*(1), 33–47. https://doi.org/10.1080/10417948009372474

Hamzelou, J. (2016, October 24). *Lying feels bad at first but our brains soon adapt to deceiving*. New Scientist. https://www.newscientist.com/article/2110130-lying-feels-bad-at-first-but-our-brains-soon-adapt-to-deceiving/

Hancock, J. T., Thom-Santelli, J., & Ritchie, T. (2004). Deception and design: The impact of communication technology on lying behavior. *CHI '04: Proceedings of the SIGCHI Conference on Human Factors in Computing Systems*, 129–134. https://doi.org/10.1145/985692.985709

Hancock, J. T., & Toma, C. L. (2009). Putting your best face forward: The accuracy of online dating photographs. *Journal of Communication*, *59*(2), 367–386. https://doi.org/10.1111/j.1460-2466.2009.01420.x

Hare, R. D. (1991). *Manual for the Revised Psychopathy Checklist* (1st ed.). Multi-Health Systems.

Hare, R. D. (1996). Psychopathy and antisocial personality disorder: A case of diagnostic confusion. *The Psychiatric Times*, *13*(2), 39–40.

Hare, R. D., Forth, A. E., & Hart, S. D. (1989). The psychopath as prototype for pathological lying and deception. In J. C. Yuille (Ed.), *Credibility assessment* (pp. 25–49). Kluwer Academic/Plenum Publishers. https://doi.org/10.1007/978-94-015-7856-1_2

Harris, P. (2000). *The work of the imagination*. Blackwell.

Harris, P. (2010, June 5). *Ted Haggard, mega-church founder felled by sex scandal, returns to pulpit*. The Guardian. https://www.theguardian.com/world/2010/jun/06/us-gay-scandal-pastor-church

Hart, C. L. (2017). *Lying in bed and other forms of sexual deception* [Paper presentation]. Southwestern Psychological Association Annual Convention, San Antonio, TX, United States.

Hart, C. L. (2019, May 16). What is a lie? Defining different elements of dishonesty. *Psychology Today*. https://www.psychologytoday.com/us/blog/the-nature-deception/201905/what-is-lie

Hart, C. L. (2021). *Mind, lies, and morality* [Conference session]. Southwestern Society of Mind 2nd Annual Meeting, Fort Davis, TX, United States.

Hart, C. L. (2022). A theory of lying and dishonesty. *Psychology Today*. https://www.psychologytoday.com/us/node/1173053/preview

Hart, C. L., Beach, R., & Curtis, D. A. (2021). *Pathological lying* [Poster presentation]. Southwestern Psychological Association 66th Annual Conference, San Antonio, TX, United States.

Hart, C. L., Beach, R., Griffith, J. D., & Curtis, D. A. (2023). *An analysis of tactics implemented while lying* [Manuscript submitted for publication]. Department of Psychology, Texas Woman's University.

Hart, C. L., Curtis, D. A., & Randell, J. A. (2023). *Development of the Pathological Lying Inventory* [Manuscript in preparation]. Department of Psychology & Philosophy, Texas Woman's University.

Hart, C. L., Curtis, D. A., Williams, N. M., Hathaway, M. D., & Griffith, J. D. (2014). Do as I say, not as I do: Benevolent deception in romantic relationships. *Journal of Relationships Research*, *5*, Article e8. https://doi.org/10.1017/jrr.2014.8

Hart, C. L., Jones, J. M., Terrizzi, J. A., Jr., & Curtis, D. A. (2019). Development of the Lying in Everyday Situations Scale. *The American*

Journal of Psychology, *132*(3), 343–352. https://doi.org/10.5406/amerjpsyc.132.3.0343

Hart, C. L., Lemon, R., Curtis, D. A., & Griffith, J. D. (2020). Personality traits associated with various forms of lying. *Psychological Studies*, *65*(3), 239–246. https://doi.org/10.1007/s12646-020-00563-x

Hartwig, M., & Granhag, P. A. (2015). Exploring the nature and origin of beliefs about deception: Implicit and explicit knowledge among lay people and presumed experts. In P. A. Granhag, A. Vrij, & B. Verschuere (Eds.), *Detecting deception: Current challenges and cognitive approaches* (pp. 125–153). Wiley-Blackwell.

Harvard Graduate School of Education. (2018, October). *Tips for encouraging honesty*. https://mcc.gse.harvard.edu/resources-for-families/tips-encouraging-honesty

Hasher, L., Goldstein, D., & Toppino, T. (1977). Frequency and the conference of referential validity. *Journal of Verbal Learning and Verbal Behavior*, *16*(1), 107–112. https://doi.org/10.1016/S0022-5371(77)80012-1

Hays, C., & Carver, L. J. (2014). Follow the liar: The effects of adult lies on children's honesty. *Developmental Science*, *17*(6), 977–983. https://doi.org/10.1111/desc.12171

Healy, W., & Healy, M. T. (1915). *Pathological lying, accusation and swindling: A study in forensic psychology*. Little, Brown and Co. https://doi.org/10.1037/14932-000

Heimlich, R. (2008, September 29). *Honesty is the best policy*. Pew Research Center. https://www.pewresearch.org/fact-tank/2008/09/29/honesty-is-the-best-policy/

Helson, H., Blake, R. R., & Mouton, J. S. (1958). An experimental investigation of the effectiveness of the "big lie" in shifting attitudes. *The Journal of Social Psychology*, *48*(1), 51–60. https://doi.org/10.1080/00224545.1958.9919267

Hendy, N. T., Montargot, N., & Papadimitriou, A. (2021). Cultural differences in academic dishonesty: A social learning perspective. *Journal of Academic Ethics*, *19*(1), 49–70. https://doi.org/10.1007/s10805-021-09391-8

Higgins, L. (2015, January 15). Munchausen won't be raised at Lacey Spears trial. *USA Today*. https://www.usatoday.com/story/news/nation/2015/01/15/lacey-spears-trial-munchausen/21817517/

Hines, A., Colwell, K., Anisman, C., Garrett, E., Ansarra, R., & Montalvo, L. (2010). Impression management strategies of deceivers and honest reporters in an investigative interview. *The European Journal of Psychology Applied to Legal Context*, *2*(1), 73–90. https://journals.copmadrid.org/ejpalc/art/b096577e264d1ebd6b41041f392eec23

Hinshaw, S. P., & Lee, S. S. (2003). Conduct and oppositional defiant disorders. In E. J. Mash & R. A. Barkley (Eds.), *Child psychopathology* (pp. 144–198). Guilford Press.

History.com Editors. (2011, March 18). *"Balloon Boy" parents sentenced in Colorado*. https://www.history.com/this-day-in-history/balloon-boy-parents-sentenced-in-colorado

Hitler, A. (1971). *Mein kampf* (R. Manheim, Trans.). Houghton Mifflin. (Original work published 1925)

Hu, C., Huang, J., Wang, Q., Weare, E., & Fu, G. (2020). Truthful but misleading: Advanced linguistic strategies for lying among children. *Frontiers in Psychology*, *11*, Article 676. https://doi.org/10.3389/fpsyg.2020.00676

Iacono, W. G. (2015). Forensic application of event-related brain potentials to detect guilty knowledge. In P. A. Granhag, A. Vrij, & B. Verschuere (Eds.), *Detecting deception: Current challenges and cognitive approaches* (pp. 81–103). Wiley-Blackwell.

Iezzoni, L. I., Rao, S. R., DesRoches, C. M., Vogeli, C., & Campbell, E. G. (2012). Survey shows that at least some physicians are not always open or honest with patients. *Health Affairs*, *31*(2), 383–391. https://doi.org/10.1377/hlthaff.2010.1137

Jaghab, K., Skodnek, K. B., & Padder, T. A. (2006). Munchausen's syndrome and other factitious disorders in children: Case series and literature review. *Psychiatry*, *3*(3), 46–55. https://www.ncbi.nlm.nih.gov/pmc/articles/PMC2990557/

Janezic, K. A., & Gallego, A. (2020). Eliciting preferences for truth-telling in a survey of politicians. *Proceedings of the National Academy of Sciences of the United States of America*, *117*(36), 22002–22008. https://doi.org/10.1073/pnas.2008144117

Jenkins, S., & Delbridge, R. (2017). Trusted to deceive: A case study of 'strategic deception' and the normalization of lying at work. *Organization Studies*, *38*(1), 53–76. https://doi.org/10.1177/0170840616655481

Jensen, K., Vaish, A., & Schmidt, M. F. H. (2014). The emergence of human prosociality: Aligning with others through feelings, concerns, and norms. *Frontiers in Psychology, 5*, Article 822. https://doi.org/10.3389/fpsyg.2014.00822

Jensen, L. A., Arnett, J. J., Feldman, S. S., & Cauffman, E. (2004). The right to do wrong: Lying to parents among adolescents and emerging adults. *Journal of Youth and Adolescence, 33*(2), 101–112. https://doi.org/10.1023/B:JOYO.0000013422.48100.5a

Jonason, P. K., Lyons, M., Baughman, H. M., & Vernon, P. A. (2014). What a tangled web we weave: The Dark Triad traits and deception. *Personality and Individual Differences, 70*, 117–119. https://doi.org/10.1016/j.paid.2014.06.038

Kahn, J. (2012, May 12). Can you call a 9-year-old a psychopath? *The New York Times Magazine*. https://www.nytimes.com/2012/05/13/magazine/can-you-call-a-9-year-old-a-psychopath.html

Kakutani, M. (2018). *The death of truth: Notes on falsehood in the age of Trump*. Tim Duggan Books.

Kalish, N. (2004). How honest are you? *The Reader's Digest, 164*(981), 114–119.

Kaplar, M. E. (2006). *Lying happily ever after: Altruistic white lies, positive illusions, and relationship satisfaction* [Doctoral dissertation, Bowling Green University]. https://etd.ohiolink.edu/apexprod/rws_olink/r/1501/10?clear=10&p10_accession_num=bgsu1147758888

Kaplar, M. E., & Gordon, A. K. (2004). The enigma of altruistic lying: Perspective differences in what motivates and justifies lie telling within romantic relationships. *Personal Relationships, 11*(4), 489–507. https://doi.org/10.1111/j.1475-6811.2004.00094.x

Kashy, D. A., & DePaulo, B. M. (1996). Who lies? *Journal of Personality and Social Psychology, 70*(5), 1037–1051. https://doi.org/10.1037/0022-3514.70.5.1037

Kassin, S. M., & Norwick, R. J. (2004). Why people waive their Miranda rights: The power of innocence. *Law and Human Behavior, 28*(2), 211–221. https://doi.org/10.1023/B:LAHU.0000022323.74584.f5

Kaya, O. (2022, December 23). *Last minute . . . fake doctor Ayşe Özkiraz wants to be a real doctor this time! Surprised by the demand in prison*. Hürriyet. https://www.hurriyet.com.tr/gundem/son-dakika-sahte-doktor-ayse-ozkiraz-bu-kez-gercek-doktor-olmak-istiyor-cezaevindeki-talebi-sasirtti-42192368

Kelley, H. H. (1967). Attribution theory in social psychology. *Nebraska Symposium on Motivation, 15*, 192–238.

Kessler, G., Rizzo, S., & Kelly, M. (2021, January 24). Trump's false or misleading claims total 30573 over 4 years. *The Washington Post*. https://www.washingtonpost.com/politics/2021/01/24/trumps-false-or-misleading-claims-total-30573-over-four-years/

Kettler, S. (2020, September 11). The story of Gypsy Rose Blanchard and her mother. *Biography*. https://www.biography.com/news/gypsy-rose-blanchard-mother-dee-dee-murder

King, B. H., & Ford, C. V. (1988). Pseudologia fantastica. *Acta Psychiatrica Scandinavica*, *77*(1), 1–6. https://doi.org/10.1111/j.1600-0447.1988.tb05068.x

King, L. W. (Trans). (2008). *The code of Hammurabi*. Yale Law School. https://avalon.law.yale.edu/ancient/hamframe.asp

Knopp, K., Scott, S., Ritchie, L., Rhoades, G. K., Markman, H. J., & Stanley, S. M. (2017). Once a cheater, always a cheater? Serial infidelity across subsequent relationships. *Archives of Sexual Behavior*, *46*(8), 2301–2311. https://doi.org/10.1007/s10508-017-1018-1

Knox, D., Schacht, C., Holt, J., & Turner, J. (1993). Sexual lies among university students. *College Student Journal*, *27*(2), 269–272. https://psycnet.apa.org/record/1993-45153-001

Kocher, M. G., Schudy, S., & Spantig, L. (2018). I lie? We lie! Why? Experimental evidence on a dishonesty shift in groups. *Management Science*, *64*(9), 3995–4008. https://doi.org/10.1287/mnsc.2017.2800

Konnikova, M. (2016). *The confidence game: Why we fall for it . . . every time*. Viking/Penguin.

Kottler, J. (2011). How well do we really know our clients? In J. Kottler & J. Carlson (Eds.), *Duped: Lies and deception in psychotherapy* (pp. 9–14). Routledge/Taylor & Francis Group. https://doi.org/10.4324/9780203858349

Kouchaki, M., & Smith, I. H. (2014). The morning morality effect: The influence of time of day on unethical behavior. *Psychological Science*, *25*(1), 95–102. https://doi.org/10.1177/0956797613498099

Kowalski, R. M., Walker, S., Wilkinson, R., Queen, A., & Sharpe, B. (2003). Lying, cheating, complaining, and other aversive interpersonal behaviors: A narrative examination of the darker side of relationships. *Journal of Social and Personal Relationships*, *20*(4), 471–490. https://doi.org/10.1177/02654075030204003

Kramer, S. R., & Shariff, A. F. (2016). Religion, deception, and self-deception. In J.-W. van Prooijen & P. A. M. van Lange (Eds.), *Cheating, corruption, and concealment: The roots of dishonesty* (pp. 233–249). Cambridge University Press. https://doi.org/10.1017/CBO9781316225608.014

Langer, W. C. (1944). *A psychological analysis of Adolph Hitler: His life and legend.* U.S. Office of Strategic Services. https://www.cia.gov/readingroom/docs/CIA-RDP78-02646R000600240001-5.pdf

Lavoie, J., Nagar, P. M., & Talwar, V. (2017). From Kantian to Machiavellian deceivers: Development of children's reasoning and self-reported use of secrets and lies. *Childhood, 24*(2), 197–211. https://doi.org/10.1177/0907568216671179

Lebelo, L. T., & Grobler, G. P. (2020). Case study: A patient with severe delusions who self-mutilates. *South African Journal of Psychiatry, 26*, Article 1403. https://doi.org/10.4102/sajpsychiatry.v26i0.1403

LeClaire, A. (2017). *The halo effect.* Lake Union Publishing.

Lee, H. (1960). *To kill a mockingbird.* Lippincott.

Lee, K. (2013). Little liars: Development of verbal deception in children. *Child Development Perspectives*, 7(2), 91–96. https://doi.org/10.1111/cdep.12023

Lee, T. B. (2016, November 16). *The top 20 fake news stories outperformed real news at the end of the 2016 campaign.* Vox. https://www.vox.com/new-money/2016/11/16/13659840/facebook-fake-news-chart

Leigh-Hunt, N., Bagguley, D., Bash, K., Turner, V., Turnbull, S., Valtorta, N., & Caan, W. (2017). An overview of systematic reviews on the public health consequences of social isolation and loneliness. *Public Health, 152*, 157–171. https://doi.org/10.1016/j.puhe.2017.07.035

Levine, E. E., & Schweitzer, M. E. (2014). Are liars ethical? On the tension between benevolence and honesty. *Journal of Experimental Social Psychology, 53*, 107–117. https://doi.org/10.1016/j.jesp.2014.03.005

Levine, E. E., & Schweitzer, M. E. (2015). Prosocial lies: When deception breeds trust. *Organizational Behavior and Human Decision Processes, 126*, 88–106. https://doi.org/10.1016/j.obhdp.2014.10.007

Levine, T. R. (2010). A few transparent liars: Explaining 54% accuracy in deception detection experiments. In C. Salmon (Ed.), *Communication Yearbook 34* (pp. 40–61). Sage.

Levine, T. R. (2014). Truth-default theory (TDT): A theory of human deception and deception detection. *Journal of Language and Social Psychology, 33*(4), 378–392. https://doi.org/10.1177/0261927X14535916

Levine, T. R. (2015). New and improved accuracy findings in deception detection research. *Current Opinion in Psychology*, 6, 1–5. https://doi.org/10.1016/j.copsyc.2015.03.003

Levine, T. R. (2020). *Duped: Truth-default theory and the social science of lying and deception*. University of Alabama Press.

Levine, T. R., Ali, M. V., Dean, M., Abdulla, R. A., & Garcia-Ruano, K. (2016). Toward a pan-cultural typology of deception motives. *Journal of Intercultural Communication Research*, *45*(1), 1–12. https://doi.org/10.1080/17475759.2015.1137079

Levine, T. R., Asada, K. J., & Massi Lindsey, L. L. (2003). The relative impact of violation type and lie severity on judgments of message deceitfulness. *Communication Research Reports*, *20*(3), 208–218. https://doi.org/10.1080/08824090309388819

Levine, T. R., Clare, D. D., Blair, J. P., McCornack, S. A., Morrison, K., & Park, H. S. (2014). Expertise in deception detection involves actively prompting diagnostic information rather than passive behavioral observation. *Human Communication Research*, *40*(4), 442–462. https://doi.org/10.1111/hcre.12032

Levine, T. R., Serota, K. B., Carey, F., & Messer, D. (2013). Teenagers lie a lot: A further investigation into the prevalence of lying. *Communication Research Reports*, *30*(3), 211–220. https://doi.org/10.1080/08824096.2013.806254

Levine, T. R., Serota, K. B., & Shulman, H. C. (2010). The impact of *Lie to Me* on viewers' actual ability to detect deception. *Communication Research*, *37*(6), 847–856. https://doi.org/10.1177/0093650210362686

Levine, T. R., Serota, K. B., Shulman, H., Clare, D. D., Park, H. S., Shaw, A. S., Shim, J. C., & Lee, J. H. (2011). Sender demeanor: Individual differences in sender believability have a powerful impact on deception detection judgments. *Human Communication Research*, *37*(3), 377–403. https://doi.org/10.1111/j.1468-2958.2011.01407.x

Lewandowsky, S., Ecker, U. K. H., Seifert, C. M., Schwarz, N., & Cook, J. (2012). Misinformation and its correction: Continued influence and successful debiasing. *Psychological Science in the Public Interest*, *13*(3), 106–131. https://doi.org/10.1177/1529100612451018

Lewin, K. (1936). *Principles of topological psychology*. McGraw Hill. https://doi.org/10.1037/10019-000

Lewis, M. (2015). The origins of lying and deception in everyday life. *American Scientist*, *103*(2), 128. https://doi.org/10.1511/2015.113.128

Lewis, M., Stanger, C., & Sullivan, M. W. (1989). Deception in 3-year-olds. *Developmental Psychology*, *25*(3), 439–443. https://doi.org/10.1037/0012-1649.25.3.439

Lie to Me. (2021). *About* Lie to Me. Fox Social. https://www.fox.com/lie-to-me/about-lie-to-me/

Lim, A., Young, R. L., & Brewer, N. (2022). Autistic adults may be erroneously perceived as deceptive and lacking credibility. *Journal of Autism and Developmental Disorders*, 52(2), 490–507. https://doi.org/10.1007/s10803 021-04963-4

Lindskold, S., & Walters, P. S. (1983). Categories for acceptability of lies. *The Journal of Social Psychology*, *120*(1), 129–136. https://doi.org/10.1080/00224545.1983.9712018

Littrell, S., Risko, E. F., & Fugelsang, J. A. (2021). The Bullshitting Frequency Scale: Development and psychometric properties. *British Journal of Social Psychology*, *60*(1), 248–270. https://doi.org/10.1111/bjso.12379

Loewen, P. J., Dawes, C. T., Mazar, N., Johannesson, M., Koellinger, P., & Magnusson, P. K. E. (2013). The heritability of moral standards for everyday dishonesty. *Journal of Economic Behavior & Organization*, *93*, 363–366. https://doi.org/10.1016/j.jebo.2013.05.001

Loftus, E. F. (1979). *Eyewitness testimony*. Harvard University Press.

Lundquist, T., Ellingsen, T., Gribbe, E., & Johannesson, M. (2009). The aversion to lying. *Journal of Economic Behavior & Organization*, *70*(1–2), 81–92. https://doi.org/10.1016/j.jebo.2009.02.010

Lupoli, M. J., Jampol, L., & Oveis, C. (2017). Lying because we care: Compassion increases prosocial lying. *Journal of Experimental Psychology: General*, *146*(7), 1026–1042. https://doi.org/10.1037/xge0000315

Lykken, D. T. (1957). A study of anxiety in the sociopathic personality. *Journal of Abnormal and Social Psychology*, *55*(1), 6–10. https://doi.org/10.1037/h0047232

Lykken, D. T. (1978). The psychopath and the lie detector. *Psychophysiology*, *15*(2), 137–142. https://doi.org/10.1111/j.1469-8986.1978.tb01349.x

Macqueen, A. (2017). *The lies of the land: An honest history of political deceit*. Atlantic Books.

Mahon, J. E. (2008). Two definitions of lying. *The International Journal of Applied Philosophy*, *22*(2), 211–230. https://doi.org/10.5840/ijap200822216

Mann, H., Garcia-Rada, X., Houser, D., & Ariely, D. (2014). Everybody else is doing it: Exploring social transmission of lying behavior. *PLOS ONE*, *9*(10), Article e109591. https://doi.org/10.1371/journal.pone.0109591

Marasa, L. H. (2018). Malingering: A result of trauma or litigation? *The American Journal of Psychiatry Residents' Journal*, *13*(3), 7–9. https://doi.org/10.1176/appi.ajp-rj.2018.130304

Markowitz, D. M. (2021). Toward a theory of prolific liars: Building a profile of situational, dispositional, and communication characteristics. *PsyArXiv*. https://doi.org/10.31234/osf.io/p3y4x

Markowitz, D. M., & Hancock, J. T. (2018). Deception in mobile dating conversations. *Journal of Communication*, *68*(3), 547–569. https://doi.org/10.1093/joc/jqy019

Markowitz, D. M., Kouchaki, M., Hancock, J. T., & Gino, F. (2021). The deception spiral: Corporate obfuscation leads to perceptions of immorality and cheating behavior. *Journal of Language and Social Psychology*, *40*(2), 277–296. https://doi.org/10.1177/0261927X20949594

Markowitz, D. M., & Levine, T. R. (2021). It's the situation and your disposition: A test of two honesty hypotheses. *Social Psychological & Personality Science*, *12*(2), 213–224. https://doi.org/10.1177/1948550619898976

Marlowe, F. (2010). *The Hadza hunter-gatherers of Tanzania*. University of California Press.

Masip, J., Sporer, S. L., Garrido, E., & Herrero, C. (2005). The detection of deception with the reality monitoring approach: A review of the empirical evidence. *Psychology, Crime & Law*, *11*(1), 99–122. https://doi.org/10.1080/10683160410001726356

Mazar, N., Amir, O., & Ariely, D. (2008). The dishonesty of honest people: A theory of self-concept maintenance. *Journal of Marketing Research*, *45*(6), 633–644. https://doi.org/10.1509/jmkr.45.6.633

Mazar, N., & Ariely, D. (2006). Dishonesty in everyday life and its policy implications. *Journal of Public Policy & Marketing*, *25*(1), 117–126. https://doi.org/10.1509/jppm.25.1.117

McCabe, D. P., & Castel, A. D. (2008). Seeing is believing: The effect of brain images on judgments of scientific reasoning. *Cognition*, *107*(1), 343–352. https://doi.org/10.1016/j.cognition.2007.07.017

McCornack, S. A., & Levine, T. R. (1990). When lies are uncovered: Emotional and relational outcomes of discovered deception. *Communication Monographs*, *57*(2), 119–138. https://doi.org/10.1080/03637759009376190

McCoy, T. (2015, March 3). Why a woman murdered her son with salt. *The Washington Post*. https://www.washingtonpost.com/news/morning-mix/wp/2015/03/03/the-rare-disorder-experts-say-drove-lacey-spears-to-murder-her-son-with-salt/

McLean, B., & Elkind, P. (2003). *Enron: The smartest guys in the room*. Portfolio Trade.

Meijer, E. H., & Verschuere, B. (2015). The polygraph: Current practice and new approaches. In P. A. Granhag, A. Vrij, & B. Verschuere (Eds.), *Detecting deception: Current challenges and cognitive approaches* (pp. 59–80). Wiley-Blackwell.

Mental Health Foundation. (2016). What is truth? An inquiry about truth and lying in dementia care. https://www.mentalhealth.org.uk/sites/default/files/dementia-truth-inquiry-report.pdf

Merriam-Webster. (n.d.). Lie. In *Merriam-Webster.com dictionary*. Retrieved April 2, 2021, from https://www.merriam-webster.com/lie

Metts, S. (1989). An exploratory investigation of deception in close relationships. *Journal of Social and Personal Relationships*, *6*(2), 159–179. https://doi.org/10.1177/026540758900600202

Meyer, P. (2010). *Liespotting: Proven techniques to detect deception*. St. Martin's Press.

Moore, A. (2019, March 2). *Abuse prevention: How to turn off the gaslighters*. The Guardian. https://www.theguardian.com/lifeandstyle/2019/mar/02/abuse-prevention-how-to-turn-off-the-gaslighters

Morell, C., & Smith, P. (2020, June 15). *After decades of police corruption, can Chicago finally reform its force?* National Public Radio. https://www.npr.org/local/309/2020/06/15/877345424/after-decades-of-police-corruption-can-chicago-finally-reform-its-force

Mosley, M. A., Lancaster, M., Parker, M. L., & Campbell, K. (2020). Adult attachment and online dating deception: A theory modernized. *Sexual and Relationship Therapy*, *35*(2), 227–243. https://doi.org/10.1080/14681994.2020.1714577

Mukundan, C. R., Sumit, S., & Chetan, S. M. (2017). Brain Electrical Oscillations Signature profiling (BEOS) for measuring the process of remembrance. *EC Neurology*, *8*(6), 217–230. https://www.ecronicon.com/ecne/pdf/ECNE-08-00256.pdf

Nagar, P. M., Caivano, O., & Talwar, V. (2020). The role of empathy in children's costly prosocial lie-telling behaviour. *Infant and Child Development*, *29*(4), Article e2179. https://doi.org/10.1002/icd.2179

Nagar, P. M., Williams, S., & Talwar, V. (2019). The influence of an older sibling on preschoolers' lie-telling behavior. *Social Development*, *28*(4), 1095–1110. https://doi.org/10.1111/sode.12367

Najdowski, C. J., & Bonventre, C. L. (2014). Deception in the interrogation room. *APA Monitor*, *45*(5), 26. https://www.apa.org/monitor/2014/05/jn

National Health Care Anti-Fraud Association. (2021). *The challenge of health care fraud*. https://www.nhcaa.org/tools-insights/about-health-care-fraud/the-challenge-of-health-care-fraud/

National Public Radio. (n.d.). *The fall of Enron collapse felt from workers' homes to halls of government*. https://legacy.npr.org/news/specials/enron/

National Research Council. (2003). *The polygraph and lie detection*. National Academies Press.

Ng, C. (2012, April 10). *Bride who faked cancer to score dream wedding, honeymoon is charged*. ABC News. https://abcnews.go.com/US/york-bride-faked-cancer-score-dream-wedding-honeymoon/story?id=16108726

Nisbett, R. E., & Wilson, T. D. (1977a). The halo effect: Evidence for unconscious alteration of judgments. *Journal of Personality and Social Psychology*, *35*(4), 250–256. https://doi.org/10.1037/0022-3514.35.4.250

Nisbett, R. E., & Wilson, T. D. (1977b). Telling more than we can know: Verbal reports on mental processes. *Psychological Review*, *84*(3), 231–259. https://doi.org/10.1037/0033-295X.84.3.231

O'Connor, A. M., & Evans, A. D. (2018). The relation between having siblings and children's cheating and lie-telling behaviors. *Journal of Experimental Child Psychology*, *168*, 49–60. https://doi.org/10.1016/j.jecp.2017.12.006

Oliveira, C. M., & Levine, T. R. (2008). Lie acceptability: A construct and measure. *Communication Research Reports*, *25*(4), 282–288. https://doi.org/10.1080/08824090802440170

O'Sullivan, M. (2008). Deception and self-deception as strategies in short- and long-term mating. In G. Geher & G. Miller (Eds.), *Mating intelligence: Sex, relationships, and the mind's reproductive system* (pp. 135–157). Lawrence Erlbaum Associates.

Oxford English Dictionary. (2021). https://www.oed.com/

Packer, G. (2018, October 12). A new report offers insights into tribalism in the age of Trump. *The New Yorker*. https://www.newyorker.com/news/daily-comment/a-new-report-offers-insights-into-tribalism-in-the-age-of-trump

Pak, E. (2021, April 14). Bernie Madoff: 6 famous victims of his Ponzi scheme. *Biography*. https://www.biography.com/news/bernie-madoff-famous-victims

Palmieri, J. J., & Stern, T. A. (2009). Lies in the doctor-patient relationship. *Primary Care Companion to the Journal of Clinical Psychiatry*, *11*(4), 163–168. https://doi.org/10.4088/PCC.09r00780

Papachristodoulou, M. (2019). *The biggest liar: Customers vs. sales people*. LinkedIn. https://www.linkedin.com/pulse/biggest-liar-customers-vs-sales-people-marios-papachristodoulou

Pareto, V. (1896). *Cours d'economie politique*. F. Rouge Libraire Editeur.

Park, H. S., Levine, T. R., McCornack, S. A., Morrison, K., & Ferrara, M. (2002). How people really detect lies. *Communication Monographs*, *69*(2), 144–157. https://doi.org/10.1080/714041710

Parker, K. (2009, September 16). Uncivil behavior should go the way of dueling. *The Baltimore Sun*. https://www.baltimoresun.com/news/bs-xpm-2009-09-16-0909150055-story.html

Parker-Pope, T. (2008, October 28). Love, sex and the changing landscape of infidelity. *The New York Times*. https://www.nytimes.com/2008/10/28/health/28iht-28well.17304096.html

Patrick, C. J. (2007). Antisocial personality disorder and psychopathy. In W. O'Donohue, K. A. Fowler, & S. O. Lilienfeld (Eds.), *Personality disorders: Toward the* DSM-V (pp. 109–166). Sage Publications. https://doi.org/10.4135/9781483328980.n6

Patrick, C. J., & Iacono, W. G. (1989). Psychopathy, threat, and polygraph test accuracy. *Journal of Applied Psychology*, *74*(2), 347–355. https://doi.org/10.1037/0021-9010.74.2.347

Patterson, J., & Kim, P. (1991). *The day America told the truth: What people really believe about everything that really matters*. Prentice Hall Press.

Paul, C., & Matthews, M. (2016). *The Russian "firehose of falsehood" propaganda model: Why it might work and options to counter it.* RAND Corporation. https://doi.org/10.7249/PE198

Paulhus, D. L., & Williams, K. M. (2002). The Dark Triad of personality: Narcissism, Machiavellianism and psychopathy. *Journal of Research in Personality*, *36*(6), 556–563. https://doi.org/10.1016/S0092-6566(02)00505-6

Pazzanese, C. (2019, April 15). Pros at the con. *The Harvard Gazette*. https://news.harvard.edu/gazette/story/2019/04/harvard-grad-studies-cons-and-how-to-avoid-them/

Peterson, C. (1996). Deception in intimate relationships. *International Journal of Psychology*, *31*(6), 279–288. https://doi.org/10.1080/002075996401034

Petty, R. E., & Cacioppo, J. T. (1986). The elaboration likelihood model of persuasion. In *Communication and persuasion: Springer series in social psychology* (pp. 1–24). Springer. https://doi.org/10.1007/978-1-4612-4964-1_1

Pflanzer, L. R. (2019). *The rise and fall of Theranos, the blood-testing startup that went from Silicon Valley darling to facing fraud charges.* Business Insider. https://www.businessinsider.com/the-history-of-silicon-valley-unicorn-theranos-and-ceo-elizabeth-holmes-2018-5

Pierce, J. R., & Thompson, L. (2021). Feeling competitiveness or empathy towards negotiation counterparts mitigates sex differences in lying. *Journal of Business Ethics*. Advance online publication. https://doi.org/10.1007/s10551-021-04776-6

Plomin, R. (2011). Commentary: Why are children in the same family so different? Non-shared environment three decades later. *International Journal of Epidemiology*, *40*(3), 582–592. https://doi.org/10.1093/ije/dyq144

Polage, D. C. (2012). Making up history: False memories of fake news stories. *Europe's Journal of Psychology*, *8*(2), 245–250. https://doi.org/10.5964/ejop.v8i2.456

Popper, N., Conger, K., & Browning, K. (2020, August 2). From Minecraft tricks to Twitter hack: A Florida teen's troubled online path. *The New York Times*. https://www.nytimes.com/2020/08/02/technology/florida-teenager-twitter-hack.html

Powell, B. (2002). *Treason: How a Russian spy led an American journalist to a U.S. double agent*. Simon & Schuster.

Premack, D., & Woodruff, G. (1978). Does the chimpanzee have a theory of mind? *Behavioral and Brain Sciences*, *1*(4), 515–526. https://doi.org/10.1017/S0140525X00076512

Quiroz, N. (2021, May 13). *Five facts about police deception and youth you should know*. The Innocence Project. https://innocenceproject.org/police-deception-lying-interrogations-youth-teenagers/

Raine, A. (2013). *The anatomy of violence: The biological roots of crime*. Pantheon/Random House.

Rappeport, A. (2021, April 13). Tax cheats cost the U.S. $1 trillion per year, I.R.S chief says. *The New York Times*. https://www.nytimes.com/2021/04/13/business/irs-tax-gap.html

Raskin, D. C., & Hare, R. D. (1978). Psychopathy and detection of deception in a prison population. *Psychophysiology*, *15*(2), 126–136. https://doi.org/10.1111/j.1469-8986.1978.tb01348.x

Raspe, E. (1785). *Baron Munchausen's narrative of his marvellous travels and campaigns in Russia*. Booksellers of Piccadilly.

Rector, K., Queally, J., & Poston, B. (2020, July 28). Hundreds of cases involving LAPD officers accused of corruption now under review. *Los Angeles Times*. https://www.latimes.com/california/story/2020-07-28/lacey-flags-hundreds-of-cases-linked-to-charged-lapd-officers-for-possible-review

Reid, J. (1947). A revised questioning technique in lie-detection tests. *Journal of Criminal Law and Criminology (1931–1951)*, *37*(6), 542–547. https://doi.org/10.2307/1138979

Reiner, R., Brown, D., & Scheinman, A. (Producers), & Reiner, R. (Director). (1992). *A few good men* [Film]. Columbia Pictures.

Renner, K. H., Enz, S., Friedel, H., Merzbacher, G., & Laux, L. (2008). Doing as if: The histrionic self-presentation style. *Journal of Research in Personality*, *42*(5), 1303–1322. https://doi.org/10.1016/j.jrp.2008.04.005

Robson, D. (2016, March 24). *Why are people so incredibly gullible?* BBC. https://www.bbc.com/future/article/20160323-why-are-people-so-incredibly-gullible

Rocca, F. X., & Lovett, I. (2020, November 10). Pope John Paul II was warned about Theodore McCarrick sex-abuse allegations, made him D.C. archbishop. *The Wall Street Journal*. https://www.wsj.com/articles/vatican-overlooked-warnings-of-sexual-misconduct-by-former-u-s-cardinal-mccarrick-report-finds-11605013875

Roggensack, K. E., & Sillars, A. (2014). Agreement and understanding about honesty and deception rules in romantic relationships. *Journal of Social and Personal Relationships*, *31*(2), 178–199. https://doi.org/10.1177/0265407513489914

Rose, P. (2004). *My prison without bars*. Rodale Press.

Rosenbaum, K. B., Friedman, S. H., & Galley, N. (2019). The act. *The Journal of the American Academy of Psychiatry and the Law*, *47*(4), 534–536.

Rosenberg, M. (1965). *Society and the adolescent self-image*. Princeton University Press. https://doi.org/10.1515/9781400876136

Roser, M., Appel, C., & Ritchie, H. (2013). *Human height*. Our World in Data. https://ourworldindata.org/human-height

Ross, L. (1977). The intuitive psychologist and his shortcomings: Distortions in the attribution process. In L. Berkowitz (Ed.), *Advances in experimental social psychology* (Vol. 10, pp. 173–220). Academic Press.

Ruedy, N. E., Moore, C., Gino, F., & Schweitzer, M. E. (2013). The cheater's high: The unexpected affective benefits of unethical behavior. *Journal of Personality and Social Psychology*, *105*(4), 531–548. https://doi.org/10.1037/a0034231

Rule, A. (1980). *The stranger beside me*. W. W. Norton and Company.

Rutenberg, J., Becker, J., Lipton, E., Haberman, M., Martin, J., Rosenberg, M., & Schmidt, M. S. (2021, January 31). 77 days: Trump's campaign to subvert the election. *The New York Times*. https://www.nytimes.com/2021/01/31/us/trump-election-lie.html

Ryan, A. (2004). Professional liars. *Social Research*, *71*(3), 733–752. https://doi.org/10.1353/sor.2004.0069

Rydell, R. J., & McConnell, A. R. (2006). Understanding implicit and explicit attitude change: A system of reasoning analysis. *Journal of Personality and Social Psychology*, *91*(6), 995–1008. https://doi.org/10.1037/0022-3514.91.6.995

Sagarin, B. J., Rhoads, K. V. L., & Cialdini, R. B. (1998). Deceiver's distrust: Denigration as a consequence of undiscovered deception. *Personality and Social Psychology Bulletin*, *24*(11), 1167–1176. https://doi.org/10.1177/01461672982411004

Sanow, E. (2011). The Reid technique of interviewing and interrogation. *Law and Order*. http://archive.reid.com/pdfs/20111213.pdf

Santos, R. M., Zanette, S., Kwok, S. M., Heyman, G. D., & Lee, K. (2017). Exposure to parenting by lying in childhood: Associations with negative outcomes in adulthood. *Frontiers in Psychology*, *8*, Article 1240. https://doi.org/10.3389/fpsyg.2017.01240

Sapir, A. (2021). *The LSI basic course on SCAN*. LSI Laboratory for Scientific Interrogation. https://www.lsiscan.com/id22.htm

Sarzyńska, J., Falkiewicz, M., Riegel, M., Babula, J., Margulies, D. S., Nęcka, E., Grabowska, A., & Szatkowska, I. (2017). More intelligent extraverts are more likely to deceive. *PLOS ONE*, *12*(4), Article e0176591. https://doi.org/10.1371/journal.pone.0176591

Satel, S., & Lilienfeld, S. O. (2013). *Brainwashed: The seductive appeal of mindless neuroscience*. Basic Books.

Schecter, A., Nathanson, K., & Connor, T. (2015, July 5). *Farid Fata, doctor who gave chemo to healthy patients, faces sentencing*. NBC News. https://www.nbcnews.com/health/cancer/farid-fata-doctor-who-gave-chemo-healthy-patients-faces-sentencing-n385161

Schein, C., & Gray, K. (2018). The theory of dyadic morality: Reinventing moral judgment by redefining harm. *Personality and Social Psychology Review*, *22*(1), 32–70. https://doi.org/10.1177/1088868317698288

Schreier, M. (2009). Belief change through fiction: How fictional narratives affect real readers. In S. Winko, F. Jannidis, & G. Lauer (Eds.), *Grenzen der Literatur: Zu Begriff und Phänomen des Literarischen* (pp. 315–337). De Gruyter. https://doi.org/10.1515/9783110210835.4.315

Schwarz, N., Newman, E., & Leach, W. (2016). Making the truth stick & the myths fade: Lessons from cognitive psychology. *Behavioral Science & Policy*, *2*(1), 85–95. https://doi.org/10.1353/bsp.2016.0009

Schweitzer, M. E., Hershey, J. C., & Bradlow, E. T. (2006). Promises and lies: Restoring violated trust. *Organizational Behavior and Human Decision Processes*, *101*(1), 1–19. https://doi.org/10.1016/j.obhdp.2006.05.005

Scott, R. (Director). (1997). *G. I. Jane* [Film]. Hollywood Pictures.

Scott, W. D. (1903). *The theory and practice of advertising: A simple exposition of the principles of psychology in their relation to successful advertising*. Small, Maynard, and Company.

Serota, K. B., & Levine, T. R. (2015). A few prolific liars: Variation in the prevalence of lying. *Journal of Language and Social Psychology*, *34*(2), 138–157. https://doi.org/10.1177/0261927X14528804

Serota, K. B., Levine, T. R., & Boster, F. J. (2010). The prevalence of lying in America: Three studies of self-reported lies. *Human Communication Research*, *36*(1), 2–25. https://doi.org/10.1111/j.1468-2958.2009.01366.x

Serota, K. B., Levine, T. R., & Docan-Morgan, T. (2021). Unpacking variation in lie prevalence: Prolific liars, bad lie days, or both? *Communication Monographs*, *89*(3). Advance online publication. https://doi.org/10.1080/03637751.2021.1985153

Setoh, P., Zhao, S., Santos, R., Heyman, G. D., & Lee, K. (2020). Parenting by lying in childhood is associated with negative developmental outcomes in adulthood. *Journal of Experimental Child Psychology*, *189*, Article 104680. https://doi.org/10.1016/j.jecp.2019.104680

Shalvi, S., & Leiser, D. (2013). Moral firmness. *Journal of Economic Behavior & Organization*, *93*, 400–407. https://doi.org/10.1016/j.jebo.2013.03.014

Shany-Ur, T., Poorzand, P., Grossman, S. N., Growdon, M. E., Jang, J. Y., Ketelle, R. S., Miller, B. L., & Rankin, K. P. (2012). Comprehension of insincere communication in neurodegenerative disease: Lies, sarcasm, and theory of mind. *Cortex*, *48*(10), 1329–1341. https://doi.org/10.1016/j.cortex.2011.08.003

Shen, Q., Teo, M., Winter, E., Hart, E., Chew, S. H., & Ebstein, R. P. (2016). To cheat or not to cheat: Tryptophan hydroxylase 2 SNP variants contribute to dishonest behavior. *Frontiers in Behavioral Neuroscience*, *10*, 82. https://doi.org/10.3389/fnbeh.2016.00082

Shesol, J. (1997). *Mutual contempt: Lyndon Johnson, Robert Kennedy, and the feud that defined a decade*. W. W. Norton & Co.

Shonk, K. (2021, August 10). *Understanding different negotiation styles*. Program on Negotiation, Harvard Law School. https://www.pon.harvard.edu/daily/negotiation-skills-daily/understanding-different-negotiation-styles/

Sicard, S. (2021, June 23). Army investigating Ft. Eustis officer for alleged cheating scandal. *Army Times*. https://www.armytimes.com/news/your-army/2021/06/23/army-investigating-ft-eustis-officer-for-alleged-cheating-scandal/

Smith, E. H. (1923). *Confession of a confidence man: A handbook for suckers*. Scientific American Publishing Co.

Smith, J. A. (2017, March 24). How the science of “blue lies” may explain Trump’s support. *Scientific American*. https://blogs.scientificamerican.

com/guest-blog/how-the-science-of-blue-lies-may-explain-trumps-support/

Smith, K. M., & Apicella, C. L. (2020). Hadza hunter-gatherers disagree on perceptions of moral character. *Social Psychological & Personality Science, 11*(5), 616–625. https://doi.org/10.1177/1948550619865051

Smith, M., Saunders, R., Stuckhardt, L., & McGinnis, J. M. (2013). *Best care at lower cost: The path to continuously learning health care in America*. National Academies Press.

Smith, M. E., Hancock, J. T., Reynolds, L., & Birnholtz, J. (2014). Everyday deception or a few prolific liars? The prevalence of lies in text messaging. *Computers in Human Behavior, 41*, 220–227. https://doi.org/10.1016/j.chb.2014.05.032

Snyder, S. (1986). Pseudologia fantastica in the borderline patient. *The American Journal of Psychiatry, 143*(10), 1287–1289. https://doi.org/10.1176/ajp.143.10.1287

Spielberg, S. (Director). (2002). *Catch me if you can* [Film]. DreamWorks Pictures.

Spohr, M. (2018, October 14). *21 kids who told bald-faced lies that in no way could be even remotely true*. Buzzfeed. https://www.buzzfeed.com/mikespohr/21-outrageous-lies-kids-told-other-kids-thatll-make-you-go

Sporer, S. L. (2004). Reality monitoring and detection of deception. In P.-A. Granhag & L. Strömwall (Eds.), *The detection of deception in forensic contexts* (pp. 64–102). Cambridge University Press. https://doi.org/10.1017/CBO9780511490071.004

Sporer, S. L., & Schwandt, B. (2006). Paraverbal indicators of deception: A meta-analytic synthesis. *Applied Cognitive Psychology, 20*(4), 421–446. https://doi.org/10.1002/acp.1190

Stanton, K., Ellickson-Larew, S., & Watson, D. (2016). Development and validation of a measure of online deception and intimacy. *Personality and Individual Differences, 88*, 187–196. https://doi.org/10.1016/j.paid.2015.09.015

Stein, J. D. (2021, April 20). Why we lie. Four men with complicated relationships to the truth explain why honesty can be hard. *Men's Health*. https://www.menshealth.com/trending-news/a36007380/why-do-people-men-lie/

Stiff, J. B. (1996). Theoretical approaches to the study of deceptive communication: Comments on interpersonal deception theory. *Communication Theory*, *6*(3), 289–296. https://doi.org/10.1111/j.1468-2885.1996.tb00130.x

Strickler, J. (2002, December 22). Public's fascination with con man isn't fake. *Star Tribune*. https://www.newspapers.com/image/?clipping_id=87154661&fcfToken=eyJhbGciOiJIUzI1NiIsInR5cCI6IkpXVCJ9.eyJmcmVlLXZpZXctaWQiOjI1MDM2NDk5MiwiaWF0IjoxNjM2MDQ0NzgyLCJleHAiOjE2MzYxMzExODJ9.86H6p2LF0Gw-HQM5ZyVlsFtK0BqKSqvi8jLOxShYoDA

Strömwall, L. A., Granhag, P. A., & Hartwig, M. (2004). Practitioners' beliefs about deception. In P. A. Granhag & L. Strömwall (Eds.), *The detection of deception in forensic contexts* (pp. 229–250). Cambridge University Press. https://doi.org/10.1017/CBO9780511490071.010

Strömwall, L. A., Hartwig, M., & Granhag, P. A. (2006). To act truthfully: Nonverbal behavior and strategies during a police interrogation. *Psychology, Crime & Law*, *12*(2), 207–219. https://doi.org/10.1080/10683160512331331328

Sun, Q., Zhang, H., Zhang, J., & Zhang, X. (2018). Why can't we accurately predict others' decisions? Prediction discrepancy in risky decision-making. *Frontiers in Psychology*, *9*, Article 2190. https://doi.org/10.3389/fpsyg.2018.02190

Sweet, P. L. (2019). The sociology of gaslighting. *American Sociological Review*, *84*(5), 851–875. https://doi.org/10.1177/0003122419874843

Swiergosz, A. M., Kasdan, M. L., & Wilhelmi, B. J. (2017). The unexpected hand patient. *Eplasty*, *17*, e16.

Talwar, V., Arruda, C., & Yachison, S. (2015). The effects of punishment and appeals for honesty on children's truth-telling behavior. *Journal of Experimental Child Psychology*, *130*, 209–217. https://doi.org/10.1016/j.jecp.2014.09.011

Talwar, V., Lavoie, J., & Crossman, A. M. (2019). Carving Pinocchio: Longitudinal examination of children's lying for different goals. *Journal of Experimental Child Psychology*, *181*, 34–55. https://doi.org/10.1016/j.jecp.2018.12.003

Talwar, V., & Lee, K. (2002a). Development of lying to conceal a transgression: Children's control of expressive behaviour during verbal deception. *International Journal of Behavioral Development*, *26*(5), 436–444. https://doi.org/10.1080/01650250143000373

Talwar, V., & Lee, K. (2002b). Emergence of white-lie telling in children between 3 and 7 years of age. *Merrill-Palmer Quarterly*, *48*(2), 160–181. https://doi.org/10.1353/mpq.2002.0009

Talwar, V., & Lee, K. (2008). Social and cognitive correlates of children's lying behavior. *Child Development*, *79*(4), 866–881. https://doi.org/10.1111/j.1467-8624.2008.01164.x

Talwar, V., & Lee, K. (2011). A punitive environment fosters children's dishonesty: A natural experiment. *Child Development*, *82*(6), 1751–1758. https://doi.org/10.1111/j.1467-8624.2011.01663.x

Talwar, V., Murphy, S. M., & Lee, K. (2007). White lie-telling in children for politeness purposes. *International Journal of Behavioral Development*, *31*(1), 1–11. https://doi.org/10.1177/0165025406073530

Talwar, V., Renaud, S., & Conway, L. (2015). Detecting children's lies: Are parents accurate judges of their own children's lies? *Journal of Moral Education*, *44*(1), 81–96. https://doi.org/10.1080/03057240.2014.1002459

Tangney, J. P., Stuewig, J., & Mashek, D. J. (2007). Moral emotions and moral behavior. *Annual Review of Psychology*, *58*(1), 345–372. https://doi.org/10.1146/annurev.psych.56.091103.070145

Taylor, D. B. (2021, July 16). Illinois bars police from lying to minors during questioning. *The New York Times*. https://www.nytimes.com/2021/07/16/us/illinois-police-deception-interrogation.html

Teasdale, K., & Kent, G. (1995). The use of deception in nursing. *Journal of Medical Ethics*, *21*(2), 77–81. https://doi.org/10.1136/jme.21.2.77

ten Brinke, L., Porter, S., & Baker, A. (2012). Darwin the detective: Observable facial muscle contractions reveal emotional high-stakes lies. *Evolution and Human Behavior*, *33*(4), 411–416. https://doi.org/10.1016/j.evolhumbehav.2011.12.003

Tenenbaum, N. (Producer), & Roach, J. (Director). (2000). *Meet the parents* [Film]. Universal Pictures.

Tetlock, P. E., & Gardner, D. (2015). *Superforecasting: The art and science of prediction*. Crown.

Teunisse, A. K., Case, T. I., Fitness, J., & Sweller, N. (2020). I should have known better: Development of a self-report measure of gullibility. *Personality and Social Psychology Bulletin*, *46*(3), 408–423. https://doi.org/10.1177/0146167219858641

Thomas, C. W. (2002, March 31). The rise and fall of Enron: When a company looks too good to be true, it usually is. *Journal of Accountancy*. https://www.journalofaccountancy.com/issues/2002/apr/theriseandfallofenron.html

Thorndike, E. L. (1920). A constant error in psychological ratings. *Journal of Applied Psychology*, *4*(1), 25–29. https://doi.org/10.1037/h0071663

Toma, C. L., Hancock, J. T., & Ellison, N. B. (2008). Separating fact from fiction: An examination of deceptive self-presentation in online dating profiles. *Personality and Social Psychology Bulletin*, *34*(8), 1023–1036. https://doi.org/10.1177/0146167208318067

Tomaszewski, M. (2021). *"My pet died" (& other lies to get out of work): 2021 study*. https://zety.com/blog/excuses-to-get-out-of-work

Tooby, J. (2017). *2017: What scientific term or concept ought to be more widely known?* Edge. https://www.edge.org/response-detail/27168

Traub, A. (2017, July 12). *When your pastor lies to your face for five years*. Medium. https://medium.com/@andytraub/when-your-pastor-lies-to-your-face-for-five-years-91b2b590c353

Treas, J., & Giesen, D. (2000). Sexual infidelity among married and cohabiting Americans. *Journal of Marriage and Family*, *62*(1), 48–60. https://doi.org/10.1111/j.1741-3737.2000.00048.x

Trovillo, P. V. (1939). A history of lie detection. *The Journal of Criminal Law and Criminology*, *29*(6), 848–881. https://doi.org/10.2307/1136489

Turner, J., & Reid, S. (2002). Munchausen's syndrome. *The Lancet*, *359*(9303), 346–349. https://doi.org/10.1016/S0140-6736(02)07502-5

Turner, R. E., Edgley, C., & Olmstead, G. (1975). Information control in conversations: Honesty is not always the best policy. *Social Thought & Research*, *11*(1), 69–89. https://doi.org/10.17161/STR.1808.6098

Tyler, J. M., Feldman, R. S., & Reichert, A. (2006). The price of deceptive behavior: Disliking and lying to people who lie to us. *Journal of Experimental Social Psychology*, *42*(1), 69–77. https://doi.org/10.1016/j.jesp.2005.02.003

Uri, Joe, & Leif. (2021, August 17). *Evidence of fraud in an influential field experiment about dishonesty*. Data Colada. https://datacolada.org/98

U.S. Department of Labor. (1988). *Employee Polygraph Protection Act*. https://www.dol.gov/sites/dolgov/files/WHD/legacy/files/whdfs36.pdf

U.S. Federal Bureau of Investigation. (2012, May 3). *Medicare Fraud Strike Force charges 107 individuals for approximately $452 million* *in false billing*. https://archives.fbi.gov/archives/neworleans/press-releases/2012/medicare-fraud-strike-force-charges-107-individuals-for-approximately-452-million-in-false-billing

U.S. Senate Select Committee on Intelligence. (1994). *An assessment of the Aldrich H. Ames espionage case and its implications for U.S. intelligence*. U.S. Government Printing Office.

Vance, M. C., Caverly, T. J., & Hayward, R. A. (2020). Underappreciated bias created by measurement error in risk factor assessment—A case study of no safe level of alcohol consumption. *JAMA Internal Medicine, 180*(3), 459–461. https://doi.org/10.1001/jamainternmed.2019.6116

Vedantam, S. (Host). (2018, April 9). Everybody lies, and that's not always a bad thing [Audio podcast episode]. In *Hidden brain*. National Public Radio. https://www.npr.org/2018/04/09/599930273/everybody-lies-and-thats-not-always-a-bad-thing

Verigin, B. L., Meijer, E. H., Bogaard, G., & Vrij, A. (2019). Lie prevalence, lie characteristics and strategies of self-reported good liars. *PLOS ONE, 14*(12), Article e0225566. https://doi.org/10.1371/journal.pone.0225566

Verschuere, B., Crombez, G., Koster, E. H. W., & Uzieblo, K. (2006). Psychopathy and physiological detection of concealed information: A review. *Psychologica Belgica, 46*(1–2), 99–116. https://doi.org/10.5334/pb-46-1-2-99

Verschuere, B., Meijer, E. H., Jim, A., Hoogesteyn, K., Orthey, R., McCarthy, R. J., Skowronski, J. J., Acar, O. A., Aczel, B., Bakos, B. E., Barbosa, F., Baskin, E., Bègue, L., Ben-Shakhar, G., Birt, A. R., Blatz, L., Charman, S. D., Claesen, A., Clay, S. L., . . . Yıldız, E. (2018). Registered Replication Report on Mazar, Amir, and Ariely (2008). *Advances in Methods and Practices in Psychological Science, 1*(3), 299–317. https://doi.org/10.1177/2515245918781032

Vicianova, M. (2015). Historical techniques of lie detection. *Europe's Journal of Psychology, 11*(3), 522–534. https://doi.org/10.5964/ejop.v11i3.919

Vohs, K. D., Baumeister, R. F., & Chin, J. (2007). Feeling duped: Emotional, motivational, and cognitive aspects of being exploited by others. *Review of General Psychology, 11*(2), 127–141. https://doi.org/10.1037/1089-2680.11.2.127

Vrij, A. (2000). *Detecting lies and deceit: The psychology of lying and the implications for professional practice*. John Wiley & Sons.

Vrij, A. (2008). *Detecting lies and deceit: Pitfalls and opportunities* (2nd ed.). John Wiley & Sons Ltd.

Vrij, A. (2015). Verbal lie detection tools: Statement validity analysis, reality monitoring and scientific content analysis. In P. A. Granhag, A. Vrij, & B. Verschuere (Eds.), *Detecting deception: Current challenges and cognitive approaches* (pp. 3–35). Wiley-Blackwell.

Vrij, A., Granhag, P. A., & Mann, S. (2010). Good liars. *The Journal of Psychiatry & Law*, *38*(1–2), 77–98. https://doi.org/10.1177/009318531003800105

Vrij, A., & Mann, S. (2006). Criteria-based content analysis: An empirical test of its underlying processes. *Psychology, Crime & Law*, *12*(4), 337–349. https://doi.org/10.1080/10683160500129007

Vrij, A., Meissner, C. A., & Kassin, S. M. (2015). Problems in expert deception detection and the risk of false confessions: No proof to the contrary in Levine et al. (2014). *Psychology, Crime & Law*, *21*(9), 901–909. https://doi.org/10.1080/1068316X.2015.1054389

Vrij, A., & Semin, G. R. (1996). Lie experts' beliefs about nonverbal indicators of deception. *Journal of Nonverbal Behavior*, *20*(1), 65–80. https://doi.org/10.1007/BF02248715

Wallace, D. (2003). *Big Fish*. Penguin.

Walter, K. V., Conroy-Beam, D., Buss, D. M., Asao, K., Sorokowska, A., Sorokowski, P., Aavik, T., Akello, G., Alhabahba, M. M., Alm, C., Amjad, N., Anjum, A., Atama, C. S., Atamtürk Duyar, D., Ayebare, R., Batres, C., Bendixen, M., Bensafia, A., Bizumic, B., . . . Zupančič, M. (2020). Sex differences in mate preferences across 45 countries: A large-scale replication. *Psychological Science*, *31*(4), 408–423. https://doi.org/10.1177/0956797620904154

Wanasika, I., & Adler, T. (2011). Deception as strategy: Context and dynamics. *Journal of Managerial Issues*, *23*(3), 364–378. http://www.jstor.org/stable/23209121

Wang, J. (2021, January 27). *Average income in America: What salary in the United States puts you in the top 50%, top 10%, and top 1%? (Updated for 2021)*. Best Wallet Hacks. https://wallethacks.com/average-median-income-in-america/

Weaver, K., & Hart, C. L. (2022). *Aversive trait predictors of impression management*. [Manuscript in preparation]. Department of Psychology & Philosophy, Texas Woman's University.

Whyte, S. (2017, September 20). *'I wanted to feel something': Inside the tangled mind of a compulsive liar.* ABC. https://www.abc.net.au/triplej/programs/hack/inside-the-tangled-mind-of-a-compulsive-liar/8965544

Wiederman, M. W. (1997). Pretending orgasm during sexual intercourse: Correlates in a sample of young adult women. *Journal of Sex & Marital Therapy*, *23*(2), 131–139. https://doi.org/10.1080/00926239708405314

Williams, S. S. (2001). Sexual lying among college students in close and casual relationships. *Journal of Applied Social Psychology*, *31*(11), 2322–2338. https://doi.org/10.1111/j.1559-1816.2001.tb00178.x

World Health Organization. (2019). *International statistical classification of diseases and related health problems* (11th ed). https://icd.who.int/

Xu, L., Chen, G., & Li, B. (2019). Sadness empathy facilitates prosocial lying. *Social Behavior and Personality*, *47*(9), Article e8371. https://doi.org/10.2224/sbp.8371

Yamagishi, T. (2001). Trust as a form of social intelligence. In K. S. Cook (Ed.), *Trust in society* (pp. 121–147). Russell Sage Foundation.

Yip, J. A., & Schweitzer, M. E. (2016). Mad and misleading: Incidental anger promotes deception. *Organizational Behavior and Human Decision Processes*, *137*, 207–217. https://doi.org/10.1016/j.obhdp.2016.09.006

Young, P. A., Eaves, L. J., & Eysenck, H. J. (1980). Intergenerational stability and change in the causes of variation in personality. *Personality and Individual Differences*, *1*(1), 35–55. https://doi.org/10.1016/0191-8869(80)90004-5

Young, S. (2010, June 4). *Kellogg settles Rice Krispies false ad case*. CNN. https://thechart.blogs.cnn.com/2010/06/04/kellogg-settles-rice-krispies-false-ad-case/

Zagorin, P. (1996). The historical significance of lying and dissimulation. *Social Research*, *63*(3), 863–912. http://www.jstor.org/stable/40972318

Zaid, M. (2002, April 16). Failure of the polygraph. *The Washington Post*. https://www.washingtonpost.com/archive/opinions/2002/04/16/failure-of-the-polygraph/07c406a5-0aa3-4e20-8dcc-89781162aaa8/

Zettelmeyer, F., Morton, F. S., & Silva-Risso, J. (2006). How the internet lowers prices: Evidence from matched survey and automobile transaction data. *Journal of Marketing Research*, *43*(2), 168–181. https://doi.org/10.1509/jmkr.43.2.168

Zhong, C.-B., Bohns, V. K., & Gino, F. (2010). Good lamps are the best police: Darkness increases dishonesty and self-interested behavior. *Psychological Science*, *21*(3), 311–314. https://doi.org/10.1177/0956797609360754

Zuckerman, M., DePaulo, B. M., & Rosenthal, R. (1981). Verbal and nonverbal communication of deception. *Advances in Experimental Social Psychology*, *14*, 1–59. https://doi.org/10.1016/S0065-2601(08)60369-X

Zvi, L., & Elaad, E. (2018). Correlates of narcissism, self-reported lies, and self-assessed abilities to tell and detect lies, tell truths, and believe others. *Journal of Investigative Psychology and Offender Profiling*, *15*(3), 271–286. https://doi.org/10.1002/jip.1511

INDEX

ABOUT THE AUTHORS

Christian L. Hart, PhD, is a professor of psychology at Texas Woman's University, where he is the director of the Psychological Science program and the director of the Human Deception Laboratory. He holds a master's degree and PhD in experimental psychology and has been a professor for almost 20 years. Dr. Hart teaches courses on deception and forensic psychology and conducts research on lie detection, pathological lying, lying within relationships, the morality of lying, and the factors that influence decisions to be honest or deceptive. He is the former president of the Southwestern Psychological Association. Prior to becoming a professor, Dr. Hart held the rank of lieutenant commander in the U.S. Navy, where he served as an aerospace experimental psychologist and taught at the Navy Test Pilot School. In addition to *Big Liars*, he has authored the reference book *Pathological Lying: Theory, Research, and Practice*, published by the American Psychological Association, and is a contributor to *Psychology Today*. His work has been featured in *The New York Times*, *The Washington Post*, National Public Radio, *London Times*, CNN, and *The Guardian*.

Drew A. Curtis, PhD, is a Texas-licensed psychologist, Rodgers Distinguished Faculty, and director of the PsyD and MS Counseling Psychology programs at Angelo State University (ASU). He is proudly serving as the executive officer and past president for the Southwestern Psychological Association and president for Psychological Association of Greater West Texas. Dr. Curtis has taught a variety of courses for more than 15 years, including abnormal psychology, psychopathology, and deception. He established and currently oversees the Clinical Science and Deception lab at ASU. His research has specifically focused on pathological lying and deception: in the context of therapy, within health care professions, intimate relationships, and parental relationships. Dr. Curtis has presented on a theoretical basis for understanding pathological lying and has collaborated with Dr. Hart on several research studies examining pathological lying. Other research has examined psychomythology of psychopathology and teaching of psychology. In addition to *Big Liars*, he authored the reference book *Pathological Lying: Theory, Research, and Practice*, published by the American Psychological Association as well as an abnormal psychology textbook, a book about psychopathology, and several papers on deception. Dr. Curtis has received various grants and awards for his research.